THE BLOOD
OF MARTYRS

THE BLOOD
OF MARTYRS

*Unintended Consequences
of Ancient Violence*

JOYCE E. SALISBURY

ROUTLEDGE
NEW YORK AND LONDON

Published in 2004 by
Routledge
29 West 35th Street
New York, NY 10001
www.routledge-ny.com

Published in Great Britain by
Routledge
11 New Fetter Lane
London EC4P 4EE
www.routledge.co.uk

Routledge is an imprint of the Taylor & Francis Group.

Library of Congress Cataloging-in-Publication Data.

Salisbury, Joyce E.
    The blood of martyrs : unintended consequences of ancient violence / Joyce E.
Salisbury.
        p. cm.
Includes bibliographical references and index.
        ISBN 0-415-94129-6 (alk. paper)
        1. Martyrdom–Christianity–History of doctrines–Early church, ca. 30-600. 2.
Christian martyrs. 3. Persecution–History–Early church, ca. 30-600. 4. Rome–
Politics and government–30 B.C.-476 A.D. I Title.
        BR1604.23. S25 2004
        272–dc22   2003022835

To Kaidyn Peter Hillesheim

CONTENTS

ACKNOWLEDGMENTS

This book represents more than twenty-five years of thinking, teaching, and writing about these early centuries of Christianity. Over the years, I have been repeatedly surprised at how many of our beliefs—and indeed simple habits of mind—were formed during the turbulent first four centuries of the Christian era, and as I've studied these ideas, I have many times come back to the martyrs who figured so prominently in the struggle of the nascent church. Here, I have taken the opportunity to present my reflections on the roots of many of our ideas.

With so many years of gestation, my list of indebtedness is impossibly long. I owe thanks to scholars as far back as my graduate studies at Rutgers University, where Professor Traian Stoianovich taught me to overlook nothing in the search for the mentalities of the past, and Professors Donald Weinstein and Rudolph Bell introduced me to the study of saints. Later, Professor Jane Tibbits Schulenburg offered unflagging support and intellectual stimulation, and recently Professor Tracy Luchetta contributed her expertise in clinical psychology in helping me understand more about torture and suicide.

Beyond these, my ideas have been shaped by many colleagues who commented on my papers at scholarly conferences on two continents, and others nearby like David Borgmeyer whose expertise in theology and excellent editorial eye were very helpful. I also have to thank a generation of students in my classes, whose questions forced me to find some answers and to develop new ideas. Paula Rentmeester provided invaluable research help in locating and obtaining the rights to the illustrations. Finally, like all medieval scholars, I have to recognize the importance of librarians all over the world who (like ancient monks and nuns) preserve the precious texts that make all this possible.

The dedication is to my new grandson, Kaidyn, who was born as I was finishing this book. I fondly dedicate it to him in the hopes that he can grow up in a world where ideas develop with civil discourse instead of violence.

INTRODUCTION

"The Blood of Martyrs is the seed of Christians." This widely quoted phrase (first written by the second-century church father Tertullian) claims that the death of each martyr stimulated the conversion of many more. In the first three centuries of Christianity, this was demonstrably true—people with little faith who were searching for spiritual truths believed that people willing to die horrible deaths must be on to something; Christians multiplied as the blood of martyrs was shed. To be fair, there were a lot of other reasons for the growth of Christianity during the Roman Empire, but that is another story.[1] In this book I look specifically at the influence of martyrdom before the fourth century when imperial decree formally ended the persecutions, and I show how the influence of the accounts of this ancient violence extended far beyond the creation of new converts.

This discussion also raises another question. How do people change their ideas? Humans are profoundly conservative when it comes to changing beliefs, and it often takes something like the dramatic witness of the martyrs to shift paradigms of thought. However, in a curious paradox, people of the ancient world also used the experience of the martyrs to maintain some old ideas—such as beliefs in magic and prophetic dreams. Thus, the blood of martyrs was an agent of change and continuity.

In the first section of this book, "The Power of the Martyrs," I recognize the influence of the accounts of martyrs and explore some of the ideas developed in this formative age that continue to affect us today. In the first chapter I set the stage by recounting the history of the age of the martyrs. I describe the Roman Empire where this struggle took place and tell of the martyrs who died, the emperors who persecuted, and the motivations that launched the age of the martyrs. (In the appendix at the back of this book I provide a chart of all these participants.) In this chapter I also explore the nature of torture itself and what it does to the people who perform it and experience it. Finally, I show how this torture and persecution caused people to see the world as a struggle of good against evil that continues to haunt our cultural memories.

Subsequent chapters take on specific themes that I suggest were profoundly shaped by the accounts of the martyrs. I look at beliefs of immortality, magic, the association of martyrs with warfare, and dreams and visions. The experience of the martyrs also helped shape Western anti-Semitism as well as views of motherhood. This unlikely pairing has nothing in common except to demonstrate how little control we have over the consequences of dramatic acts. Finally, Section 1 ends with a chapter called "The Blood of Sacrifice," which shows how (for better or worse) the very old idea of blood sacrifice entered into the Christian world.

In the second section of the book, "Controlling the Martyrs," I demonstrate that even as early as the fourth century, Christian leaders recognized how influential martyrs were and how difficult it was to direct that influence. In one chapter I look at violence of Christians against Christians, as each side tried to claim the mantle of martyrdom. In another chapter I consider how accounts of martyrs' deaths were changed for theological and political purposes; anything as powerful as martyrdom cannot help but be subject to propaganda. Finally, in the last chapter I show how fourth-century attempts to control martyrdom led to a prohibition of suicide that moved into modern laws. (Yes, physician-assisted suicide is banned because of the blood of martyrs.)

MEMORIES AND TEXTS

Before I begin the narrative, I must say something about our sources of information on martyrs, because what was most influential was not the death of any martyr but people's recollection of the death. It is memory, not the past, that transforms the future, and memory was preserved in texts. Witnesses to a martyr's death, or people who heard about a death, wrote down an account of it so survivors would not forget. Throughout this book, we shall see that the words they chose and the incidents they selected mattered more than the blood that was shed, so here I want to introduce the major texts that will appear and reappear throughout the book.

The earliest accounts of martyrs were preserved in correspondence written on scrolls, tucked in leather pouches, and circulated with Christians who traveled through the Roman Empire. Travelers stopped and read the accounts at churches, where the faithful made copies and continued to read them. It is impossible to overstate the significance of these texts; they were given as much respect as the letters of Paul, and since the canon of scripture had not yet been defined, many believed the words of the martyrs were messages from God.

Perhaps the most influential series of letters outside Scripture were written by Ignatius, Bishop of Antioch. Ignatius was arrested in about 107 and sent in chains to Rome to be martyred in the arena. As he journeyed from Antioch to Rome, he was greeted enthusiastically by the faithful along the way, and in response to their entreaties, he wrote many letters to those who watched with sadness as their beloved leader went calmly to his martyrdom. There are fifteen letters attributed to him, but probably only seven are authentic, and among them was a letter to a young bishop of Smyrna, Polycarp, who later became a martyr in his own right.[2]

The second most influential account of a martyrdom was a letter telling of the death of Polycarp (Ignatius's correspondent) who died as an old man in his eighties in 155. Ancient writers credited him with having studied with apostles who had known Jesus. Probably as a boy he had heard the preaching of the apostle John in Ephesus, and some traditions suggest that it was John himself who awarded the bishopric of Smyrna to Polycarp. The bishop served in Smyrna for nearly fifty years, and during that time, he gained a reputation for being an excellent pastor and a fierce guardian of orthodoxy. As subsequent churchmen struggled to establish uniform beliefs, the careful record of the orthodox bishop's martyrdom remained popular and a prototype for many other accounts.[3] A third early account was a letter written to Christians in modern Turkey relating in much detail the arrest and deaths of martyrs in Lyons (in modern France) in 177.[4] All these letters establish a vocabulary and a way of understanding martyrdoms that would shape many of the future texts. Throughout this book I will draw from these rich and influential works to see how Christians in the future made sense of the martyrdoms of the past.

Beyond the influential letters, the accounts of the martyrs take two forms. The first form is the "acts," which purport to recount the trials of the martyrs. These are probably not verbatim transcripts of the court proceedings but are based on witnesses' recollections; most retell the dialogues between the confessors and the judges. These *acta* were heavily rewritten over the centuries and must be used with caution as historical sources. (In chapter 9 I discuss how the Acts of Vincent were substantially modified to meet changing theological ideas.) A second form of martyr accounts were "passions," which were descriptions of the last days and death of a martyr. Some of these are highly imaginative, but others, such as the "Passion of Perpetua," record an authentic firsthand account of the diary of the martyr's last days. Throughout this book readers will come to know many of the acts and passions of the martyrs.

In addition to these accounts of individual martyrs, the most important text is Eusebius's *History of the Church from Christ to Constantine*, which recounts the victory of the church over the forces of Rome. Eusebius was born about 260 and died about 339. Therefore, he lived through the worst of the persecutions and was able to celebrate the victory of the church under Constantine. Not only is his firsthand account invaluable in its details, he also had access to the great libraries of the age and included letters, edicts, and martyrs' acts within his history. Many of the primary sources that would otherwise have been lost remain thanks to Eusebius's care. (In the appendix at the back of this book I list the martyrs described by Eusebius so readers can see the influence of this renowned eyewitness to church history.)

Creation of texts on martyrs continued well beyond the end of the persecutions. Hundreds of *acta* were composed in the fourth and fifth centuries to celebrate the anniversaries of the deaths of martyrs, and legends continued to be written for centuries afterward. How many of these were accurate, or even preserved the memory of real martyrs? We have no idea, but one thing is certain—the faithful believed and treasured the accounts, so the narratives themselves became highly influential as Christians read them annually on the feast day of the saint (usually the day of his or her death). For example, the poet Prudentius, who lived in Spain in the early fifth century, composed a series of poetic versions of the passion of martyrs, and his were recited annually on the martyr's feast day. These poetic versions were influential because, as we will see in chapters 7 and 9, the poetry added a symbolic dimension to the accounts, and some of the poetic images took on a reality of their own.

In addition to these sources, each major city had a list of martyrs whose festivals they celebrated, and these martyrologies at least give us the names of the early martyrs even if we have no surviving accounts of their deaths. The Martyrology of Carthage alone contained eighty-six entries.[5] The congregations had such love and veneration for these accounts that many people treated the texts with the same respect they accorded holy scripture, and they celebrated the saints' feast days with the same joy and awe that surrounded other festivals of the church calendar.

A final source of our information about the continuing importance of martyrs comes from visual evidence: drawings, illustrations in manuscripts, and paintings from the ancient world to the present all testify to people's desire to remember the extraordinary deeds of these early Christians. Most of these portrayals are explicit, indeed too graphic for modern sensibilities. The illustration that opens chapter 1, for example, was a drawing done in the sixteenth century to show tortures that the ancient Christians experienced, and the early twentieth-century translator of the work reminds us that the illustrations may be at first repellent, but then we are to lead to an enhanced admiration for the passion of the ancients.[6] I hope readers of this work will share this view and look at the illustrations as the ancients did—with awe for the blood of martyrs that was spilled in the early battles for the soul of the Roman Empire.

As I explore various ways the violence of the ancient world influenced many of our attitudes, I will repeatedly refer to these letters, acts, passions, and pictures. After all, what was enduring was not the deaths themselves but people's recollections of the brave witnesses; historians always study not only the past but also the memories of the past, for the latter are more influential than the former.

Periodically throughout this book, I draw parallels with modern examples. I ask readers' indulgence as people as varied as Jim Jones, David Koresh, and Palestinian suicide bombers appear in a narrative about ancient martyrs. My thesis is that martyrs matter, and they matter for a long time, even to our modern headlines. By exploring the roots of these ideas we may perhaps understand our world a little better. I have to admit a second purpose for writing: I do not think we need martyrs any more (if we ever *needed* them at all). It is time to recognize that faith is not compromised by discourse, that ideas can change without bloodshed, and that differences are not cause for killing. Unfortunately, that day is not yet here; so for now, I invite readers to explore the intersection of faith, blood, and the legacy of the unintended consequences of the age of the martyrs.

THE POWER OF
THE MARTYRS

This sixteenth-century drawing of tortures is based on the Passions of the martyrs. Drawings like these created more than a millennium after the end of the persecutions show the continued fascination with the martyrs' ordeals.
Martyrs being tortured in the following ways:
A. Hung from the wooden horse and scorched with the flame of torches
B. Suspended by the feet from a pulley and tortured with torches.

THE STRUGGLE BETWEEN
EVIL AND GOOD

n 19 July 64 a great fire broke out in the city of Rome. It began amid shops between the Palatine and Caelian hills, and the fire immediately became so fierce it could not be contained. It blazed rapidly through the low parts of the city then began to climb the seven hills. The palaces of the rich burned as did the wooden tenements of the poor, and witnesses told of the panic that ensued. Women, children, and the elderly were trapped in flaming narrow streets and screams of the helpless rose over the roar of the flames, while rumors spread that some people were openly hurling torches to keep the fire blazing as it consumed more and more of the city. Finally, after burning for five days, the fire was contained by the erection of a huge firebreak around the flames. When the smoke settled, Romans could see with horror that of the fourteen districts of the city, only four were left unburned. Three were completely leveled, while the remaining seven had only a few half-burned houses left.[1]

The unpopular emperor Nero opened the public buildings for the homeless and brought in food to provide for the newly destitute Romans, but his popularity did not increase. People muttered that he had started the fire so he could make room for a new huge palace for himself. Others said that he appeared on a private stage and sang of the destruction of Troy as he watched the fire burn.[2] Roman priests offered prayers and sought to propitiate the gods and goddesses who had so far guarded the city so well, but popular sentiment was not satisfied. As Tacitus wrote, "But all human efforts, all the lavish gifts of the emperor, and the propitiations of the gods, did not banish the sinister belief that the conflagration was the result of an order."[3]

Nero then hit on an ingenious way to deflect anger and suspicion: he accused Christians of starting the fire. Tacitus does not tell us why he selected Christians, writing only that he selected a "class hated for their abominations" who followed "Christus," a man killed "at the hands of one of our procurators, Pontius Pilatus."[4] Nero may have selected Christians because as a new sect they had little support among the large population of Rome. He may also have been influenced by his wife Poppaea's favoritism to the Jews, many of whom fiercely objected to Christians (see chapter 5). Whatever his motives, Nero introduced the first persecution of the Christians by Romans, and he did so in spectacular fashion.

Nero had his soldiers arrest everyone who claimed to be Christian, then tortured them to get names of others in the Christian community. In this way, he arrested hundreds of people. Nero turned their execution into a spectacle designed to please the crowds who had so recently turned their anger on the emperor himself. He had some Christians covered with the skins of beasts and attacked by dogs. Others were crucified or tied to wooden torches and burned alive to illuminate the night. These "executions" were conducted in Nero's own gardens, and he mingled with the spectators in the costume of a charioteer. Once again, Nero's excesses offended some of the crowd. Tacitus, who had no sympathy for Christians, noted "even for criminals who deserved extreme and exemplary punishment, there arose a feeling of compassion; for it was not, as it seemed, for the public good, but to glut one man's cruelty, that they were being destroyed."[5]

Tacitus had no idea how significant this event was; he reported it as one more bizarre example of the excesses of a cruel and corrupt emperor. The historian rapidly moved on to tell of other more momentous events. But this was a turning point, for the age of martyrdom had begun. Christian communities were no longer quarreling in the synagogues with their Jewish relatives. Now, they had to prepare themselves to confront the power of Rome.

Many of the faithful remembered this horror of persecution when so many were brutally killed, but the most influential articulation of the struggle between good and evil that began in Nero's garden was written in about 95 by a man named John who had been exiled to the island of Patmos by Emperor Domitian. While on this rocky island off the coast of modern Turkey, John recorded his visions of the upcoming struggles, and these visions, which came in magnificent and frightening images, became the final book of the New Testament—The Revelation to John: The Apocalypse, known as the Book of Revelations.

The Book of Revelations recognized that the age of martyrs had dawned: "For men have shed the blood of / saints and prophets" (Rev. 16:6), and in this struggle, Christians were set against the power of the state. In John's vision, a beast rose out of the sea that was "allowed to make war on the saints and to conquer them" (Rev. 13:7), and most commentators identify this beast with the Roman Empire. The "number" of this beast—666—probably referred to Emperor Nero (the sum of the letters in his name).

John's visions were probably written for Christians outside Rome who had heard of the horrible events. His visions were intended to inspire hope among Christians who John believed would face more persecutions. He promised that God was guiding the struggle and that it would end in victory. Furthermore, the revelation promised justice: The martyrs were in heaven—"I saw the souls of those who had been beheaded for their testimony to Jesus and for the word of God, and who had not worshiped the beast. . . ," and unbelievers who had persecuted them would be "thrown into the lake of fire" (Rev. 20:4, 15). This book foretold the struggles that were to come and promised an ultimate victory in which Christians would prevail. However, as people interpreted the powerful and compelling images, John's revelation did more: it cast the struggle between the faithful and the unbelievers into a cosmic battle between good and evil in which the state was evil. As we will see in chapter 8, the cosmic vision had long-standing consequences long after the age of martyrs was ended. When John wrote of his vision, however, the martyrdoms had just begun. The struggle was still new, and even though John fiercely drew the battle lines, Rome did not yet realize it was engaged in a war.

After the violence under Nero, the emperors did not officially persecute Christians for almost another 150 years. That is not to say that there were no martyrdoms during that time, for there were, but the persecutions were local and took place when provincial officials chose to prosecute. The random nature of these persecutions between 64 and 203 has led to much discussion about what constituted the legal basis for the persecutions, and the answer has remained somewhat elusive, or at least unsatisfying.

Some Romans spread scandalous rumors about their Christian neighbors. The Christian North African Minucius Felix in about 240 listed some of these shocking charges in order to refute them: He said that Christians were accused of gathering together with "the lowest dregs of society, and credulous women." They met in the dark and despised the temples. They disdained present tortures, yet "dread those of an uncertain future." They threatened the whole world with destruction, and finally in violation of all propriety, they committed incest, cannibalism, and indulged in orgies after secretive love feasts.[6] One can see hints of a badly misunderstood reality within these accusations, for there actually were secret Eucharistic feasts at which Christians who called themselves "brother and sister" exchanged kisses of peace while expecting the destruction of the world.

Christians universally denied the charges of criminal behavior. The church father Tertullian wrote with characteristic sarcasm: "Who has detected the traces of a bite in our blood-steeped loaf? Who has discovered, by a sudden light invading our darkness, any marks of impurity, I will not say of incest, in our feasts?"[7] Tertullian was right; none of the trials of martyrs accused them of these charges, although one early martyr (Attalus) was clearly reacting to these rumors when he shouted to the crowd as he was being slowly burned to death: "Look you, what you are doing is cannibalism! We Christians are not cannibals, nor do we perform any other sinful act."[8] Another martyr, Lucius, cried out to the judge as his fellow Christian was condemned: "What is the charge? He has not been convicted of adultery, fornication, murder, clothes-stealing, robbery, or of any crime whatsoever; yet you have punished this man because he confesses the name of Christian?"[9] Rome had to decide what their crime was.

Romans were deeply—and rightly—proud of their legal traditions. By the time of the empire, Roman law had developed into a complex system, which was unique in the ancient world because Roman jurists not only wanted to maintain the stability of the state but they also wanted to provide justice. Consequently, when confronted with Christians, Roman authorities were careful to look at the prevailing laws, and they were troubled by the lack of clear direction.

The legal situation was complicated by the fact that in the early empire, citizens and noncitizens were subject to different laws. Citizens were governed by civil law (*ius civile*), while others were subject to their own laws and customs, which came to be called the *ius gentium*, or law applying to other nations. Different magistrates administered these two different kinds of laws, so when Christians were arrested, judges first had to ascertain whether they were citizens, then they were tried in the appropriate courts. The penalties for citizens and noncitizens differed, which also determined the legal form of execution. As we shall see, this question of legal status would shape the experience of the martyrs.

The Roman desire for justice and legality led to discussions about the proper treatment of members of this new religious sect. There is a famous correspondence between Pliny the Younger and Emperor Trajan from 112 that addressed the ambiguity of the charges against Christians. By 112, there had been enough sporadic charges brought to the attention of the authorities that Pliny, as a careful provincial governor, wanted an imperial ruling about how to handle these Christians. Pliny told the emperor how the matter had progressed: a number of people came to him and denounced others—both citizens and noncitizens—of being Christian. Since Pliny had never before confronted such a trial, the governor did not know whether the crime was one simply of being a Christian (the "name" itself) or whether they were indeed guilty of vile crimes, as the previously mentioned rumors indicated. These Christians pleaded guilty to the name and were sent off to be executed.

The situation then became more complicated for Pliny. The accusations spread and a large number of people were accused, some of whom were clearly innocent and others who said they had once been Christians but were no longer. Pliny forced the accused to sacrifice by pouring a bit of wine and burning incense before the imperial statue and cursing Christ. Those who performed these rituals were freed. Pliny, however, was made more curious about this cult, and he investigated the matter further to see if they were guilty of any crimes. After questioning people, he found nothing illegal in the life of these people, and even after torturing two Christian slaves (identified as deaconesses) to determine the "truth," he still found no illegality. They carefully avoided all crime and simply met before daybreak to sing and worship God.

Yet, Pliny found something disagreeable at best in their obstinate refusal to perform the Roman sacrifices for the health of the emperor. Pliny called this a depraved superstition that was intolerable, but the legality of his trials was unclear to him. Thus, he stopped all proceedings until he received a ruling from the emperor. Trajan's answer was decidedly lenient. The emperor forbade anonymous accusations as contrary to the spirit of his reign, so the governor need not seek out Christians. However, if an obstinate Christian came to the attention of the governor, he should be punished, but if an accused Christian was willing to sacrifice, then all his or her previous "crimes" or associations were forgiven.[10]

Trajan's ruling was practical but somewhat inconsistent. In his clear analysis, the fourth-century historian Eusebius noted what many believed: "This meant that though to some extent the terrifying imminent threat of persecution was stifled, yet for those who wanted to injure us there were just as many pretexts left."[11] Tertullian, a little less than a century after the letter was issued, commented with scorn at the legal difficulties implicit in the opinion: "How unavoidably ambiguous was that decision! . . . So you condemn a man when he is brought into court, although no one wanted him to be sought out. He has earned punishment, I suppose, not on the ground that he is guilty, but because he was discovered for whom no search had to be made."[12] In many ways, Tertullian was right. What was the crime that brought Christians to the attention of the authorities? It was not the crime of not sacrificing because that came *after* the charges as proof of innocence. No, the charge was simply that of the "name," and throughout the records of the martyr trials, their profession of the name Christian was enough to condemn them. A group of North African martyrs in 180 are representative. The dialogue is sparse and to the point:

The proconsul Saturninus said to Speratus: "Do you persist in remaining a Christian?"

Speratus said: "I am a Christian." And all agreed with him.

The proconsul then read the decision: "Whereas [all] . . . have confessed that they have been living in accordance with the rites of the Christians, and whereas though given the opportunity to return to the usage of the Romans they have persevered in their obstinacy, they are hereby condemned to be executed by the sword."[13]

There was no evidence presented, nor were additional crimes charged; the name was enough. Some of the reported trial records include more dialogue with the judge and confessor arguing the merits of each side, but there is never any doubt that the end is as the dialogue between Speratus and Saturninus portrayed.

Trajan's successor, Hadrian (who ruled from 117 to 138), also issued an edict restricting persecution of Christians. His letter urged his provincial governors to rely strictly on the law, not on rumor or popular demand for persecutions. He wrote, "If then the provincials can so clearly establish their case against the Christians that they can sustain it in a court of law, let them resort to this procedure only, and not rely on petitions or mere clamor." He further urged the governors to prosecute people who brought charges against Christians for their own financial gain.[14] Both Trajan and Hadrian demonstrate that from 64, the persecutions that created martyrs did not originate from imperial policy. Instead, they were local matters stimulated usually by controversy among neighbors.

In 177, a persecution broke out in Lyons in Gaul, and we know many details about this horrible event from a letter by an eyewitness written to inform churches in Asia of the persecution. Christians in Lyons were made unwelcome by their pagan neighbors—they were forbidden to go to the baths, to the forum in the center of the city, indeed, to be seen anywhere at all.[15] Were these Christians immigrants from the East (which would explain why the letter relating their fortunes would have been sent back) and thus perceived as foreigners bringing in an unusual cult? Probably, but we cannot know for sure. Nevertheless, we do know the anger of the people of Lyons against their Christian neighbors escalated. The Christians were marched into the forum, interrogated by city officials while the whole population of the town watched, and then imprisoned until the governor arrived. When the governor questioned them, many confessed the name "Christian," which was enough to cause them to be arrested. When one claimed Roman citizenship, the governor—like Pliny before him—thought he'd better consult the emperor on the matter.

The response came back from Marcus Aurelius: the Roman citizens among the Christians were to be beheaded, and the rest to be sentenced to the beasts in the arena.[16] The witness's letter tells how the crowd was delighted that they would witness a spectacle, and it gives a detailed picture of the deaths of dozens of men and women in the arena at Lyons. This martyrdom is typical; between 64 and 250, the sources repeatedly tell of the crowds urging the provincial governors to try Christians in their communities. Since the legality of the charges was sufficiently ambiguous for governors to worry, why were the Christians brought to their attention?

The answer is almost shockingly simple. Christians were perceived by their pagan neighbors to be antisocial in the deepest meaning of the word. They were creating their own society within the Roman one, and their loyalties were to each other rather than to the family structures that formed the backbone of conservative Roman society. Their faith led them to renounce parents, children, and spouses, and Romans believed this actively undermined the fabric of society. In fact, it did.

Furthermore, Christians refused to offer appropriate reverence to the gods of Rome by offering sacrifice. Romans were deeply religious (or superstitious depending on your point of view). A number of ancient writers noted that Romans were set apart from others of the ancient world precisely for their piety. Cicero may serve to summarize their views when he wrote, "If we care to compare our national characteristics with those of foreign people, we shall find that . . . in the sense of religion, that is, in reverence for the gods, we are far superior."[17] In this passage rendered in English, we use the word *reverence*, but the Latin word *cultus* implies much more than reverence; it really emphasizes correct action, that is the repeated performance of the ritual acts—specifically sacrificing to the deities. This respect for religious rituals led to much proliferation of cultic activities. Romans were so religiously conservative, or perhaps we should say careful, that they were unwilling to abandon any religious rituals. The Romans deeply believed that these religious rituals—including sacrificing for the well-being of the emperor—had ensured their safety and prosperity.

Thus, we can perhaps understand the great offense the Christians gave when they refused to participate in the cultic activities that had been at the defining heart of Rome. By their unwillingness to participate in the very activities that secured the safety of society, Christians were again perceived as antisocial. One of the trial records from the second century expresses this sentiment precisely. The governor conducting the interrogation of Christians responded to their claims of spirituality by articulating the Roman position: "We too are a religious people, and our religion is a simple one: we swear by the genius of our lord the emperor and we offer prayers for his health—as you also ought to do."[18] Christians were setting themselves apart from Romans.

One would think that Jews, who were equally monotheistic, would also have fallen afoul of Roman cultic requirements. While many Romans were suspicious of Jewish unwillingness to share in the empire's religious life, Jews at least had the virtue of following an age-old religion of their fathers. The Roman Tacitus (who did not like Judaism) wrote, "This worship is upheld by its antiquity."[19] Romans were proudly conservative in that they believed that people should follow the "ways of their fathers," so they respected the rights of Jews to do so. Christians, on the other hand, were rejecting the ways of their ancestors—the Jews—as well as rejecting the rites of their neighbors. Because of their adamant embrace of this new religion, Christians alienated both Romans and conservative Jews (as we will see further in chapter 5).

Thus, between the persecution of Nero in 64 and 250, arrests were sporadic and generated locally. Charges usually stemmed from two main sources: (1) local disturbances during which pagan Romans brought charges against Christians and (2) less often, governors who looked for criminals to execute in the amphitheater to please a crowd. Obviously, these two motives were not mutually exclusive; an angry crowd could be happily appeased by executions that took the form of a spectacle, just as Nero's spectacular persecution quelled the anger over the fire. In about 210, Tertullian summarized the idiosyncratic nature of the persecutions in a letter to a North African governor urging him not to begin a new cycle of persecutions. In this letter, Tertullian gave examples of previous governors who exerted their authority in varying ways. One thought of a verbal formula that allowed Christians to answer in a way that was consistent with both Christian belief and Roman requirements. (Unfortunately, he did not include what must have been a fascinating phrase!) Another governor freed a Christian without making him sacrifice, and yet another dismissed the case because he perceived that the charge grew from neighborly malice.[20]

If the underlying causes of the arrests were vague and inconsistent, the result of an arrest was clear: death, usually in the arenas in which Romans celebrated spectacles and ritually asserted their power. As the incident in Lyons showed, the sentence of death varied a bit. Roman citizens were supposed to be beheaded, which was a merciful death accorded to citizens. Noncitizens were sentenced to be executed in public by the flames or the beasts, but in reality there were many instances of citizens being sentenced to the beasts. These public executions were usually conducted in the amphitheaters large and small that were one of the hallmarks of Roman cities throughout the empire, and the greatest was the Colosseum in Rome itself.

These magnificent structures that towered over any other in the town were much more than entertainment centers. Here Romans gathered to watch rituals that ensured that the state and the emperor were firmly in control—chaos was at bay. A day at the amphitheater began in the morning with some hours of animal hunts during which hunters killed thousands of exotic animals brought from all over the empire. At this event spectators could readily see that Rome not only controlled vast areas that could deliver leopards, ostriches, elephants, giraffes, and many other species to Rome itself but also that Rome through its animal controllers and hunters could control nature itself. Nothing was too fierce for the hunters. The afternoon was reserved for the main event, the gladiator battles.

Gladiators were condemned criminals or enslaved enemy soldiers. They deserved death, but had been given a reprieve, a right to earn life again through their brave facing of death. The gladiators took a terrible oath to be burned (i.e., branded), to be chained up, and to be killed by an iron weapon,[21] and they appeared with full ceremony in the amphitheaters bravely and repeatedly to face death. This highly popular entertainment was also a sacred ritual. Gladiator deaths began as a blood sacrifice given for the dead, and now they sacrificed their blood for the glory and power of Rome. (I will pursue this idea of sacrifice in more detail in chapter 7.) Spectators came to watch to overcome their own fear of death.[22]

Between the two major events, criminals were brought into the amphitheater to be sentenced to death through the beasts or the flames. During these executions, Rome demonstrated its control over those who threatened the social order, and Christians fit this category. While Christian sources emphasize this part of the day's events, for pagan Romans watching, the execution of criminals was the least interesting part of the spectacle. Romans expected gladiators to show how to die bravely, and they equally expected Rome's criminals to die badly. A few Christians when faced with the beasts in the arena did grow afraid and renounce their faith,[23] but by far the greater number stood firm and faced their painful deaths without flinching. When Christian martyrs bravely and indeed cheerfully met their deaths during the midday executions, Romans were shocked because their understanding of human behavior had been violated.

One group of martyrs, for example, "marched from the prison to the amphitheater joyfully as if they were going to heaven."[24] When faced with this perceived anomaly, some Romans were moved to convert to Christianity, wanting to share the same disdain for death. Others, however, were angered. During the case of the martyrs in Lyons in 177, when the martyrs "stood firm" the "mob was infuriated with them,"[25] and this kind of rage was repeated through many of the martyrdoms. We can perhaps only understand this degree of anger when we consider how much it violated Romans' view of the world in which gladiators accepted death and criminals fought it. The public executions of the Christian martyrs caused Romans to reconsider their realities.

The deaths described in the arena showed the Christians withstanding much pain. The best martyrs could hope for was a swift kill by a leopard or a lion for the big cats killed quickly and efficiently. Bears and boars on the other hand dragged and ripped at their victims, as did bulls who tossed and gored victims who were usually bound in nets to immobilize them.[26]

All the accounts of the martyrs tell of their steadfast witness to the faith in the face of drawn-out painful deaths. It is these accounts that have made readers gasp with sympathy and artists portray the terrible sufferings of the martyrs (as many of the illustrations in this book show). Their resilience would not have seemed so miraculous if their ordeals had not been so excruciating, so to understand the influence the martyrs have had, we must look as the ancient Romans did and not recoil (too much) from the graphic descriptions. The deaths in the arena in the first two centuries were bad enough, but things got worse in 249 with the advent of Emperor Decius, when the perceived struggle between good and evil escalated.

ESCALATING PERSECUTIONS

In part, the third-century persecutions grew from an imperial decree by the Emperor Caracalla, who in 212, extended citizenship to all free persons in the empire. Caracalla probably had no religious motives for his act, indeed many of his contemporaries thought he was simply trying to increase the tax base because all citizens had to pay a tax. However, once the distinctions between citizen and noncitizen were erased, many Romans believed that the privilege of citizenship came with religious obligations.

The empire faced many crises during the mid-third century. There were civil wars with scores of claimants to the imperial throne, and each was backed by his own army. As if that were not trouble enough, the borders of Rome seemed fearfully permeable and hundreds of thousands of barbarians from the north swept into the empire while Persians threatened from the east. During these dark times, Romans turned even more fiercely to their traditional religious practices. In 248, as part of a ritual desire to ensure Rome's prosperity, an emperor who ruled briefly (Philip the Arab) celebrated the one-thousandth anniversary of the founding of Rome. "Millenarian celebrations" began during which residents celebrated for three days and nights, and smoke arose from all the altars of the pagan temples as the faithful sacrificed in celebration of the past one thousand years and in hope of another one thousand years to come. During these celebrations, Romans could not help but see that

Christians did not share their joyous festivals, and they really noticed how many Christians there were.

In the years before 250, the church had grown remarkably. North Africa had at least ninety bishops and a well-organized hierarchy to support them. In Rome alone, there were 155 clergy and more than fifteen hundred widows being supported by the charity of the church.[27] Many of the new converts were wealthy and influential, and more important, highly visible in the community. These were the people who did not celebrate the millennium, and their neighbors noticed. When plague struck in 249 and added to the misery of the age, religious Romans looked once again for someone to blame.

Decius became emperor at the end of 249, and he planned to restore Rome to its old glory. On 3 January 250, he solemnly performed the annual sacrifice to Jupiter on the Capitol, and furthermore he ordered that his example be followed in the capitals of every city in the empire. The sacrifice was to be performed by everyone (not simply suspected Christians) and involved sacrificing to the deity and eating the sacrificial meat. Those who sacrificed received a written certificate proving their loyalty.

When the emperor took his stand against Christian worship, it appeared that the battle foretold by John in Revelations was fulfilled. Now many Christians believed that the struggle between good and evil had really been launched, and tragically it appeared that all too many Christians quickly leaped to the side of evil. Some who were summoned were so frightened for their lives that they quickly sacrificed. Others who were concerned about their jobs and public positions came forward quickly to prove they were good, loyal citizens.[28] Even in Carthage, which had been a center for early Christianity, so many people rushed to the marketplace in their haste to perform the sacrifice that all could not be accommodated in one day. By evening the magistrates had to delay the sacrifices and cause the Christians to come back the next day.[29] The mass defections posed a much greater threat to the church than the persecutions that had taken relatively few lives in the previous century and a half.

Ironically, perhaps, the very fact that so many lacked the courage to become martyrs led to an enhanced respect for those Christians who did stand firm. Some—like the church father Origen—were arrested, tortured, then released. These became known as "confessors" and were given as much or more respect as priests. Martyrs who died for their faith probably numbered no more than a few hundred throughout the empire, but their witness was much admired—particularly in contrast to the many who lapsed. By the end of 250 the persecution was over; Decius died in battle the next year, and Christian leaders were left to reassemble their congregations after the frightening conflagration that had tested the faithful and found many wanting.

Over the next fifty years there were occasional local persecutions, but Christians around the empire experienced peace, and the congregations reassembled. Provisions were made to restore the "lapsed," (those who had renounced their Christian faith) and as the stories of brave martyrs circulated, the church grew. In North Africa alone, the number of bishops probably doubled.[30] However, most of the newly enrolled converts were no more ready to undergo martyrdom than they had been in 250. Eusebius noted the problem with the new congregations: "But increasing freedom transformed our character to arrogance and sloth."[31] Perhaps people thought the struggle was over, but in fact the final test—the Great Persecution—was about to begin.

Diocletian became emperor in 285 when the empire was experiencing continued crises on many fronts: invasions, plague, economic troubles. The emperor was rather dour and autocratic by nature and seemed to have believed that with his word and his will he could save the empire. He surrounded himself with trappings of autocracy, for now people had to approach him and prostrate themselves on the ground. He required his subjects to address him as Lord (*Dominus*) and obey unfailingly. His plan to bring peace and order to the empire involved bringing about uniformity and obedience throughout. He set prices, wages, and jobs, and it is thus not surprising that he turned to religious obedience as well.

On 23 February 303, Diocletian began a persecution that was to be the final struggle for the allegiance of the empire, and many believed that here finally was the struggle John had predicted. Diocletian knew the power of the blood of martyrs, and he ordered none to be shed.[32] Instead he wanted to recall Christians to do their duty as loyal Romans, and stop practicing the new religion. This persecution at first was aimed at the organization of the church, its influential members, its buildings and scriptures. With his autocratic inclinations, Diocletian believed if you cut off the head the rest will die. Eusebius described the early stage of the struggle:

> I saw with my own eyes the places of worship thrown down from top to bottom, to the very foundations, the inspired holy Scriptures committed to the flames in the middle of the public squares, and the pastors of the churches hiding disgracefully in one place or another, while others suffered the indignity of being held up to ridicule by their enemies.[33]

Many Christians (and their leaders) fled the cities into the hills to wait out the storm, but the pressure only increased. During the summer, a second edict was promulgated that said all bishops and other Christian leaders should be arrested and forced to sacrifice. This created further chaos because of the large numbers involved. Prisons had not been built to hold so many, so there was no room for real criminals—murderers and grave robbers.[34] At one point, the Romans gave up on prisons (they never built many anyway) and fell back on their traditional punishment of criminals: sending them to the mines to be worked to death, usually in less than a year. At one point, a government official offered (sarcastically?) to grant a "humane" solution to the controversy: he issued an order that soldiers should "hack out one eye with a sword and cauterize it with fire, and render the left foot useless by branding-irons applied to the joints" and then send these Christians to work in the province's copper mines.[35] This decree shows a certain desperation; the idea of treating Christian citizens like criminals just was not working.

Therefore, this decree was quickly followed by another that said if the prisoners offered a sacrifice, they should be released, but if they refused, "they should be mutilated by endless tortures."[36] The persecution that began against buildings and books now began to create martyrs in larger numbers than ever before. The blood of martyrs was spilled again, once again paradoxically giving heart to the frightened Christians who watched their brave deaths. By this decree, the persecutions of Diocletian introduced a new, horrible element in the history of the struggle for the soul of the empire: torture. To understand the experience and victory of the martyrs, we need to look more closely at the psychology of torture (which unfortunately still applies in the twenty-first century).

In its origins (and in much modern usage), torture was a legally regulated way of seeking evidence in criminal cases. The Roman jurist Ulpian (third century) wrote, "By torture we are to understand the torment and suffering of the body in order to elicit the truth."[37] Under Roman law (and the Greek law that preceded it) slaves had to be tortured to use their testimony since the ancients assumed that slaves would not tell the truth otherwise. Therefore, when Pliny questioned the two Christian slaves to find out about their practices, he had to torture them for their testimony to be accepted in law.

In the early martyrdoms (before 250), torture seldom appears, and when it does, it adheres to the rules of Roman law—it is applied to slaves to seek evidence. In the account of the martyrs of Lyons, the two slaves Blandina and Sanctus were severely tortured. Witnesses were amazed that the small woman, Blandina, withstood so much torture—"her whole body was mangled and her wounds gaped"—but her confession remained the same: "I am a Christian: we do nothing to be ashamed of."[38] This testimony is reminiscent of the torture of the slave by Pliny to determine the activities of Christians. Sanctus, too, was tortured to "force him to utter something improper," but he refused even to give his name, birthplace, or nationality to the questioners, instead insisting, "I am a Christian."[39] After this inquiry, the Christians were condemned to the beasts in the arena, and their painful deaths continued.

With the persecutions of Decius and even more under Diocletian, the circumstances had changed. These persecutions intended not simply to execute those who came to the attention of the authorities but to force everyone to conform to the cultic worship of the empire. The same reasons that led to the expanded executions led to the increase in torture—the central authority and the empire itself was weakened. When power slips, those who want to hold it try extralegal means to do so, and this was as true in the third century as it is today. Thus, torture was used not just to extract evidence (which was legal) but to compel behavior. In the late third century, Diocletian issued an edict designed to bring the laws into conformity with practice: he said that all Christians should lose their privileged status (as citizens) and thus be subject to torture.[40]

Many Christians believed this meant the intensification of the struggle between the two great powers—Rome and Christ—that had been foretold. Eusebius explained the edict concisely: "if the prisoners offered sacrifice they should be allowed to go free, but if they refused they should be mutilated by endless tortures."[41]

What this meant in practice was that judges and other officials could resort to torture to try to make Christians sacrifice on the altars of Rome, and the sources tell of the terrible suffering that the Christians experienced. One man in Nicomedia was brought in and commanded to sacrifice. When he refused, he was stripped and whipped. Then his torturers mixed vinegar with salt and poured it over his wounds that were so deep even the bones showed. Finally, they put him on a slow fire to torture him further without killing him until he would perform the sacrifice. He "stuck immovably to his determination, and victorious in the midst of his tortures, breathed his last."[42] Experiences like this are recounted many times in the sources, varied only by the torturers' brutal creativity in devising new and different torments, like those described by the ancient historian:

> But words cannot describe the outrageous agonies endured by the martyr.
> . . . They were torn to bits from head to foot with potsherds like claws till
> death released them. Women were tied by one foot and hoisted high in
> the air, head downwards, their bodies completely naked without a morsel
> of clothing, presenting thus the most shameful, brutal, and inhuman of
> all spectacles to everyone watching. Others again were tied to trees and
> stumps and died horribly; for with the aid of machinery they drew
> together the very stoutest boughs, fastened one of the martyr's legs to
> each, and then let the boughs fly back to their normal position; thus they
> managed to tear apart the limbs of their victims in a moment. In this way
> they carried on, not for a few days or weeks, but year after year.[43]

Christians and Romans alike found the resilience of the martyrs (and confessors, because some did survive the torture) to be miraculous. They believed God imbued their very bodies with supernatural grace to withstand the tortures, which had long-standing implications for Christian views of the body (which I will explore in depth in chapter 2).

However, beyond the miraculous, modern studies on the psychology of torture may also shed light on what both the torturers and the victims were experiencing.

The point of torture is to inflict pain, so much pain that it dominates the victim's world. As someone experiences such overriding pain, one's reality contracts so that all he or she feels is the body in pain. Nothing else matters as much as the pain,[44] and the victim disassociates from all the things that seemed to matter so much before. For modern torturers, this achieves the purpose of extracting information and betraying loyalties not simply to avoid pain but because nothing matters anymore besides the body's feelings. This experience parallels that of people who are dying, for as the body gives way, it becomes the center of the patient's experience and the world recedes.

At the same time, the torturer experiences a transformation during the process, but instead of his world contracting, it expands. The torturer feels more powerful in direct proportion to the degree the victim is forced to contract his world into one existing solely of bodily pain.[45] The torturer's power is complete at the moment when the victim gives the required information, or in the case of the martyrs, performs the required sacrifice. Victims will have given up the things that had connected them to the world, the things that had once seemed important enough to suffer for.

Unfortunately, through most of history when torture is practiced as a mechanism of state authority, it often works. Even Galileo confessed that the earth did not rotate around the sun. He confessed not just to stop the torture but, perhaps more insidiously, because it just did not matter anymore if the universe was heliocentric. Under extreme pain, one's deep commitments leave, and perhaps ultimately this is as great a suffering as the bodily pain itself.

This is what the Romans under the late persecutions tried to do—torture people so they no longer cared enough about their faith to adhere to it—but in most cases it did not work. It appears that if a Christian were going to recant, it happened more often under the threat of torture rather than under the torture itself. While divine intervention may have helped sustain the victims (which is what the sources claimed), I believe that the dynamic of the torture itself contributed to the martyrs' resolve. The Romans were trying to do exactly the opposite of what torture accomplishes: they wanted the Christians to *re*associate with the world, that is the world of Rome and its gods. Instead, torture *dis*associates people from the world. The more pain the confessors experienced the more they focused on the next world rather than this one. You can torture people *out* of loyalties, not *into* them.

The text of the martyrdom of Montanus and Lucius show that within the Christian communities, confessors knew of this disassociation and the way it helped them withstand torture. A confessor experienced a vision in which the martyr Cyprian appeared to him. He asked Cyprian if the final death blow was painful. Cyprian replied "It is another flesh that suffers when the soul is in heaven. The body does not feel this at all when the mind is entirely absorbed in God."[46]

The dissociation from worldly concerns is demonstrated in many of the accounts of the martyrs, including that of Irenaeus, Bishop of Sirmeum, who was arrested during the persecution of Diocletian. Irenaeus was tortured until he was bruised and bloodied, then his family was brought in to plead with him. (During these early years bishops could marry.) His children kissed his feet and begged, "Father have pity on yourself and on us!" His wife, too, was weeping and pleaded with him, but Irenaeus was unmoved. As the text said, "He was gripped by a much stronger passion . . . and made no reply to anyone; for he was in haste to attain the hope of his heavenly calling." Later, when his torturer questioned him about his wife and children, the martyr claimed to have no family.[47] The martyr's detachment was so complete that he even "lied" to the torturer, violating the Roman notion that the truth emerged under torture. Yet, the exchange is exactly what one might expect from complete disassociation with the world that goes on in torture.

The tortures were fierce and frightening to those who watched.

> Things that would make the hearer shudder were done. . . . Pointed reeds were driven into the fingers of both hands under the ends of the nails; in other cases lead was melted over a fire and the boiling seething mass poured down their backs, roasting the vital parts of the body; others endured in their private parts and bowels sufferings shameful, merciless, and unmentionable, which the noble judges, upholders of the law, showing off their brutality as proof of their cleverness, most ingeniously devised. . . .[48]

The more the torturers escalated the torments, the more the Christians disassociated from this world and focused on the next—to the comfort of the faithful and the frustration of the pagans. Since the tortures were not working, power did not flow in expected ways to the tormentors. In fact, the reverse was true: the pagans lost power by their inability to persuade through cruelty. As Eusebius noted, "In this state of affairs some died under their tortures, shaming their adversary by their unshakeable determination."[49] Through this public failure (since most of the tortures were public), pagan Romans were shamed, lost power, and the Christians gained respect and strength. The expected relationship between torturer and tortured was reversed in the case of the martyrs, and Christianity grew.

As the deaths increased, so did the resistance of surviving Christians. Many were convinced that Rome was the evil power that first raised its head during the persecutions of Nero, and Diocletian's vision of a restored, dignified pagan empire disappeared in the flames and blood of persecution. After a decade of persecution, the church was stronger than ever, and both pagan and Christian witnesses to the persecutions knew that too many good and honorable people had been killed. They also knew that the courage of Christian martyrs marked a strength of purpose that was lacking in the pagan temples.

The final failure of the brutal persecution initiated by Diocletian marked the end of the great struggle between the faith and Rome that was initiated by Nero and described in cosmic terms in the Book of Revelations. Torture is the last resort of regimes fading in power, and by increasing the Christians' focus on the next world, Rome lost the battle for this one. All that was lacking to bring about a final Christian victory was a leader. He arrived in the person of Emperor Constantine.

In 312 Constantine gathered an all-too-small army and marched on competing claimants to the throne. Constantine's forces were outnumbered about three to one, and it seemed his rival Maxentius would clearly win what looked like a foolhardy challenge by Constantine. However, purportedly on the evening before the battle, Constantine saw a cross in the sky with the writing, in Greek, "By this sign, conquer." This was confirmed by a vision that night that told him to put the monogram for Christ on the armor of his troops. Miraculously—the Christians said—Constantine won the battle at the Milvian Bridge, just north of Rome. With that victory, Constantine secured sole power in the west. Constantine acknowledged his debt to Christ, and in 313 signed the Edict of Milan that proclaimed toleration of Christianity throughout the empire. The age of the martyrs was over; Christ had defeated Rome and Christians everywhere shared Eusebius's euphoria: "Thus all men living were free from oppression by the tyrants and released from their former miseries. . . . There was unspeakable happiness, and a divine joy blossomed in all hearts. . . ."[50]

These centuries of struggle brought about the victory of Christianity in large part through the blood of martyrs. If this were the whole story, however, this book would end here. What ensured that the martyrs' struggles would influence much more than the establishment of the church were the texts that preserved the memory of their deeds. As the fourth-century church father Augustine perceptively observed, the past does not exist. Instead, it continues ever-present in our memories.[51] The deeds of the martyrs were extraordinary–indeed miraculous–but it is the memory of their deeds that continued to haunt the world.

Shrouded bodies rise from the grave in the background, while in the foreground, birds and beasts regurgitate body parts so they can be restored to the eaten at the Resurrection. Eleventh-century mosaic on the west wall of the cathedral at Torcello, near Venice. Published with the permission of the *Ufficio Beni Culturali* of Venice, Italy.

RESURRECTING
THE FLESH

On the third day He rose again from the dead and ascended into heaven." This statement from the Apostles' Creed expresses the central mystery of Christianity. Jesus was crucified to death, and he was buried in a stone tomb in a Jewish cemetery. The third day after his death, his tomb was discovered empty and subsequently Jesus appeared to his disciples. He spent time with them on earth before he ascended bodily into heaven. In this miracle, Christians saw the promise of their own victory over death, as Paul said in his letter to the Romans: "If the Spirit of him who raised Jesus from the dead dwells in you, he who raised Christ Jesus from the dead will give life to your mortal bodies also through his Spirit which dwells in you" (Rom. 8:11). I've stated this miraculous good news in its simplest form here, but the narrative raises as many questions as it answers. What part of the human is resurrected? What form will we take? What degree of identity will we have in the next life? People still discuss these questions, and early Christians debated them with the same vigor as modern ones. For the medieval world (and many in the modern church) the answers were shaped by the experience of the martyrs.

Jesus' resurrection and Christians' subsequent analysis of it took place within a context of ancient understandings of what makes up a human being. Greeks believed the self was made up of body and soul, and the great philosopher Plato articulated the relationship in a way that had a long-standing influence. Plato believed that the body and soul were profoundly opposite. The body was formed of matter and was thus changeable and mortal. The soul on the other hand was incorporeal, eternal, and unchangeable. Thus, the very property of the soul was immortality—that was neither a divine gift nor a miracle—and the expectation at death was that the immortal soul would escape from the flesh that had entrapped it and resume its incorporeal state.

Romans believed death brought the risk of pollution to the family and anyone else in the vicinity, so corpses were carefully buried outside the city, away from the living. Romans believed in a spiritual persistence of the dead, which translated into ancestor worship during which ancestors guarded the living. This relationship with the dead was mutual, however, because the immortality of the deceased depended on the existence of descendants to celebrate an ongoing cult for the dead. After their contacts with Greeks, many Romans adopted the Platonic notion of the immortality of the soul, which could serve to explain their own ancestor veneration.

In earliest Judaism, body and soul were more intimately united, and there was no expectation of an afterlife for either one. However, by the second century B.C., some Jewish thinkers seemed to provide for the possibility of some form of afterlife. For example, the Essenes, who were a spiritual community of Jews living in Qumran by the Dead Sea, believed with Plato that although bodies are perishable, souls will endure and receive either reward or punishment in the afterlife. The first-century Judaic-Roman historian Josephus offered a lyrical description of the Essenes's view of the soul that probably reflects the view of many early Judeo-Christians.

> It is their unshakable conviction that bodies are corruptible and the material composing them impermanent, whereas souls remain immortal forever. Coming forth from the most rarefied ether they are trapped in the prison-house of the body as if drawn down by one of nature's spells; but once freed from the bonds of the flesh, as if released after years of slavery, they rejoice and soar aloft.[1]

By the time of Jesus, Jewish thought was split on the subject of the afterlife: Pharisees were a party of pious Jewish laymen who believed firmly in the strict adherence to Jewish law as expressed in Torah (the Jewish Scriptures). The Pharisees represented the religious leadership of the mass of Palestinian Jews, and their influence on early Christianity was profound. The Pharisees, unlike the Essenes, believed in an afterlife that included the resurrection of the body on Judgment Day. They looked to the scriptures in the Book of Daniel, which they believed predicted this final judgment: "And many of those who sleep in the dust of the earth shall awake, some to everlasting life, and some to shame and everlasting contempt" (Dan. 12:2).

The third influential group of Jews during the time of Jesus were the more traditional Sadducees who were drawn from the wealthy, aristocratic families. Looking back to the earliest Jewish traditions, Sadducees strictly rejected as unscriptural resurrection of the body or even the immortality of the soul. Josephus succinctly summarized their position on this subject: "The permanence of the soul, punishments in Hades, and rewards they deny utterly."[2] The gospels confirm Josephus's description, for they describe Jesus arguing with the Sadducees, "who say there is no resurrection." Jesus claimed the contrary, reprimanding the Sadducees for their error (Mark 12:18–27; Matt. 22:23–33; Luke 20:27–40).

The apostle Paul, too, came into confrontation with the Sadducees over this issue when he was arrested for preaching in Jerusalem. He looked for popular support, crying out "Brethren, I am a Pharisee, a son of Pharisees; with respect to the hope and the resurrection of the dead I am on trial" (Acts 23:6). His statement triggered a controversy between the Pharisees and Sadducees who were present, "For the Sadducees say that there is no resurrection nor angel, nor spirit; but the Pharisees acknowledge them all" (Acts 23:8).

Thus, by the time of Jesus' resurrection, there had already been a lot of discussion about life after death, so Christian analysis had to engage these opinions. The resulting decisions about the resurrection have influenced a number of Western ideas far beyond the limited scope of the afterlife. After all, to decide what part of an individual will rise from the dead goes directly to the question of self-identity—what is it that makes us who we are? People contemplating resurrection also had to confront the question of justice in order to decide just what would be rewarded and punished. Issues of identity and justice remain at the core of many of our beliefs whether we believe in an afterlife or not, and to understand our modern attitudes, we have to look to the age of the martyrs.

As they considered an afterlife in the context of Greek and Jewish thought, Christians emphasized a new feature—the Second Coming of Jesus. For Christians, there are essentially two turning points in our futures. The first turning point is our own death, and the second is the triumphal return of Jesus when all the dead will rise again. As Paul wrote in his letter to the Thessalonians, "For the Lord himself will descend from heaven with a cry of command, with the archangel's call, and with the sound of the trumpet of God. And the dead in Christ will rise . . ." (1 Thess. 4:16). The expectation of the Second Coming brought about a twofold reflection: what would happen to the faithful with their death, and what would happen with the Second Coming?

Many early Christians believed with the Pharisees that the soul and body were joined and both would sleep until the final judgment.[3] They looked back to the Hebrew Scriptures book of the prophet Ezekiel, which described a field of dry bones. God told the prophet to call the bones to life, "and behold, a rattling and the bones came together, bone to bone. And as I looked there were sinews on them, and flesh had come upon them, and skin had covered them." Then they received God's breath and the restored bodies came to life again (Ezek. 37:7–10). Early Christians expecting the imminent return of Christ looked to his pulling together their bones and restoring them to life. However, as hopes for an immediate Second Coming receded, visions of the afterlife changed, and Greco-Roman ideas that separated body and soul came to the fore.

By the late third century, most Christians joined the Greeks in holding that the soul was immortal but that the body had to fall in order to rise again.[4] Christians who had absorbed these ideas of Plato soon displaced the Judaic ideas of the Pharisees, and the immortality of the soul became such a central part of Christian belief that the fourth-century historian, Eusebius, identified those who believed the contrary as heretics. He described a sect called the Helkesaites, who held "a doctrine far removed from the truth, namely, that at the end of our life here the human soul dies for a time along with our bodies and perishes with them; later, when one day the resurrection comes, it will return with them to life."[5] Christian Platonists forcibly argued with these heretics and persuaded them of the immortality of the soul. Thus, by the third century, the orthodox position had become that only the body died when the soul departed. This answered the question of what happens when the faithful die—the soul departs and waits for the final judgment when Christ would come again.

The second question—what happens to the body and soul at the last judgment—was more difficult and generated more controversy. There are essentially three possibilities: (1) only the soul is judged, (2) the soul reenters a transformed body for judgment, and (3) the soul reenters the same body it left for judgment. As I discuss the history of these options, we will see that it was largely the experience of the martyrs that determined that the third choice became the orthodox position. This idea about the resurrection affects Western notions about self, justice, death, and life.

RESURRECTING THE SOUL

By the second century, there were many communities of Christians throughout the Roman Empire, but they did not all remember the message of Jesus in the same way, nor did they even agree on which writings preserved the good news of Christ's message. Some of these groups came to be called "gnostics," and in the second and third centuries orthodox Christians believed gnostics posed a serious threat to the growing church.

Like orthodox Christianity, gnosticism was spread by teachers who traveled and preached. While these teachers differed in various particulars of doctrine, they all believed they possessed secret revealed knowledge that brought truth that was deeper than that possessed by average Christians. The term *gnostic* derives from the Greek for "knowledge," so the term emphasizes the possession of secret truths that only the teachers can reveal. One of the great gnostic teachers was Valentinus, who moved from Alexandria to Rome in about 140. He had such a reputation for holiness and wisdom that he was almost elected bishop but later was expelled as a heretic. Valentinus and his followers wrote a number of treatises that have been preserved in the greatest collection of gnostic writings—the Nag Hammadi texts found in 1945 in Egypt. Within these gnostic scriptures, we get a glimpse of many of the beliefs of gnostic Christians—including how they perceived death and the afterlife.[6]

Gnostics believed that the purpose of a Christian life was to enlighten the soul so it would understand that our goal here is to transcend this material world (which they devalued completely) and focus on higher spiritual truths. The texts reveal a complex mythology that describes a pre-cosmic struggle during which many divine emanations were created in descending order. The struggle ended with the creation of the world during which some sparks of divinity were trapped in the flesh.[7] This precreation hierarchy causes the entrapped spirit, usually identified as the soul, to yearn for ever-higher truths as it lifts itself up through the emanations to more and more wisdom. The gnostic path was a solitary one taken by each soul, as the gnostic *Gospel of Thomas* writes, "Blessed are the solitary and the chosen, for you will find the Kingdom. For you are from it, and to it you will return."[8] The gnostic quest was a strictly spiritual one, outside historical events and largely irrelevant to the struggle with the Roman Empire. Similarly, the gnostic view of Jesus' death and resurrection was different from that of the orthodox.

With their rejection of the flesh, most gnostics downplayed Jesus' crucifixion and death. In the gnostic *Apocalypse of Peter*, for example, the author describes a vision of crucifixion in which Jesus is seen happily in the air watching his own bodily death: "He whom you saw being glad and laughing above the cross, he is the Living Jesus. But he into whose hands and feet they are driving the nails is his fleshly part, which is the substitute."[9] In this interpretation, it is the soul or spirit that matters, not the flesh that entraps it, so Jesus' spirit could watch the mutilation of his body with indifference. The gnostic, Valentinus, claimed that the flesh was no more than a "leather tunic" to be discarded as a suit of old clothes. Indeed, some gnostics described the clothing that Adam and Eve put on at their Fall was their very flesh that encased the soul.[10] Jesus was not a human at all but a spiritual being who adapted himself so humans could see him,[11] and his resurrection was a spiritual one, not one of the body. Therefore, believers could and should hope for a comparable resurrection that would leave the flesh and body behind.

Since gnostics believed Christ's physical death was less significant than his spiritual ascendance, they also believed that martyrdom, which the orthodox saw as an imitation of Christ's suffering, was pointless. One gnostic writer believed it simplistic to think that "through suffering of one hour they purchase for themselves eternal life." Of course, this is exactly what the orthodox Christians believed of martyrdom. Furthermore, this gnostic author ridiculed the idea of martyrdom as a human sacrifice (as discussed in chapter 7) because such a belief makes God into a cannibal who desires flesh.[12] Few gnostics joined the ranks of the martyrs, because they saw no point to it.

This is not to say that gnostics did not believe in a resurrection—after all, Christ's rising from the dead was at the core of Christian faith. Instead, they believed the resurrection was a spiritual one that was almost irrelevant to bodily death. In fact, some gnostics said that death is really the ignorance of God (thus the individual is "dead" to God) and "buried in error" as he would be in the grave.[13] Salvation—the Kingdom of God—did not exist in some longed-for future, it was an internal transformation during life.[14] Then, after death the soul would just continue the ascent that had begun in life as it returned to its origin in the Creator.

Another group of Christians, the Docetists, also devalued the body in favor of the soul. Declared heretical, Docetism shared with the gnostics the belief that Christ's humanity was only a disguise worn by the heavenly Redeemer. They believed that the flesh and blood that witnesses to the crucifixion saw were only an illusion, and that Christ felt no bodily pain. Therefore, at Christ's resurrection, his body continued to be an illusion, and it was his divine spirit that ascended into heaven. They concluded, therefore, that in imitation of Jesus, only our souls will be resurrected, leaving the body behind.

Both these beliefs offered no praise for martyrdom—what is the point in enduring suffering in a body that you will leave behind? Ignatius of Antioch (described in chapter 1), the influential second-century martyr, addressed these points directly in his letter to the faithful of Tralles, near Ephesus. He wrote this correspondence as he was in chains being led to his own martyrdom, and Christians asked him to write to them so they could treasure the final wisdom of the confessor. In this letter, Ignatius wrote in strongest terms against the Docetists who preached compellingly in Asia Minor. Ignatius wrote that if they were right and that Christ's sufferings "were not genuine" there would be no meaning to his own martyrdom:

> If this is so, then why am I now a prisoner? Why am I praying for a combat with the lions? For in that case, I am giving my life for nothing; and all the things I have ever said about the Lord are untruths.[15]

However, the blood of the martyrs and the respect they garnered by their sufferings ensured that the views of the gnostics and the Docetists would not prevail.

Why did it matter? Why couldn't Christianity simply accept the belief held by ancient Greco-Romans (and frankly most modern people) that the soul departs at death and goes on to its reward? The answer turns on the issues of identity and justice. Most people believed as Plato did that the soul is immortal and imperishable: "When death approaches a man, the mortal in him dies, as it seems, but the immortal part goes away undestroyed, giving place to death. . . . Soul is immortal and imperishable, and in fact our souls will exist in the house of Hades [the dark shadowy underworld where the Greeks believed dead souls went]."[16] If the soul is immortal, then it preexisted the body and entered it at some point. (Throughout the Middle Ages thinkers disagreed on when the soul entered—some arguing for at the moment of quickening in the womb, others at birth, and yet others at baptism.) If the same soul then leaves at death, what did the life experience of the individual add to the soul? How does the soul acquire the identity of an individual unless one's memories remain with it? And if the soul did not maintain the identity it acquired during a lifetime, how would we recognize our loved ones in the afterlife? Furthermore, what is the point of rewarding or punishing a soul that lacked identity? There would be no justice in that, and as we saw in chapter 1, the Book of Revelations promised justice for those who prevailed in the struggle between good and evil that was represented by the age of the martyrs. No, most Christians (with Ignatius of Antioch) wanted justice in the afterlife, and thus the body, too, would have to be resurrected. But what kind of body?

RESURRECTING THE BODY

Since the resurrection was the defining moment for early Christians, it is not surprising that people asked the apostle Paul what they might expect. As he wrote in his letter to the Corinthians, "But some one will ask, 'How are the dead raised? With what kind of body do they come?'" (1 Cor. 15:35). Within his answer, Paul established the position that the resurrected body would be dramatically different from the body that had died. The dead body is like a seed that dies but when it is resurrected it will grow into a similar body (for it sprang from the "seed" of the original flesh), but it would be different. As Paul explained,

> For not all flesh is alike, but there is one kind for men, another for animals, another for birds, and another for fish. There are celestial bodies and there are terrestrial bodies; but the glory of the celestial is one, and the glory of the terrestrial is another. . . . So is it with the resurrection of the dead. What is sown is perishable, what is raised is imperishable. It is sown in dishonor, it is raised in glory. It is sown in weakness, it is raised in power. It is sown a physical body, it is raised a spiritual body. If there is a physical body, there is also a spiritual body. (1 Cor. 15:35, 42–44)

He goes on to say that this miracle takes place "in the twinkling of an eye, at the last trumpet," and at that moment the perishable flesh will be raised as immortal flesh (1 Cor. 15:50–54), but he leaves no doubt that the flesh will be transformed. He says, "I tell you this, brethren: flesh and blood cannot inherit the kingdom of God, nor does the perishable inherit the imperishable" (1 Cor. 15:50). Something radically different would be raised to Paradise.

This position satisfies people's desire for preservation of identity, because the new spiritual body would sufficiently resemble the original one so that we will be able to recognize one another on the last day. Furthermore, this body might well preserve the memories and experiences accumulated during a lifetime. In addition, such a reconstituted body might also justly receive punishment and reward for its remembered acts during this life. However, it was a difficult concept for people in the ancient world (and the modern as well) who were familiar with the idea of an immortal soul but uncertain about an immortal body.

The third-century controversial, yet brilliant, church father, Origen, offered an analysis of the resurrection of a transformed body that seemed to reconcile the Platonist notion of immortal soul with Paul's idea of a spiritual body. Origen was a firm believer in the preexistence of souls that through their free will had fallen from God. In this fall, the earth was created and souls were given our earthly bodies. (Many Christians thought these ideas sounded suspiciously like gnostic thoughts, but unlike the heretics, Origen's ideas remained grounded in the experience of the historical Jesus.) The earthly body offers the soul the ability to continue to express its free will and earn salvation. Origen held that after death, the soul would receive a spiritual body, but it would not resemble the earthly one it had acquired as a consequence of the Fall.[17]

Since the soul adopts a body suitable to its surroundings, Origen believed the body had to change to accommodate the different circumstances of the afterlife. He said when the soul comes into the world at birth, "it casts off the integuments which it needed in the womb; and before doing this, it puts on another body suited for its life upon earth."[18] Upon its resurrection, the soul would also assume an appropriate body—a spiritual one "capable of inhabiting the heavens" with no predictable, discernable shape.[19] In a different tract, Origen suggested the resurrected bodies of the saved will become "like the bodies of angels, ethereal and of a shining light." He further suggested that our spiritual bodies will be without age or sex and might even lose all memory of the relationships of earth.[20]

Here Origen moves closer to the Platonic position that emphasizes soul over body, for without sex, age, or memory, how can the soul preserve the identity it acquired during life? Some later Christians followed the implications in Origen's thought to extremes that he perhaps did not, for the Second Council of Constantinople in the sixth century condemned Origen for claiming that our bodies would be resurrected as spheres instead of in the shape of bodies.[21]

Other ancient writers tried to be even more specific about the nature of our resurrected bodies and how they would be transformed. Gregory of Nyssa in the third century, for example, wrote of the body as "globules of mercury, which spring quivering into an indistinguishable mass at the resurrection."[22] God then reassembles these globules into a different—more spiritual—body that lacked genitals, intestines, degrees of weight (being fat or thin), or anything else that was specifically necessary to the brutishness (or changeability) of this world.[23] By insisting that the atoms of the original body would be rearranged, Gregory emphasized more than Origen had the necessity to preserve the identity that somehow lay within the original body. The fourth-century writer Cyril of Jerusalem added an image that I particularly like: our transformed bodies will "shine like iron in fire or glowworms on a summer night."[24]

Both Origen and Gregory scrupulously tried to bridge the gap between old (and highly respected) Platonist ideas of the immortal soul and the dramatic Christian news of the resurrection of the body. Most likely, people who held these views (including Paul) imagined resurrected spiritual bodies as similar to ours, yet transparent—"immaterial"— lacking internal organs and the other necessities of life on this earth that many in the ancient world found crude and disgusting. These spiritual bodies more likely resembled what many imagine as ghosts—spirits who visually resemble the bodies they once inhabited but who are not bound by the physical realities of this world that bind our bodies. And if Cyril is right, we will shimmer with self-contained light in the dark of the universe.

Some of the biblical references to Jesus' resurrected body seemed to support this idea of a transformed body, for he could pass through closed doors (John 20:19) and he warned Mary Magdalene not to touch him for he had not yet "ascended to the father" (John 20:17). In the gospel of Luke, as soon as the apostles recognized the risen Jesus, he vanished from their sight (Luke 24:30), which suggests a spiritual body. As we will see in the following section, there are other scriptural passages that support other interpretations of the resurrected body, but those who shared with Paul and Origen the notion that our new bodies would be dramatically different from these existing ones found comfort in the passages from John.

This model of a resurrected transformed body satisfies the need to preserve identity, because a spiritual body could be recognizable and could remember its experience on earth. Furthermore, such a body could justly be rewarded or punished at the final judgment fulfilling the promises within scripture. What this model failed to consider—or embrace—was the experience of the martyrs. As we have seen in the descriptions and in the illustrations included in this book, their sufferings were profoundly physical. Their tortures called attention to every part of their body, and their resilience and victory was a physical one. Could a belief in resurrected spiritual bodies give sufficient credit to the tortured flesh that had defeated the Romans?

RESURRECTING THE FLESH

The fourth-century irascible church father, Jerome, vigorously attacked the idea of the resurrection of transformed spiritual bodies. He said, "You, [heretic] say 'body' and do not mean 'flesh' at the same time, [for you wish to deceive] the ears of the ignorant. Believe me, your silence is not simple. For 'flesh' has one definition, and 'body' another. . . ."[25] Jerome's strong attack focuses the discussion on what is meant by body. As we have seen, men like Origen (and even Paul) imagined bodies that scarcely resembled our earthly flesh, but those who treasured the suffering of the martyrs would not accept this definition.

As we saw in chapter 1, torture focuses the victim's attention on the body (or in Jerome's definition, on the flesh), and this concentration was expressed in many of the recorded acts and passions of the martyrs. For example, the account of Pionius's martyrdom shows his awareness and appreciation of the fleshly body that served as the avenue to his martyrdom:

> Hastily he went to the amphitheater because of the zeal of his faith, and he gladly removed his clothes as the prison-keeper stood by. Then realizing the holiness and dignity of his own body, he was filled with great joy; and looking up to heaven he gave thanks to God who had preserved him so; then he stretched himself out on the gibbet and allowed the soldier to hammer in the nails.[26]

This language is extraordinary in its praise of the body and its "holiness and dignity." There is nothing here of the disgust that served as a subtext to the discussions of the resurrection of the soul or of spiritual bodies. Pionius sees his flesh as a matter of pride, as the mark of his humanity.

Similar praise was included in the acts of Marian and James, in which the narrator cast scorn on the torturers: "Impious pagans, you could do nothing to God's temple, the coheir with Christ! You hung up his body, beat his sides, racked his bowels, and yet our Marian with his faith in God, grew great in body as well as soul."[27] Here the body is further dignified as God's temple that shared in the victory of Christ. Even Marian's bowels—that were so conspicuously omitted from spiritual bodies—were dignified through the suffering. The text adds an additional detail by claiming that Marian's suffering enhanced not only his soul but his body as well. Through texts like these, Christians began to envision a heaven in which their earthly flesh would be rewarded.

This idea was stated explicitly in the account of the martyrdom of Phileas, which recorded a purported dialogue between the martyr and his judge. There is no reason to think that the dialogue reflected exactly what went on in the trial, but the account did express what Christians who lovingly read the account believed:

> Phileas said: "I have said that you may receive in the body the recompense for the good deeds it has done for God." "The soul alone," said Culcianus, "or the body as well?" "The soul and the body," said Phileas. Culcianus said: "This body?" "Yes," said Phileas. Culcianus said: "This flesh will rise again?" In his amazement he asked once again: "This flesh will rise again?" Phileas said: "This flesh will rise again . . . [in] eternal life."[28]

Many in the Roman world were as astonished as the judge Culcianus at this new idea: this very flesh would be victorious over death.

Christians who believed in the resurrection of the flesh looked to passages in the Bible different from those quoted by people who looked forward to a spiritual body. The most popularly quoted text among these Christians was the story of "doubting Thomas," the apostle who couldn't believe his eyes when he saw Jesus, thinking him a ghost. Jesus said to him, "Put your finger here, and see my hands; and put out your hand, and place it in my side" (John 20:27). Thus, Thomas and many subsequent Christians were persuaded that Jesus' resurrected body was solid; he was not just a ghost or spirit.

A more detailed account of Jesus' corporality was found in the gospel of Luke in which the apostles saw Jesus and they were frightened:

> [They] supposed that they saw a spirit. And he said to them, "Why are you troubled, and why do questionings rise in your hearts? See my hands and my feet, that it is I myself; handle me, and see, for a spirit has not flesh and bones as you see that I have." And while they still disbelieved for joy, and wondered, he said to them, "Have you anything here to eat?" They gave him a piece of broiled fish, and he took it and ate before them. (Luke 24:36–44)

In this passage, Jesus' resurrected body is very much like his living flesh—it is solid and it bears the wounds of the crucifixion in his hands and feet. Most significant, he eats fish, which proclaimed to future theologians that the resurrected body contained stomach and bowels, all denied by proponents of a spiritual body.

Armed with this biblical evidence and the bloody witness of the martyrs, early Christian writers developed a complex theology of the resurrection of the flesh. They meant not only the soul, or a spirit imbued with the soul, but the very flesh that shared the soul's earthly journey. If Christ's body, complete with wounds, stomach, and intestines, was resurrected, then that promised the same for the faithful.

Perhaps not surprisingly, the early theologians who passionately loved the sacrifice of the martyrs also were most adamant in their insistence on the resurrection of the flesh, and the most important of these was Tertullian, who wrote prolifically in Carthage, North Africa, at the turn of the third century. Tertullian was a convert to Christianity, and he came to his new religion with an intensity that combined with his literary talents and legal training to make his writings profoundly influential to the growing church in the western part of the empire. (This is particularly true since Tertullian wrote in Latin, unlike the eastern fathers who preferred Greek. Thus his works had an immediate circulation in the Latin-speaking west.)

Tertullian loved martyrs and martyrdom. He believed God's spirit was most visible in the arena of Carthage where martyrs were tested, and his writings are full of encouragement to imprisoned Christians urging them to joyfully embrace their salvation through the baptism of blood in the violence in the arena. Late in his life, Tertullian witnessed the lull in persecutions at the beginning of the third century, and he was disappointed that the dramatic battle between good and evil seemed to have ended. He wrote with exasperation, "I should not be surprised if people were not figuring out how they could abolish martyrdom . . . ,"[29] and of course he was right that many Christians were happy to embrace their faith without being haunted by the spector of persecution. Without a doubt, Tertullian wished that he could have died a martyr's death, but he was not to be chosen.

His passion for martyrdom shaped many of his writings, including those that most specifically developed a theology of the resurrection of the flesh. His major works on this subject include *On the Flesh of Christ*, *On the Soul*, and *On the Resurrection of the Flesh*. In addition, Tertullian spent much of his energy writing against gnostics, who, as we have seen, advocated a flesh-rejecting resurrection of the spirit. Through these passionate tracts written in clear Latin, Christians saw the theoretical link between the blood of the martyrs in the arenas and their own resurrection of the flesh.

Like others in the ancient (and modern) world, Tertullian believed human identity to consist of body and soul; however, for him (unlike the gnostics and Origen) the soul possessed many characteristics of a body. It "possessed corporality," which means it was made of a substance, as he wrote, "For *nothing* it certainly is, if it is not a bodily substance."[30] He claimed that after God breathed a soul into an infant, the soul "spread itself throughout all the spaces of the body; and . . . impressed itself on each internal feature. . . . Hence, by this densifying process, there arose a fixing of the soul's corporeity. . . ."[31] The soul then grows and changes with the body's growth taking on the identity of the body that imprinted it. In a sense, for Tertullian, the soul very much resembles the transformed bodies of Paul and Origen, for in response to a question about what color the soul is, Tertullian says it is an "etherial transparent one."[32] If Origen and Tertullian saw the same ghost, the first would identify it as the resurrected saved body and the second would claim it was the corporeal soul.

For Tertullian, death was the separation of the soul from its body, for he agreed that the soul was immortal and indivisible.[33] The ghostly soul that kept the shape and imprint of its body went immediately to an afterlife. Echoing modern Islamic beliefs, Tertullian claimed that martyrs went directly to paradise to receive their reward, and they were the only souls who could do so. "The sole key to unlock Paradise is your own life's blood."[34] The suffering of the martyrs was so intense that Tertullian's fierce sense of justice required that they receive immediate reward.

The rest of the souls went to Hades and began accounting for their deeds on earth. Since souls are immortal, they do not need to wait for the resurrection of the flesh to begin to be punished for what they had done in partnership with the flesh.[35] Of course, as even Tertullian noted, this model raised the question of why there had to be a resurrection of the flesh at all if the corporeal soul was already being punished or rewarded after death? The theologian answered his critics by falling back again to his deep sense of justice. The soul participated in sins by its will or its thought—all the intangibles that lead us to action. The body on the other hand performed those acts, so the body had to be resurrected on the last day to participate in the promised justice.[36]

For Tertullian, identity consisted of both soul and body: "Now since the entire man consists of the union of the two natures" and thus justice requires the reward and punishment to the whole person: "he should be judged in his entirety."[37] Tertullian's legal mind envisioned God as a judge, and he had complete confidence in His justice: "Now we are not permitted to suppose that God is either unjust or idle. Unjust, however He would be, were He to exclude from reward *the flesh* which is associated in good works. . . ."[38] Tertullian found it impossible and "unworthy of God . . . that this flesh of ours should be torn by martyrdom, and another wear the crown."[39]

Therefore, on the last day, the bodies would be resurrected and rejoin their souls to complete the justice that God promised in the Book of Revelation to those who engaged in the struggle of good against evil. For Tertullian this struggle was that of the martyrs against Rome, but later Christians would see the struggle as our own paths to negotiate the temptations of this life.

Since his souls looked very much like transformed bodies, what kind of bodies did Tertullian envision would rise out of the dust of their graves? First of all, these resurrected bodies would retain their identity, and this included all the visual characteristics that defined us in this life, even if we will not need them in the afterlife. Tertullian addressed in detail questions about why we would need teeth and stomachs and bowels when we will not eat, hands when we will not work, or sexual organs when we will not procreate. Through these answers, he made sure he negated the imagined resurrection of a bodyless soul of the gnostics. He claimed that all our organs either can serve different functions in the afterlife—a mouth can praise God instead of eating—or can simply continue as marks of our identity. Our teeth make our mouths look more attractive so we will have them after the resurrection.[40] All our memories will be preserved, since they, too, are part of our identity.[41] We would not be who we are without all our parts and thoughts. As Tertullian summarizes, "And so the flesh shall rise again, wholly in every man, in its own identity, in its absolute integrity."[42]

Tertullian's definition of identity as residing in our flesh continues to echo in modern ideas far divorced from questions of resurrection. For example, for many people issues of race or ethnic identity lie in our "blood"—our genetic background. For others such attributions lie in cultural characteristics or spiritual associations, thus locating identity within the soul or spirit rather than in the flesh and blood. Adults who had been adopted as children who search for birth parents are longing for identity of the flesh, and generally those who do not search identify with their cultural parents. Examples can multiply, but these might serve to show how our struggles with identity often remain embedded in our flesh.

Ancient discussions of resurrection of the flesh inform important ideas even beyond identity. At the same time Tertullian was arguing for the resurrection of the flesh after death, he made a case for the excellence of the flesh that we bear during life. Through such arguments, theologians' opinion of our living bodies was resurrected from the negative rejection of the flesh as a simple prison for the spirit. Tertullian argued that although the living body was admittedly frail and subject to pain—"wounds, and fever, and gout"[43]—it is much more than this. People who focus on our weaknesses are thinking about the substance of this frail flesh, not the "dignity and skill of the maker."[44] Tertullian argues that the great ideas generated by the spirit are made manifest only through the flesh. Wonderful speeches are possible only with the mouth; great arts are created with the hands, and in fact everything excellent in life exists because the flesh has made substantial the ideas of the mind. Tertullian quite rightly claims that Christianity gave the flesh new dignity: if Christ put flesh on to save us and if God chooses to resurrect it, then the flesh must be central to both our lives and our salvation.[45] Through works like these, Christianity was saved from being only a religion of the spirit, and the blood of the martyrs helped dignify the flesh.

The last creative act of the flesh in this life is dying,[46] and for Tertullian dying meant dissolution and decay. The body dissolves into its tiniest parts but does not disappear. The image of death that he (and many others) used most frequently was digestion.[47] Martyrs' flesh was consumed in the arena by beasts, but that was a visible metaphor for all the dead that are digested into decay from "the devouring fires, and the waters of the sea, and the maws of beasts, and the crops of birds and the stomach of fishes, and time's own great gullet itself."[48] Even when the cadaver is respectfully placed in the grave, it is consumed by worms (that inhabited most living bodies anyway). As Augustine claimed, "All men born of the flesh, are they not also worms?"[49] Death was only the final victory of the small creatures who had lived in and on the body of the human host.[50]

Thus, death is dissolution by digestion, and even many of the images of hell drawn throughout the Middle Ages portray hell as a great mouth that consumes the damned. Salvation, then, is a victory over decay, and it is this victory that was the most astonishing miracle. In one of Ignatius's letters, he used images that were shocking as they embraced the reality of death as digestion: "Leave me to be a meal for the beasts, for it is they who can provide my way to God. I am His wheat, ground fine by the lions' teeth to be made purest bread for Christ. Better still, incite the creatures to become a sepulcher for me; let them not leave the smallest scrap of my flesh. . . ."[51] The martyr was willing to confront and conquer one of the greatest fears of the ancients, to be eaten by beasts instead of receiving a decent burial. The Romans watching wondered how God could reassemble these pieces of flesh that had been consumed and spread beyond the confines of a peaceful grave.

Tertullian reprimanded people who believed that although God was powerful enough to create the world in the first place, he is not able to reassemble the bits of flesh that were consumed by death. "For if God produced all things whatever out of nothing, He will be able to draw forth from nothing even the flesh which had fallen into nothing."[52] Once Tertullian had demonstrated that the resurrection of the flesh was central to God's plan, this last miracle of reassembling the lost pieces was a small miracle indeed for the Almighty. Many of the images of resurrection include animals and fishes regurgitating the flesh they consumed on the last day, and these images vividly testify to the victory of this flesh over digestion, decay, and death itself.

Most of the medieval theologians after Tertullian continued and built on the theology of the resurrection of the flesh, but none defended it with such passion (and detail) as this fierce proponent of martyrdom.[53] There could be no justice if the flesh was not resurrected to share with the soul its reward, and there could be no identity without the body that shared in the choices made by the soul in this life. The fourth-century bishop, Augustine, who was the most influential theologian of all, summarized these principles, and promised that the martyrs' bodies will be restored at the resurrection but that the scars left from the tortures they experienced will remain as badges of honor: "For in those wounds there will be no deformity, but only dignity, and the beauty of their valor will shine out, a beauty *in* the body and yet not *of* the body."[54]

Here, in the end, is the victory promised by the crucifixion of Christ and the suffering of the martyrs—identity preserving even our glorious scars and justice rewarding the deeds that earned those scars. Through these theologians, Christians rejected the idea that the soul alone would escape this body, leaving it behind. Nor would they accept the idea of a transformed body that imperfectly resembles the living flesh. No, for Christians for at least the next millennium and a half, the flesh as well as the soul would be vindicated at the end of time. However, perhaps not surprisingly, early Christians began to venerate the sanctified remains of the flesh here on earth.

REMNANTS OF HEROIC FLESH: RELICS

The pagan world was dramatically separated from the Christian world in its attitude toward cadavers. Decaying bodies were considered polluting and were burned, buried, or both as soon as possible, away from the cities that were the spaces of the living. The Greek playwright, Euripedes, poetically summed up ancient views when he wrote, "It is not right for me to look upon the dead, and stain my eyesight with the mists of dying men."[55] The ancient dead were to be carefully and quickly shut away to keep decay away from the living. Ancient Roman tombs were respectfully and discretely tended by families, and the living mourned and separated themselves from the tragedy of death. The pagan Celsus in the second century stated the strongly felt pagan position: "For what sort of human soul is it that has any use for a rotted corpse of a body? . . . [C]orpses should be disposed of like dung, for dung they are."[56]

Christian martyrs changed all that. The faithful who watched the brave resilience of the martyrs knew beyond a shadow of doubt that God had given the martyr's body the strength to withstand his or her ordeal. The account of the martyrdom of Pionius describes the miraculous events that occurred when his body was burned: "[It was like] . . . that of an athlete in full array at the height of his powers. His ears were not distorted; his hair lay in order on the surface of his head; and his beard was full as though with the first blossom of hair. His face shone once again—wondrous grace!"[57] Readers of this account were reassured that even the flesh of the martyrs was holy.

When the martyr's soul went quickly to its reward, his or her body remained on earth waiting for the final judgment when its soul would reclaim it, but during this sojourn, people believed the flesh retained the power that God had given it during its ordeal. This caused Christians to treasure bodily remnants in ways that caused pagans much disgust. After Marian's mother had watched her son be decapitated for his faith, she was happy at the strength of his flesh, and "again and again with religious devotion she pressed her lips to the wounds of his neck."[58]

Perhaps a mother could be forgiven for this extravagant display, but this behavior extended to people unrelated to a martyr. For example, a wealthy Carthaginian woman, Lucilla, had purchased a bone of a martyr. She took it to church with her and kissed it before she took the Eucharist.[59] Another pious Carthaginian noblewoman, Megetia, came with passion to the shrine of Saint Stephen, whose bones had recently been moved to near Carthage. There was an iron grill protecting a cubicle that contained the relics so people could see but not touch the precious bones. When Megetia came, she was carried away with the "longings of her heart . . . [and] her whole body." She beat herself against the grill until it collapsed and she "pushed her head inside and laid it on the holy relics resting there, drenching them with her tears."[60]

This kind of passionate attachment to the martyr's remains led Christians to seek out these holy remnants to preserve their power. For a typical example, after Fructuosus and his companions were burned, their fellow Christians waited until night fell then stealthily entered the amphitheater with flagons of wine to quench the flames on the still-smoldering bodies. Then "each collected the ashes of the martyrs, so far as he could, and claimed them for his own."[61]

As Christians rushed to preserve and venerate the bodies of the holy dead, pagan Romans tried to prevent it. After the martyrdoms in Lyon in 170, the authorities swept the ashes of the martyrs into the river Rhône "so that not a single relic of their bodies might be left on earth."[62] At another time, after the death of the martyr Vincent, the officials tried to feed his remains to wild animals, and when that failed, to sink them in the sea (see chapter 9). During some persecutions, Christians were forbidden to enter the burial areas of Christians.[63]

Not only were these efforts designed to prevent the bodies of martyrs from stimulating further worship and conversion but they reflected the pagan frustration at such "unseemly" behavior. The emperor Julian (who ruled from 360–363) was known as the "Apostate," because he tried to restore pagan worship after the Christian victory under Constantine and his successors. Julian tried to legislate traditional Roman burial practices to keep Christians from venerating relics, and his complaint about Christian processions show the deep change that had come into the lives of the men and women of antiquity:

The carrying of the corpses of the dead through a great assembly of people, in the midst of dense crowds, staining the eyesight of all with ill-omened sights of the dead. What day so touched with death could be lucky? How, after being present at such ceremonies, could anyone approach the gods and their temples?[64]

For all of Julian's expression of horror at the pollution that he believed accompanied the handling of body parts, he was too late. By 360, burial shrines of martyrs were a central part of Christian worship, and processions displaying relics were a popular form of Christian celebration.

Cemeteries outside the walls that had been ignored by pious Romans became centers of the ecclesiastical life of pious Christians. Martyrs' bodies were buried with great ceremony to become centers of worship, and people vied to have the holy dead buried near their own burial chambers. The living made pilgrimages to these burial places and focused their spiritual longings on the spirit-filled bones the martyrs had left behind.[65] The topography of ancient cities had been transformed and shrines for the bones of the dead became part of the landscape of the living.

In Rome, the most dramatic example of this shift in the burial spaces is the great catacomb system—the Christian burial ground beneath the city itself. In the second century, Christians began to bury their dead in these tombs, which became a venerated community of the Christian dead. There are more than sixty catacombs in Rome with hundreds of miles of galleries with niches to receive the dead. Christians wanted to be buried together and near the remains of martyrs. To walk in these deep hallways is to vividly experience the respect the Christians brought to the remains; Roman disgust for dead bodies was replaced with the veneration of the remains.

The faithful guarded and venerated the flesh of martyrs as part of their belief in Christ's resurrection and part of the hope for their own. But almost immediately, people began to believe that these powerful relics performed miracles (see chapter 3). Augustine in his monumental work *City of God* wrote with wonder at the power of relics. He asked, "How is it that the martyrs, who were slain for the faith that proclaims this resurrection, have the power to work such marvels?"[66] He is not sure exactly of the mechanism that permits the miracles, but he is sure that the miracles reaffirm the promise of the resurrection of the flesh.[67]

With Augustine, then, the evidence of the martyrs' witness comes full circle. Their death in the flesh proved the necessity for its resurrection, and the miraculous power remaining in their relics offered the final proof for believers that the martyrs' flesh—and our flesh—like Christ's would be resurrected on the last day. Furthermore, medieval (and many modern) Christians believe that like the martyrs, our identity resides in our flesh and it is our flesh that will experience God's full justice.

St. James magically appearing before Christian forces to kill Muslims. The late date of the sculpture shows the endurance of the idea of the warrior martyr who magically fights for the faithful. In this case, martyrdom is transformed from victim to warrior. "Santiago Matamoreos" sculpture in the cathedral at Santiago de Compostela. 18th century. Photo by L. Meuris.

3

MAGIC AND THE
WARRIOR MARTYR

A t the time of Jesus and the apostles, people were seeking truth among many competing deities. How could one know which deity offered true hope and salvation? In fact, what most people in the Roman Empire (and perhaps today) sought was a way to bridge what seemed a huge chasm between humans and their deities. The second-century writer, Plutarch, called this search a "longing for the divine,"[1] but how would one know that the separation between this world and the next had been spanned? For many (both educated and not), the proof of the presence of the divine lay in magic that briefly seemed to overturn the rules of this world, proving that the gods had intervened. (At this point, I do not draw a distinction between magic and the miraculous—both overturn the rules of nature,[2] but as we shall see, the difference between miracles and magic was defined during early centuries of Christianity.)

Jesus himself combined the miraculous with his message as he traveled and preached. As the gospel of Matthew says, "And he went about all Galilee, teaching in their synagogues and preaching the gospel of the kingdom and healing every disease and every infirmity among the people" (Matt. 4:23–25). This pattern of proving the message by the magic continued after Jesus' crucifixion.

After Jesus' ascension into heaven, the apostles traveled and preached of the good news of His message. While some were persuaded by apostolic rhetoric, more came to belief through the magical or miraculous "signs" that accompanied their travels. For example, the Book of Acts tells of the apostle Philip's travels to Samaria where many people "gave heed to what was said by Philip, when they heard him and saw the signs which he did. For unclean spirits came out of many who were possessed, crying with a loud voice; and many who were paralyzed or lame were healed" (Acts 8:6–7). As this account shows, the most common miracle was healing, whether mental illnesses ("unclean spirits") or physical problems; the natural world of pain and suffering was suspended in the presence of the divine that accompanied the apostles.

The story of Philip's travels continues with a description of a competing "magician," Simon Magus (which means "the magician"), and the account is instructive for a number of reasons. At the most basic level, it shows a worldview in which magic played an instrumental role; in addition, in later church history, Simon comes to take a large place in the history of Christian thought. Finally, and most significant for this book, Simon defines the dividing line between acceptable and unacceptable magic–between sorcery and miracle. Simon had practiced magic in Samaria before Philip came to the region, and he had a great reputation, "because for a long time he had amazed them with his magic" (Acts 8:11). Simon's reputation was so great that people said of him, "This man is that power of God which is called great" (Acts 8:10), which meant that he accomplished the goal of bringing the divine into the realm of this world.

However, even Simon was impressed with Philip's deeds–"seeing signs and great miracles performed, he was amazed"–and Simon was baptized and followed the apostle (Acts 8:13). When the apostles Peter and John heard that Philip had baptized many in Samaria, they came to visit the new congregations in that region. When they arrived, they performed another sort of miracle. They laid their hands on the newly baptized and prayed that they might "receive the Holy Spirit; for it had not yet fallen on any of them. . . . Then they laid their hands on them and they received the Holy Spirit" (Acts 8:16–17).

It is hard to know exactly what happened when the Holy Spirit entered the new converts; centuries later, Eusebius described some miraculous gifts that were manifested in the early communities as the Spirit descended on the faithful: "Some have foreknowledge of the future, visions, and prophetic utterances; others, by the laying on of hands, heal the sick and restore them to health; and . . . dead men have actually been raised and have remained with us for years."[3] His account probably mirrors the experiences of the earlier congregations, which claimed the baptized acquired some of the magical powers that the Apostles possessed. However, the most common manifestation of the presence of the Spirit was glossolalia (speaking in tongues) or other prophetic utterances.[4] These manifestations seemed to prove the presence of the divine in the early Christian communities, and Simon Magus coveted the power to bring on these manifestations.

Simon said to the apostles, "Give me also this power, that any one on whom I lay my hands may receive the Holy Spirit," and he offered them money in exchange for the spiritual gift. Peter was furious at the assumption that Simon could "obtain the gift of God with money" (Acts 9:19–22). It was from this incident that later churchmen would coin the word *simony*, naming the purchase of church offices after this biblical magician who first tried to buy grace with silver.

While the biblical story of Simon Magus ends here, other ancient sources develop his story in much greater detail. The apocryphal acts of the apostles Peter and Paul write in detail about two trials of magical strength between Peter and Simon. The two appear before Nero–the emperor we discussed in chapter 1 who introduced the struggle between good and evil–and it is perhaps not surprising that this emperor is chosen to preside over the test between good and evil magic. According to the texts, Simon performed an astonishing number of magical feats: he made bronze serpents move, statues laugh and walk, and he shifted his own shape to appear as a boy, an old man, and even a woman. He jumped into fires unharmed, became invisible, passed through walls, and even flew. Peter remained unimpressed, and he achieved his final victory during Simon's demonstration of his flying abilities. As Simon flew from a high tower built by Nero for the show, all watchers were impressed until Peter told the angels who supported Simon to release him and he crashed to the ground. In one version Simon died from the fall and in another he only broke his leg.[5]

This popular story offered a number of lessons for Christians for the next millennium and beyond. First, the story argued that magic existed; God provided for supernatural powers to be used on earth. Second, whether the magic was good or bad depended on the motive of the practitioner. Simon Magus used his magical powers to enhance his own status. He wanted to be revered as a God himself, and according to the apocryphal writings, the blasphemous Nero waited three days for the dead Simon to be resurrected as Christ had been.[6] The apostles, on the other hand, used their powers only in recognition that they were simply vessels through which God's power flowed. It is in this latter form that magic acceptably enters Christian thought.

Simon was called a heretic, and he became associated with gnostics as a holy man who possessed secret knowledge. As Ireneaus wrote, Simon had "feigned faith, supposing that the apostles themselves performed their cures by the art of magic, and not by the power of God." For Ireneaus and others, Simon became the first of many heretics, who were marked by pride and magic.[7]

The evidence in scripture convinced many Christians that magic accompanied the gifts of the Spirit. Like Jesus, the apostles healed the sick, drove out evil spirits, and even raised the dead. However, questions remained about the role of magic after the age of the apostles had ended. Ancient Romans had a deep suspicion of magic and it was regularly prohibited,[8] and some deeply pious pagan Romans found Christian belief in magic a distraction from serious spiritual searching. Celsus, for example, said, "[T]hose who have had anything to do with philosophy . . . are above such trickery."[9] After the age of the apostles, would there be a place for magic in Christian worship? The answer to this question (like so many others) was found in the blood of the martyrs.

MAGIC IN MARTYRDOM

Like Celsus, most Christians rejected magic as unworthy of the new religion. The martyr Ignatius of Antioch wrote, "Everywhere magic crumbled away before it [the Incarnation]; the spells of sorcery were all broken, and superstition received its death-blow."[10] Here begins the separation between magic and miracle, because as we have seen in the previous chapters, the martyrs, and those who watched them suffer, believed firmly that their resilience was miraculous, and power remained in their bodies when they died. In the minds of the faithful, however, the difference between magic and miracle lay in the struggle between

Peter and Simon Magus: if the magical power came from an individual to the enhancement of his or her own glory, it was sorcery. If a person was only a vessel through whom God's power flowed, the glory was given to God, and it was miraculous. Of course, for many in the ancient world, this was too fine a distinction to make much difference, but it was sufficiently large to permit magic to enter Christian worship.

This contrast appears in an unusual way in a dialogue preserved in the Passion of Saint Maxima. As Maxima was questioned by the proconsul Anulinus, she claimed that both of them are magi (magicians), but she a good magician, not an evil one:

> Maxima responded: "So am I the daughter of a magus, the way you are a magus?"
>
> Anulinus the proconsul said: "How would you know whether I am a magus?"
>
> Maxima responded: "Because the Holy Spirit is in us but an evil spirit manifests itself in you."[11]

In this exchange, Maxima contrasts Christian and Roman in the terms of good against evil that we explored in chapter 1 but adds the idea that both sides are helped by the supernatural.

When the martyrs went to their death, none (that I know of) claimed the ability to perform miracles. Even Maxima who claimed she was a magus did not offer to challenge the proconsul in a contest of magic. However, most martyrs (perhaps all) fully expected to receive miraculous power at the time of their confession, and they believed that this power might be available to help the surviving Christians. As Maxima said, "The Lord is fortifying me against you,"[12] and like so many other martyrs, Maxima bravely went to her death in the amphitheater.

Martyrs may not have claimed the ability to perform magic, but they, like other Christians, believed the Bible promised that even tokens that had touched holy bodies could perform miracles: "And God did extraordinary miracles by the hands of Paul, so that handkerchiefs or aprons were carried away from his body to the sick and diseases left them and the evil spirits came out of them" (Acts 19:11–12). As Cyprian prepared for his martyrdom by decapitation, he placed his tunic on the ground and stood on it as he waited for the executioner. The faithful who were watching, threw their handkerchiefs on the tunic so they would catch his blood and become powerful, miraculous, relics.[13] If handkerchiefs that had touched Paul would perform miracles, such cloths with the blood of martyrs would be equally powerful. (See chapter 7 for a discussion on the power of sacrificial blood.)

The witnesses to the martyrdoms were not the only ones who treasured magical relics. The martyrs, too, seemed to recognize the power that would come after their death. The martyr Saturus was mauled by wild animals in the amphitheater of Carthage, but he did not immediately die. While he was waiting for the gladiator to come give him the death blow, Saturus asked the guard for his ring, dipped it in his own blood, and returned it to the guard "as a record of his bloodshed."[14] Like Saturus, the martyrs knew well how their remains would be treasured and used to perform miracles.

It is not surprising that Christians believed relics of martyrs were miraculous, but perhaps surprisingly, their persecutors did too. An account of a Persian martyr, Tarbo, offers a fascinating, if grisly, story of the belief in magic in the ancient world and its intersection with martyrdom. Christianity spread primarily through the Roman Empire and thus most of the martyrs came from the Mediterranean world. However, there were some Christians in the east, in the towns of modern Iraq and western Iran, and some of these Christians came into confrontation with the Persian Empire where the predominate religion was Zoroastrianism. In the fourth and fifth centuries (after the Roman Empire had stopped persecuting Christians) some died bearing witness in the east.[15] In about 341, the Christian virgin Tarbo was arrested with two of her companions, and a summary of her passion is as follows.[16]

The Persian queen fell ill, and since she favored Jews in her kingdom, she consulted them for the cause of her illness. These advisors made their "customary false accusation" against the Christians, Tarbo and her sister and servant. (See chapter 5 for a discussion of the anti-Semitism within many of these accounts.) The queen readily believed she was a victim of evil magic, and the women were brought in for interrogation. The judge accused Tarbo of sorcery: "You deserve to die, seeing that you have brought these evil effects upon the person of the queen, the mistress of the entire orient." Tarbo replied as strongly as any of the western martyrs: "What false charges are you bringing against us that are quite out of keeping with our way of life?" She denied the charge of sorcery, quoting scripture in support of her position: "The following is written down for us: 'If a sorcerer should be found, he is to die at the hands of this people.' How, then, could we perform sorcery? Sorcery is in the same category as the denial of God; in both cases the sentence is death."

The judge acknowledged that he knew sorcery was against their law, but he said the women practiced it because they had been angered over the martyrdom of their brother: "You have gone so far as to transgress your own law, performing sorcery on the queen, despite the fact that you are not allowed to do this, as you yourself have said." The women were arrested even though they persistently denied practicing any sorcery. The judges offered to marry the women and thus save their lives, but the Christian virgins dedicated to Christ refused. In their rage, the judges brought a false verdict, "saying that they were indeed witches." The king offered to withhold the death penalty if the women would worship the sun and thus prove they did not really know how to cast spells. The women, of course, refused.

The Persians watching the proceedings began to clamor for an execution: "These women should perish from beneath the face of the heavens; they have cast spells on the queen and she has fallen ill." The king then gave permission for the women to be executed in any way the Persian priests decreed. Now the priests—the magi—decided to employ some magic of their own, using the magical qualities of the martyrs' blood. They said the women's "bodies should be cut in two and that the queen should pass between the two halves, after which she would be healed."

The execution proceeded. "They took the three holy women outside the city and drove into the ground two stakes for each woman and they stretched them out, attaching them by their hands and feet, like lambs about to be shorn. Thereupon they sawed their bodies in halves, cut them up into six portions, placing them in six baskets, which they suspended on six forked pieces of wood; these they thrust into the ground, three on each side of the road. These were shaped like half crosses, carrying half a body each." The magic ritual (and the account of the martyrs' passion) was concluded as they brought the queen along that road and "made her get out in between the bodies." We are not told if the queen was indeed healed from her illness, but we are simply told that the whole court continued to the king's summer residence in the mountains, so the reader is left to conclude that the relics of the martyrs' bodies did their work.

This gruesome story summarizes many elements about the ancient belief in magic. All (including Christians) believed that sorcery existed. The Christian women denied that they would engage in magic through their own efforts; they were not like Simon Magus, but all the Christians—including the many readers of the Passion—believed in the efficacy of the martyrs' blood to heal. As we saw in chapter 2, Christians throughout the ancient world—east and west—believed martyrs' relics could heal the sick. In fact, this was a kind of democratization of healing. All Christians, rich and poor alike, could take advantage of the magical power of martyrs' remains—one did not have to be the queen of the whole orient to take advantage of a magical cure.

The need to find meaning, indeed magic, in sacrifice appears even in the twenty-first century during the war on terrorism in Afghanistan. As early as January 2002 when the dust had hardly settled from our bombs, many Afghans began slowly, yet repeatedly, to gather at mass graves of Taliban and al Qaeda soldiers who had been killed in battle. People brought their sick and their petitions as they hoped the remains of the dead would magically help them. One elderly man explained "they are martyrs to Islam."[17] The feelings and hopes are the same across so many millennia: remains of the holy dead can bridge the chasm between this world and the divine and bring the power of the supernatural to the natural world. If echoes of these sentiments continue today, you may be sure that they existed even more strongly in the ancient world where people expected magic to prevail.

RELICS AND MIRACLES

As we saw in chapter 1, during the age of martyrdom, the faithful carefully guarded the precious relics away from Roman authorities who wanted to destroy them. For example, during the torture of Vincent in the fourth century, many people came to "moisten linen cloths with blood that oozes from his wounds to keep as relics in their homes for generations yet to come."[18] After the fourth century, when Christianity became the accepted religion, the relics were brought out from private care to a public function—they were incorporated into shrines where the faithful could gather in community to venerate the martyr and hope for blessings. At first, relics were placed in sanctuaries separate from parish churches so the veneration of the martyr was seen as separate from the gathering of the faithful in communion. We can see this distinction in a letter written in 410 by Pope Vigilius to a bishop in northern Spain in which he describes how some churches have relics, and are thus called sanctuaries, and others do not.[19]

This separation of spheres of influence between martyrs' relics and parish priests was not to hold; it was a competition useful neither to the church nor to the community of the faithful. Slowly sanctuaries were converted to churches and the faithful gathered near the martyrs' relics to worship. For example, the Ninth Council of Toledo in Spain, convened in the seventh century, decreed that all religious buildings (including martyrs' shrines) must be served by an appropriately ordained priest.[20] By the ninth century in the west, all church altars were required to contain relics to be consecrated. In the east, if a priest wanted to celebrate the mass on an unconsecrated altar, he draped it with a cloth that contained martyrs' relics sewed into each corner. The magic that people believed was contained in the martyrs' remains guaranteed that God was present in the church celebration.

Not surprisingly, there came to be a great traffic in relics, since churches quickly began to compete for precious relics to enhance the power of their holy spaces. This movement of body parts often seems ghoulish to modern sensibilities, but to fourth-century Christians it was positively miraculous. Augustine wrote the following in a sermon to be delivered on St. Stephen's day: "His body lay hidden for so long a time. It came forth when God wished it. It has brought light to all lands, it has performed miracles."[21] God, not human agency, caused someone to discover the tomb of a reputed martyr, and God caused the revelation because he knew the needs of the faithful. Thus, the movement (called "translation") of relics was cause for celebration and awe. When Stephen's coffin appeared, a witness described the magic that accompanied it:

> At that instant the earth trembled and a smell of sweet perfume came from the place such as no man had ever known of, so much that we thought that we were standing in the sweet garden of Paradise. And at

that very hour, from the smell of that perfume, seventy-three persons were healed.[22]

As this description shows, the translation of relics began to be regarded with almost the same reverence as the death of the martyr. The remains were the powerful remnants of the holy dead, and it is perhaps not surprising that such popularity sometimes led to confusion. There is a wonderfully poignant letter from the seventh-century bishop, Braulio, to a priest, Iactatus, responding to the priest's request for relics. Braulio admitted to having a roomful of holy bones, but he could not identify them: "As for the relics of the most revered apostles, which you have asked me to send, I truthfully reply that I have not a single martyr's relics so preserved that I can know whose they are." He goes on to explain that his predecessors had feared that the valuable relics might be stolen so they removed all the identifying labels "to make them indistinguishable" so no one would take them in the rush of the relic trade.[23]

To modern ears, this account of a room of unidentifiable bones sounds somewhat implausible. Why would people save bones if they did not know what martyr's deeds they recalled? Even Gregory of Tours in the sixth century acknowledged that people "give more attentive veneration to those saints of God whose combats are read aloud."[24] Thus, if the name and deeds were forgotten, it was more difficult to venerate the relics—but it was not impossible. That people had forgotten the deeds, even the name of the martyr, was a human flaw, a failure of human memory. It did not mean that the sacred bones were any less powerful, for that was a divine matter. Braulio could happily send anonymous relics to his parish priests because his faith in the bones was secure even if human memory could no longer identify them. It was this sort of relic traffic based on faith rather than documentation that led to the abuses of the later Middle Ages, when for example three churches boasted of having the head of John the Baptist.

These problems would come to light much later. For the fourth and immediately subsequent centuries, the main problem remained finding enough sacred bones to meet the demand. While many martyrs had died, by the fourth century there were many more Christians who longed for the comfort of proximity to remains of the holy dead. With the end of the age of martyrdom, new holy men and women began to be added to the roles of the venerated; saints joined martyrs as recipients of special power from God.

Isisdore of Seville, an influential seventh-century encyclopedist, explained that there were two types of martyrdom: one by "visible passion" and the other by "virtue hidden in the soul."[25] The latter were men and women who essentially *lived* "martyrdom" by ascetic renunciations. From the third century, the Christian world included people who left their communities to seek God on their own. As a contemporary chronicler wrote, "A holy man and an unconquerable warrior in order to exercise and prove himself, desires to find tribulation and misery."[26] An aspiring "soldier of Christ" fought twin demons of natural forces: externally he faced cold, storms, and wild beasts; internally he coped with lust, hunger, thirst, fatigue, and fear. If he failed, he retreated from the wilderness to resume his life within a community—and was forgotten by history. If he persevered, his reputation for holiness grew and in time he was recognized as a man through whom the power of God flowed. At his death, the faithful preserved his relics as carefully as they did those of martyrs who died with "visible passion." Some women, too, took this route of ascetic renunciation, but more often, women achieved holiness through sexual renunciation. (This is discussed more fully in chapter 7.)

As Christianity spread from the communities of the faithful to the countryside, people were more often than not converted through the magical power of a Christian holy person—either alive or dead. Now, the Catholic church recognizes people as saints only after a careful investigation of their lives and recognition of miracles done through their intercession, and the miracles have to be documented carefully. In the early Middle Ages, the process was much more simple. When churchmen heard of miracles occurring at the shrine of a local martyr or holy person, he was less interested in exploring the origins or orthodoxy of the entombed than he was in assembling evidence of miracles to demonstrate holiness. When presented with such examples, churchmen argued inductively that such evidence of God's grace meant that the individual must be a saint. Arguing from the miraculous to the orthodox helped populate the Mediterranean world with magical relics.

Thus, through the magic conducted at the martyrs' and saints' tombs, the early Christians adopted the ancient dependence on magic that even the pagan Celsus had disdained as unworthy of a spiritual search, and in many ways this was true. God was in his heaven, presiding over cosmic forces, but he seemed to have delegated the day-to-day dispensing of divine generosity to saints' relics through whom his power flowed.

For many Christians, faith was less a faith in an omnipotent God than in a mediating saint, and since this faith depended on a relationship (between God and His saint) that was out of the control and beyond the comprehension of earthly petitioners, it may have been less reassuring than the older form of worship in which gods were more directly accessible. The only way anyone could assess the standing of a local saint with God was to observe the number of miracles performed through a saint's intercession. Cults rose and fell on the basis of miraculous productivity, and villagers were always receptive to rumors of more powerful saints who were perhaps closer to God. In the transition from pagan to Christian, the blame for misfortune was inverted spatially. Pagans accused a distant abstract "fate" for misfortune, leaving their local gods largely intact; Christians accused local saints, leaving the distant all-powerful God untouched by their anger. This relationship fueled the hunt for relics, because people were always willing to acquire the remains of a saint who seemed particularly full of God's blessing and power.

The miracles reported at the tombs were many. Most popular were the healings, and the faithful came to the tombs just as the ill flock to the shrine at Lourdes today or the Afghans come to the burial of the Taliban fighters. As a form of medical petition, the faithful asked to exorcize demons that seemed to inhabit the troubled. The fourth-century pilgrim Paula vividly described those (whom we might call mentally ill) who approached ancient tombs for cures:

> She shuddered at the sight of so many marvelous happenings. For there she was met by the noise of demons roaring in various torments, and, before the tombs of the saints, she saw men howling like wolves, barking like dogs, roaring like lions, hissing like snakes, bellowing like bulls; some twisted their heads to touch the earth by arching their bodies backwards.[27]

Other miracles addressed more mundane problems. For example, Saint Emilian reputedly stretched a beam that a peasant had cut too short so that it grew to the right size, saving the man the labor of cutting another. Other saints commanded storms to cease, crops to grow, or water not to dampen precious books.[28]

While the church accepted beneficial magic that helped the faithful, it consistently forbade "black magic" as a remnant of paganism and unworthy of the beneficent Christian God. For example, saints might stop storms, but it was forbidden for "enchanters and invokers of tempests, who, by their incantations, bring hailstorms upon vineyards and fields of grain."[29] The dead could be resurrected in an act of grace, but bringing back the dead for magical purposes—necromancy—was forbidden.[30] These distinctions looked back to the original struggle between Simon Magus and the apostle Peter. Magic that came from God through the relics of the holy dead was good; magic that was generated by a magician to satisfy his or her own desires was bad. This was the bargain struck in the age of the martyrs between the growing church and people who had come to depend on magic in their hours of need, and this bargain lasted for more than a thousand years until people began to depend on science instead of magic.

Magic and miracles from healings to stopping storms to exorcisms were largely in response to petitions from individuals. However, a more powerful magic was one that brought benefit to a whole community, and in the ancient world (as perhaps in the modern one) communities most needed help in war. When martyrs got involved in warfare, the battles were perceived as holy wars. This was true of Muslim followers of Muhammad, Christian crusaders, and modern, misguided, self-defined "self-martyrs" in Palestinian lands.

There were a number of examples of saints who got involved in battle. For example, the medieval chronicler Paul the Deacon told of the battle in which Duke Ariulf of Spoleto was defended in battle by a fierce, unknown protector who saved his life. When the duke went to church, he saw a picture of the martyr Sabinus, and recognized the man who had miraculously fought with him.[31] The fame of warrior martyrs spread far. For example, in the sixth century, Gregory of Tours wrote of the installation in Bordaux of the finger bone of the Persian martyr Sergius. The fame of the finger relic had spread so far that even the French king had heard that an eastern king had won battles by attaching the finger bone to his own hand. The French king tried to acquire the bone for his own use in war, but the finger bone was destroyed in the ensuing struggle over possession.[32] Throughout the Middle Ages, however, the most important warrior martyr was the apostle James the Elder, who is most popularly remembered by his Spanish name Santiago.

THE WARRIOR MARTYR:
SAINT JAMES OF THE STARRY FIELD

When Jesus began his ministry, he called together the twelve whom he chose to be his apostles and to whom he gave the power to preach and "cast out demons." The first three he named—Simon, James the son of Zebedee, and John the brother of James—were considered the most important apostles by early Christians. Jesus gave each a "surname" that demonstrated their character: Simon became Peter, the "rock" that future popes would claim served as the foundation of the church. James and John were named "sons of thunder" (Mark 3:13–15, 17), perhaps for their fiery enthusiasm and preaching, because a thirteenth-century account wrote of James, "the sonority of his preaching, which terrified the wicked, aroused the slothful, and won the admiration of all by its loudness."[33] This James, who is known as the elder or greater to distinguish him from the other apostle James, became the first martyr of the Christian faith.

During the mission of the apostles, the king of Judea, Herod Agrippa (who had been made king by Emperor Claudius in A.D. 41), began to persecute Christians—"Herod the king laid violent hands upon some who belonged to the church"—and his most famous victim was James, whom he killed with a sword (Acts 12:1–2). The year of his martyrdom was A.D. 62, but scriptures offer no more information on the martyrdom of James, recounting nothing of his burial nor the location of his remains.

James suddenly was in the news in 2001 with the discovery of an ossuary (a limestone burial box for bones) dating from the first century A.D. The box has an inscription in Aramaic (the language Jesus spoke) that says "James, son of Joseph, brother of Jesus." This discovery received a lot of publicity because at first, experts concluded that this archaeological find might actually be the original repository of James's remains, for the language, script, and form of ossuary is consistent with other finds dating from this period.[34] Susequent studies, however, suggest that this burial box is nothing more than a highly-skilled forgery. It appears that scholars will be debating this find for some time to come, which shows how this ancient martyr still captures the imagination of the modern audience. If this is indeed James's ossuary, scholars and theologians alike will have to reconsider the fortunes of James, the warrior martyr of Spain. If it is a fake, why would someone go to all this effort to force such a reconsideration? In either case, the long-dead martyr once again found his way into the headlines. However, the ancient audience had no such doubts: the religious landscape of the medieval world was shaped by a different account of the remains of James, the first martyr.

About the sixth or seventh centuries, accounts began to be written that claimed James had done missionary work in Spain before he returned to Judea to meet his death. Did these accounts recall an oral tradition that had been lost from the written texts? Probably not. Indeed, the most plausible motive for the growth of the association between the martyr James and Spain was the desire for the western regions to claim the authority of an apostolic tradition to balance the growing reputation of Rome, which claimed the martyrdom of Peter and Paul.

The need for another apostle in the west became even more important after the late seventh-century spread of Islam, which divided up the Mediterranean world into Christian and Muslim. The spread of Islam dates from A.D. 622, when the Prophet Muhammad fled from the Arabian city of Mecca to Medina, where his message began to take root. A mere one hundred years later, the armies of Islam had spread the new religion from Arabia to India in the east and to Spain in the west. By 711, all of the Iberian peninsula was conquered by Muslims except the mountainous northwest corner–the province of Galicia–where the Christian kingdoms maintained a precarious hold in the hills. Many Christians now saw a new battle of good against evil unfolding, where Christians in Spain struggled against an overwhelming force. Some believed new martyrs were created as Christians fell in battle fighting Islam, and in these perilous times, Christians needed supernatural help.

In the early ninth century (814 according to some accounts), a poor shepherd named Pelayo had a vision in which he was guided to a field under a brilliant canopy of stars. Pelayo and his companion shepherd reported the vision to Theodemir, bishop of the nearby city of Iria

Flavia. The bishop examined the site and found a small shrine that purportedly contained the bones of James the Elder along with two of his companions martyred with him. Theodemir built a chapel on the site, and he was buried alongside these precious relics at his own death in 847. (His tombstone has been found in excavations in the cathedral.) The cult of Saint James—"Santiago"—was established here at the field of stars—"Compostela" (the probable but controversial derivation from the Latin *campus stellae*).[35]

How did the bones of James the Elder supposedly get from Judea all the way across the Mediterranean to the remote hills of Galicia? A legend rapidly arose to explain the presence of the much-needed relics located in the battleground between Christians and Muslims.[36] An account that began to circulate in the ninth century claimed that after the apostle's death, his disciples placed James's body in a small boat at night and set out to sea with neither rudder nor steersman. The boat, bearing the corpse along with the disciples was guided by angels and sailed westward across the Mediterranean, through the stormy straits of Gibralter into the Atlantic Ocean. Then the hand of God guided it northward up the coast of the Iberian peninsula until it reached the province of Galicia. The mountainous coast there is rough and indented with deep fjords where the steep hills descend almost into the sea. The boat entered one of the fjords and came to rest at the end of the inlet. The disciples moved the body of the saint out of the boat and placed it on a large rock, which purportedly turned soft as wax and shaped itself into a stone sarcophagus to hold the body.

The disciples then approached the pagan queen of the region—named Lupa, which means she-wolf– to tell her of the miraculous translation of the relics to Galicia and to ask her to appoint a place to bury the saint and create a shrine. The evil queen set obstacles in their path. She first sent them to the king who threw them into prison, but the doors miraculously opened and freed them. Then the queen offered them oxen to yoke and bring the sarcophagus, but the oxen she pointed out were savage bulls. However, the legend claims the oxen miraculously turned tame in the presence of the relics and submitted to the yoke. They pulled the stone sarcophagus directly into the middle of the queen's palace. Seeing the miracle, the queen converted to Christianity and transformed her palace into a church for Saint James.

The body of James supposedly landed in Galicia on 25 July 62, four months after his martyrdom, which was about the right amount of time for a journey across the whole Mediterranean. The celebration of his saint's day takes place on 25 July, which shows the translation of relics had become more significant than the martyrdom itself. In the turmoil of the fall of the Roman Empire, the legend claimed that people forgot about the relics and the holy shrine of Saint James until the eighth century, when the shepherds were led to the starry field to discover the relics that could magically help them in their struggle against the Muslims.

Before I continue the account of the miraculous deeds of Saint James of the starry field, I should perhaps comment on the historical probabilities surrounding this legend. Since there is no mention of the translation of James's body in scriptures nor in other early writings, it seems implausible at best, and if the ossuary found in Judea is the burial box of James, it further reduces the probability. Galicia in the fourth through sixth centuries (before the Muslim conquests) had a vital Christian community, with travelers that went as far as the Holy Land and regular exchange of letters with Christian centers. None mentioned the shrine, but the explanation is that by the fourth century its location had been lost. The scholar Henry Chadwick offers a more logical explanation of the shrine in Galicia: it was the burial place of the heretic, Priscillian.

Priscillian was a popular preacher in northern Spain in the mid-fourth century, and he had a great reputation for magic, for an ancient chronicler wrote that he "practiced magical arts from his boyhood." At his trial in 385, he admitted to chanting "magical incantations over the first fruits [of the harvest]," and was reputed even to be able to raise the dead.[37] Like Simon Magus and the apostles, Priscillian's following grew in proportion to his magical abilities. Also like Simon Magus, the orthodox church found him guilty of leading the faithful astray, and he was tried in Trier before Emperor Maximus in 385. Priscillian and two companions were found guilty of sorcery and gnosticism and were decapitated. Their remains were brought back to Spain and buried with much ceremony in a secret spot in Galicia, and as the ancient chronicler writes, the faithful "began to reverence him as a martyr."[38]

In time, the heresy was forgotten,[39] but I suggest that his burial site was remembered as a holy space where miraculous things occurred.

When the shepherds were led to the starry field, they may have been responding to long-remembered reverence for the spot. Modern excavations have shown there to be a fourth-century necropolis of Christian graves at the site, and excavations at the shrine itself have revealed three decapitated bodies.[40] Were these relics the bodies of the apostle James and his companions or the heretic Priscillian with his? Faith promises the former and logic dictates the latter, but for the subsequent history of Spain and its reconquest from the Muslims, it makes no difference. The faithful began to flock to the shrine, seeking spirituality and miracles, and from the twelfth century until the Reformation in the sixteenth century, the pilgrimage to Santiago de Compostella dominated consciousness of Western Europe.

By the twelfth century, the reputation of Saint James had grown enough to draw pilgrims numbering in the thousands from Scandinavia, England, Germany, and especially France to cross the Pyrenees and proceed across northern Spain to the shrine of Santiago. A detailed book was written in the twelfth century to tell about the pilgrimage and the glorious miracles performed by the martyr and saint. This *Book of Saint James* (*Liber Sancti Jacobi*) served to increase the fame of the pilgrimage and draw even more people to the far reaches of the Iberian peninsula. Once pilgrims arrived, they wore cockleshells on their clothing as emblems of their pilgrimage, and artwork consistently shows Saint James wearing the cockleshell as part of his identity.

Santiago's reputation for the miraculous grew with the many pilgrims who came to the shrine. In addition to some cures, Santiago was known for freeing prisoners and raising the dead. However, his principal reputation hinged on his military help to Christians during their battles to reconquer the peninsula from Muslims. In fact, the thousands of pilgrims who came annually across Spain brought money and soldiers that helped Christians in their reconquest, but Christians focused less on these practical results of the traffic to the shrine than on the magical help Santiago brought in battle.

The apostle known for his thundering preaching voice in Judea had become a warrior thundering from the sky on a white warhorse to battle the infidel with his sword. Christians believed they saw Santiago appear regularly on the battlefield, leading them to victory. He became known as St. James the Moorslayer. (*Moor* referred to North African

Muslims who had invaded Spain.) The illustration that accompanies this chapter shows Saint James attacking Muslims at the siege of Granada in 1492 when the Muslims were finally expelled from Spain, but this is just one of many portrayals of the martyr as warrior. For Christians at war with Islam, this was a magic stronger than any other—a martyr who fought alongside them with sword in hand.

The victory in 1492 did not end Santiago's wars. That year saw Spain's soldiers cross the Atlantic to explore and claim new worlds, and Saint James went with them. People claimed the warrior saint appeared with his armies as they fought against the natives of South America and the influence of his cult is profound. There are more than 150 towns in the New World named after Santiago, most visibly the capital of Chile. His iconography is widespread and there are many local celebrations of his cult.[41] As late as the twentieth century, Santiago was believed to have fought in the wars of the new world. In a war between Guatemala and El Salvador, Santiago fought with the Highland Maya—soldiers claimed they saw him fly above them on his white horse urging them on with his sword.[42] The warrior martyr continued to be invoked when soldiers needed supernatural help.

In spite of these centuries of warfare in which the faithful believed they were led by a warrior-martyr, it is worth stepping back a moment to consider the logic of this. Martyrs defeated the pagan Roman Empire not by the sword but by the strength of their convictions. Like Gandhi and Martin Luther King Jr., they tranquilly accepted all the violence that was thrown at them and emerged victorious through their persistence, not through retribution. The transformation of victims to warriors arose from the human hope for magic to help human struggles. It seemed a small step to move from a prayer for a healing to a prayer for help in a battle, especially if the battle seemed to be a holy war, a war between good and evil—just the sort of battle the martyrs had initially won. Yet, this small step from hope to magic transformed the idea of martyrdom from witness to warrior and unleashed Santiago onto battlefields both ancient and modern.

Painting of the martyrdom of Polycarp (1966). The painting captures both his death as well as his prophetic dream in which he saw himself in flames. Photo used by permission of Canton Baptist Temple, Christian Hall of Fame, Canton, Ohio.

4

DREAMS AND VISIONS

our old men shall dream dreams and your young men shall see visions" (Joel 2:28). The biblical prophet promised this as one of the positive signs of the coming last judgment, and he was not alone in identifying dreams and visions as longed-for phenomena. People believed that in dreams we can lift the veil between humanity and divinity. We spend a third of our lives sleeping, during which our mind's eye sees things that are familiar and strange, comforting and frightening. What do we make of such visions? In the nineteenth century, Freud established the theory that dreams reveal only the mind of the individual dreamer; they offer no larger truth than the experience of the sleeper. In *Interpretation of Dreams*, Freud wrote, "[Dreams] give us knowledge of the past. For dreams are derived from the past in every sense."[1]

Through most of history (and often today), however, people believed that dreams were not just reflections of an individual's past but instead sometimes a source of deep spiritual and prophetic truths. A vivid example of modern reliance on prophetic dreams emerged in the testimony of John Walker Lindh, the "American Taliban" who was captured in 2002 during our war in Afghanistan. Lindh believed that when he and his comrades were trapped in a cave, one of his companion Taliban soldiers dreamed that someone would come for them in seven days. They counted each setting sun until the seventh day, when indeed they were rescued.[2] Even after his imprisonment, Lindh remained convinced this dream was a divine revelation, and his experience is not unique; many less visible dreamers today seek messages and solace in dreams.

As we saw in chapter 3, in the early centuries of Christianity, people longed to be closer to the divinity in searching for magic. In the same way, ancient people (like modern ones) longed for dreams to communicate with the spiritual world, and not surprisingly the experience of martyrs contributed to the growing dream wisdom.

Throughout this discussion, I draw no distinction between sleeping dreams and visions that might take place during a waking state. People in the ancient world could not tell the difference between a vision granted in sleep or in a trance, nor can I. Sometimes a visionary seemed possessed by a god—this could happen whether the prophet was in a trance or asleep, and who could tell the difference between the two? Either way, with the body in repose, the soul seemed accessible to the supernatural, which generated the dreams and visions that were so valuable to the ancients longing for truth.

PAGAN DREAMS

In the second century A.D.—just when Christianity was spreading and martyrdoms became more frequent—many pagans were searching for gods' messages in dreams, and this century saw the compilation of much dream wisdom. One such seeker of dreams was the orator Publius Aelius Aristides, who was born in the Asian province of the Roman Empire (modern Turkey) in 118. Aristides was talented and educated and a skilled orator. A successful future seemed ensured for the young man, but first he wanted to travel to satisfy his curiosity. He first toured Greece and then Egypt, where he became ill with a lingering sickness that was to change his life.

Physicians were unable to help Aristides, so he turned to the gods. First he prayed to Sarapis, the Egyptian healing god, but receiving no help, he journeyed back to Asia. While soaking in a warm spring in Asia in 144, Aristides received a dream or vision from Asclepius, the predominate god of healing in the ancient world. In addition to telling him to walk barefoot outdoors, the god admonished him to keep a record of his dreams.[3] This autobiography of dreams (a genre called oneiric auto-biography) is called the *Sacred Tales* and is a remarkable document, influential in its own times and fascinating for modern readers. Through this record that spanned sixteen years (twenty-six years of Aristides's life with a ten-year gap in the record), we can see the importance of the dream world to ancient pagans and follow the psychology of one dreamer.

Once Aristides was called to Asclepius for a cure, he went to the great temple of that god at Pergamum. There he joined many other petitioners who sought cures, and the main vehicle for healing information was a dream. Aristides and others performed the rite of "incubation," which simply meant they spent the night in the temple seeking a dream message. Assisted by servants or friends, petitioners entered the temple, took a ritual purifying bath, and made a burnt offering to the god. Finally, they lay down on a pallet inside the temple and the priest extinguished the lights and told the petitioners to go to sleep. In the morning, the petitioners and the staff of the temple discussed the kind of advice indicated in any dreams, and afterward, petitioners were sent forth to try to fulfill the dream prescriptions.[4]

Many of the "cures" seem inappropriate at best to modern ears. These included fifty-mile walks, bathing in frigid water, bleeding, enemas, and enforced vomiting. Here is one typical example of one of Aristides's dreams and the subsequent prescription:

> I dreamed that some Parthians had got me in their power, and one of them approached me and made as if to brand me. Next he inserted a finger in my throat and poured in something, according to some native custom, and named it "indigestion." Later, I recounted these things as they had appeared in the dream. And the audience marvelled and said that the cause of my thirst and inability to drink was this, that my food turned sour. Because of this, vomiting was indicated and the Parthian ordered that I abstain from bathing today and produce one servant as a witness of this. No bathing, and vomiting, and comfort.[5]

Through this oneiric account, we can see the dream, his discussion of it with the other dream-seekers, and his subsequent interpretation and action—no bath that day and enforced vomiting. While Aristides felt better briefly, none of these cures solved his illnesses, which seemed to include a weakening cough and digestive problems. (Of course, modern physicians would cringe at the bulemic behavior of repeated vomiting and know that such activity would only ensure continued stomach disorders.)

After reading this example of a dream and cure, no one should be surprised that Aristides remained ill, and yet he stayed for two years in Pergamum at the temple soliciting dreams, recording them, and following their instructions. Why did he continue to seek dreams? The answer lay in the dreams themselves, not in the results obtained. Aristides wrote with joy of the presence of the deity in his dream world: he began his *Sacred Tales* by claiming to celebrate "the achievements of the Savior [Asclepius], which I have enjoyed to this very day." He ended his account by suggesting that some raise the question of why solicit cures when health eludes, and his response (delivered in a dream) was that you stay "until God himself stands by you and makes an utterance. Strike out the dead part of your soul, and you will know God."[6] Through dreams, Aristides felt himself connected with a divinity—blessed by god with visions—and because of this blessing, his actual health mattered little.

Beyond his belief in the presence of the divine in dreams, Aristides's experience offers us a second important lesson about the pagan dream world: dreams need analysis and interpretation. The seekers at the temple of Asclepius shared their dreams with each other and with trained officials to help them understand the message within the dream. The ancients (along with many moderns) knew that the message of dreams is often buried in symbol and not clearly available.

Roman children raised on reading Virgil's *Aeneid* (which followed Homer) learned that there were two kinds of dreams: true and false. "There are two gates of sleep, one of which is said to be of horn, by which an easy egress is given to true spirits; the other is gleaming, wrought of dazzling ivory but the shades send by it false dreams to the upper world."[7] The key to knowing the difference between a true and false dream lay in the skill of an interpreter, so the ancient world saw a proliferation of oneiromancers—those who claimed to be able to interpret a dream. One cannot help but wonder whether Aristides would not have recovered more quickly if his oneiromancers had interpreted his dreams as recommending a little more rest and a little less purging.

But here is the central problem of dreams: how does one know what they mean?

A rough contemporary of Aristides in the second century produced a monumental work by a skilled dream interpreter, Artemidorus, who compiled the existing wisdom on the subject. This work yields extensive information on the study of dreams in the ancient world. For all oneiromancers, proper interpretation of a dream depended on knowing its origin, for example, whether it came through the gate of horn or of ivory. The Roman orator Cicero developed this typology more fully by arguing that some dreams originated with the individual's spirit, others came from immortal spirits that filled the air, and the third (and best) kind came from the gods who addressed themselves to sleeping individuals.[8] In this structure, the first key for interpretation was to sort out the origin of the dream and ignore those dreams that did not derive from the gods.

Not surprisingly, dream analysis developed increasingly complex studies of the origins of the dreams, and by the mid-second century, Artemidorus had developed a rather complicated analysis of the origin and types of dreams. First, he agreed with Plato that all dreams came through the soul and that some dreams predicted the future and some did not. Nonpredictive dreams usually derived from the soul itself, and Plato claimed these came from disordered bodily states,[9] such as indigestion following a large meal. Nonpredictive dreams are also familiar to us as ones that review the day's preoccupations. Artemidorus believed these dreams were inconsequential, needing no interpretation and fading upon awakening. Thus the first task of the oneiromancer was to separate the relevant from the irrelevant dreams. For example, some might have eliminated Aristides's dream of indigestion as coming from his diet rather from a deity. So even at this first level, dream analysis was fraught with the possibility for error.

More important kinds of dreams came through the soul from the gods, and these were predictive or instructive, such as the medical dreams followed by Aristides. For all of Aristides's preoccupation with his health, however, everyone agreed that the most important dreams were those that predicted the future, not those that promised cures. Artemidorus explained, "For the god presents to the dreamer's soul, which is by its very nature prophetic, dreams in response to future events."[10] These were the dreams that generated the most interest and were the most important, both to pagans and to Christians.

Even after determining that a dream was predictive, an analyst had to proceed to a second level of complexity. Some true dreams were obvious and direct in their meaning, while others hid their meaning behind allegory. Plato had explained that only pure souls could receive direct predictive dreams from the deity; impure souls received their message through an allegory,[11] so a dream analyst had to help interpret allegorical dreams of an impure soul (and most people's souls were impure). Of course, one can immediately see the problem here: how do you know a dream is an allegory? For example, does a dream of a shipwreck predict the event directly, or does it refer to a dramatic shift of fortune on land? Artemidorus's work was written to help interpret only allegorical dreams that brought messages from the gods, so if the analysis was applied to the wrong kind of dream, the conclusion would be incorrect.

The complexities of even these variables was such that it is easy to see that dream analysis was always subject to mistakes. Artemidorus even added that one had to consider the character, occupation, social status, and gender of the dreamer before hazarding an interpretation. Not surprisingly, most of the successful analysis of prophetic dreams were done in retrospect—after an event occurred, people claimed dreams that had foretold it. Thus, people continued to believe that gods sent predictive dreams to souls even while they could not make certain decisions about their future based on such dreams. The problem lay not with the gods' message but with the interpreter. Perhaps that was why Aristides could continue to praise the dreams sent by the god even while his health did not improve. What was most important was his connection to divinity, even if the human interpretations did not always measure up.

These problems of prediction also generated a certain—understandable—suspicion of oneiromancers. It was simply too easy for some to take advantage of people's desire to understand these precious messages from the gods and equally easy to be wrong. One of the major challenges for Christian thinkers was to preserve dreams as vehicles for God's grace while rejecting the interpreters of these dreams. The experience of the martyrs was instrumental in this transition from pagan to Christian dream wisdom.

CHRISTIAN DREAMS

At the end of the second century—just a few decades after Aristides's remarkable oneiric autobiography and Artemedorus's compilation of dream wisdom—the church father Tertullian wrote the first Christian explanation of dreams. In his "Treatise on the Soul," Tertullian wrote about the relationship between souls, sleep, and dreams. He claimed that bodies need rest and sleep, which offers that a cessation of senses provides that rest. Souls, however, have no need for rest, because they are immortal. As he explained, "Nothing immortal admits any end to its operation; but sleep is an end of operation."[12] Thus, while the mortal body sleeps in imitation of its long rest after death, the soul stays active and wanders in imitation of its separation from the body after death. During the cessation of sensory stimulus, souls receive dreams that sometimes a person remembers after awaking.

Tertullian drew from pagan dream analysis to explain the kinds of dreams souls receive, and like his pagan predecessors, he focused most on the origin of a dream. Favoring Cicero's explanation, Tertullian believed dreams originated from three different sources. First, "the soul itself apparently creates [dreams] for itself from an intense application to special circumstances." These are the dreams that Artemidorus and others counted as inconsequential; dreams that we recognize derive from our daily lives. Second, Tertullian believed most dreams came from demons who sent messages to deceive humans, flatter them, and lure them into misbehavior. Finally, the church father claimed some dreams were sent by God, who had promised (as we saw in the opening biblical quote) that believers might see visions and utter prophecies. These dreams were rare but very precious, and Tertullian acknowledged the value of these dreams for "the greater part of mankind get their knowledge of God from dreams."[13] Aristides demonstrated the proof of this statement, for he was certain of the presence of Asclepius in his dreams.

Like so many in the ancient world, Tertullian longed for dreams from God. He offered recommendations to "contribute to efficient dreaming," which suggests that Christians might solicit dreams like Aristides and the other petitioners had done when looking for dreams from Asclepius. Tertullian claimed there were a number of variables that could be controlled to affect dreams. First, is the time of night: "Dreams are more sure and clear when they happen towards the end of the night, because then the vigor of the soul emerges." (This is logical, since we are more likely to remember the dreams we have just before waking.) Tertullian also believed summer was more conducive to important dreams, for the soul "hardens" in the winter and is "enervated" by the lushness of fall. He also recommended sleep positions; for example, one should not sleep on the right side because doing so "wrenches" the intestines. Finally, sobriety and fasting made the soul more receptive to divine dreams and visions.[14]

Of course, all these methods for soliciting dreams did not solve the underlying problem of ascertaining the veracity (or the origin) of the dream. Christians worried if they were being deceived by demons sending misleading messages through dreams. Into the fourth century, church fathers, like the influential Augustine, were warning the faithful that dreams from God are very rare[15] and that it was too easy to be led into wrong beliefs by misinterpreted dreams. Augustine was even highly suspicious of the dream revelations that pointed believers to the burial places of martyrs. He wrote, "For the altars that are established everywhere by dreams and by the vain pseudorevelations of all sorts of men are something to be condemned absolutely."[16] These are strong words indeed, for it would be just such a revelatory dream that would establish the influential shrine of Saint James (discussed in chapter 3). The fact that Augustine's warnings carried little weight meant that people were too certain that God spoke through dreams to ignore these messages. How could Christians reconcile the value of dreams with the problems of interpreting them? In response to this dilemma, Christian dream theory developed in a new direction.

As we have seen, pagan dream interpreters like Artemidorus claimed to be able to offer the meaning of a dream to the dreamer. However, Christians included oneiromancers in forbidden categories along with magicians and soothsayers (as we saw in chapter 3). A church council (The First Council of Ankara) convened in 314, linked dream interpretation with other kinds of prohibited divination, writing, "All who observe auguries or auspices or dreams or divinations of any kind according to the custom of the pagans . . . shall do penance for five years."[17] Dream interpreters were placed in bad company indeed by such prohibitions.

Instead, Christians offered another source for dream interpretation: within the dreamer's mind. If God cared enough to send a revelatory dream, He would also provide the interpretation, thus rendering professional dream interpreters irrelevant. In the second century (contemporary with the pagan dream literature I've been discussing) two influential texts were circulating in the Christian communities: *Second Esdras* and the *Shepherd of Hermas*. Although when the canon of scripture was established these two works were not included, many second-century Christians valued them as inspired and gave them equal weight with other sacred books. (These two books are now included in the collection called apocryphal texts, meaning that while they were as early as some of the biblical works, they are not included in the established canon.) These two books offered a new way of dream interpretation.

The *Second Book of Esdras* (renamed the *Fourth Book of Esdras* in the sixteenth century after the Council of Trent) was written near the end of the first century. The main part of the work is a series of seven revelations that the dreamer is led to understand by the angel Uriel, who also appears in the dreams.[18] Here we can see that the dream interpreter (and the interpretation) was present within the dream itself and was accessible to the dreamer.

This message was even more clear and direct in the *Shepherd of Hermas*, which was written in the middle of the second century and was extraordinarily popular. In this text, Hermas was led to wisdom through five visionary dreams. Hermas also had dreams within the dreams of spiritual dream guides who interpreted the dreams for him. Through the interpretations, Hermas grew in spiritual understanding until his final vision, when he saw a shepherd. In the dream, he is told that the shepherd has "been sent by the most venerable angel to dwell with you for the rest of your life."[19]

Hermas concluded with Ezra that when God selects his vessel, he empowers that person with the ability to interpret the dream. Many Christians, influenced by texts like these, renounced the pagan practice of consulting dream interpreters and relied on their own interpretation. The question for Christians then became not what was the meaning of a dream but whether the dreamer was worthy to have a true vision. If the dreamer was worthy, God would give the dreamer the correct interpretation. How to know who was selected for a prophetic dream? One easy answer was confessors. People whom God had chosen for martyrdom were believed to be filled by the Holy Spirit. Thus, believers accepted their dreams as having been sent by God. Martyrs' dreams were recorded, preserved, and read with the same care accorded to ancient oneiric accounts like that of Aristides. Consequently, the experience of martyrs enhanced the reputation of dreams just as their dreams contributed to their own reputation for holiness.

MARTYRS' DREAMS

One of the first blessings granted to many of the confessors who had recently been arrested was a comforting, prophetic dream. Such a dream or vision confirmed that God would be with them in their upcoming ordeal, and the faithful preserved their dream records with care. The account of the martyrs Marian and James records the euphoria with which martyrs received these comforting dreams:

> O sleep more intense than all our waking hours! How happily he sleeps this sleep who is awake by faith! For that sleep had dulled merely his earthly members, for only his spirit could see the Lord. How joyful, how uplifted must we believe the souls of the martyrs were when just as they were on the point of suffering . . . they were permitted to hear and see Christ beforehand, offering himself for his dear ones at every place and every time.[20]

For the martyrs, dreams were one of the surest signs of God's grace, and believers trusted that these dreams had meaning for them as well, so they were saved. What messages did they hold for the Christian communities?

As the complicated dream books show, pagan dreams that people believed had been sent by the gods could cover a range of subjects. Dreams might instruct a believer: Aristides was given medical advice, others were told where to find lost items, and yet others were offered business recommendations. The most important of the pagan dreams, however, were those that predicted the future, like the famous (yet easily misinterpreted) predictions proclaimed by the oracle at Delphi. Even the ancient Hebrews recognized the importance of prophetic dreams, such as those of pharaoh that Joseph (acting as oneiromancer) interpreted as warning of seven years of famine (Gen. 41).

When we analyze the dreams in the accounts of the earliest martyrs, the range of messages in the dreams has been dramatically restricted. Virtually all the confessors' dreams that are recorded were prophetic, predicting their own death and salvation. For example, Renus who was imprisoned with a number of Christians fell asleep and dreamed that each of his companions was brought forth to execution. One of his companions recorded the dream: "As each of us advanced one by one, a lamp was carried in front of him. . . . And after he had seen us pass by with our lamps he awoke." Renus then interpreted his dream to his fellow confessors saying that the lamps signified that each was walking guided by the lamp of God.[21] A similar (though better known) dream was that of Polycarp, who before he was arrested dreamed his pillow caught on fire. He then interpreted the dream himself, saying, "I must be going to be burnt alive."[22] When the martyr was sentenced to the flames, his prophetic dream came true, which enhanced his reputation for holiness, as well as proving that dreams come true.

Occasionally dreams of impending martyrdom were very complex. In the early third century, a young Roman woman–Perpetua–was imprisoned for her faith. While waiting for execution, she kept a diary in which she recorded her dreams. This oneiric record contains four remarkably detailed dreams. The most famous was her last dream that she received the night before her appearance in the amphitheater to die by the beasts. I will relate this extraordinary dream in the young martyr's words:

> Pomponius the deacon came to the prison gates and began to knock violently. I went out and opened the gate for him. He was dressed in an unbelted white tunic, wearing elaborate sandals. And he said to me: "Perpetua, come; we are waiting for you." Then he took my hand and we began to walk through rough and broken country. At last we came to the amphitheater out of breath, and he led me into the center of the arena. Then he told me: "Do not be afraid. I am here, struggling with you." Then he left.

I looked at the enormous crowd who watched in astonishment. I was surprised that no beasts were let loose on me; for I knew that I was condemned to die by the beasts. Then out came an Egyptian against me, of vicious appearance, together with his seconds, to fight with me. There also came up to me some handsome young men to be my seconds and assistants.

My clothes were stripped off, and suddenly I was a man. My seconds began to rub me down with oil (as they are wont to do before a contest). Then I saw the Egyptian on the other side rolling in the dust. . . . We drew close to one another and began to let our fists fly. My opponent tried to get hold of my feet, but I kept striking him in the face with the heels of my feet. Then I was raised up into the air and I began to pummel him without touching the ground. Then when I noticed there was a lull, I put my two hands together linking the fingers of one hand with those of the other and thus I got hold of his head. He fell flat on his face and I stepped on his head. The crowd began to shout and my assistants started to sing psalms. Then I walked up to the trainer and took the branch [of victory]. He kissed me and said to me: "Peace be with you, my daughter!" I began to walk in triumph towards the Gate of Life. Then I awoke.[23]

After this extraordinarily complicated dream, Perpetua analyzed its meaning with simple clarity: "I realized that it was not with wild animals that I would fight but with the Devil, but I knew that I would win the victory."[24] Once again, like the simple dreams of Polycarp or Renus, Perpetua's conclusion was that the dream foretold her coming martyrdom.

A skeptic might say that these dreams were not particularly prophetic—they were simply products of preoccupied minds that were focused on what they knew would happen to them. But the confessors, and the Christians who preserved the dreams, saw it differently. As we have seen, successful martyrdom was not a foregone conclusion. Some Christians were unable to withstand the struggle and renounced their faith at the last minute. These dreams promised the confessors that they were indeed chosen for martyrdom and that they would withstand the test. In this way, these dreams were seen as prophetic.

A second category of prophetic dreams recorded by people on the eve of their martyrdom pointed to their salvation after their death.

Christians treasured these dreams as images of the afterlife that were granted to the chosen souls of the living martyrs. Perpetua's first dream foretold not only her martyrdom but it also gave an image of the heaven that awaited her. For Perpetua, heaven was an "immense garden" presided over by a kindly gray-haired shepherd. There she was welcomed by "thousands of people clad in white garments."[25] Perpetua's vision contributed to the range of images Christians had of heaven. In the *Book of Revelation*, John had seen heaven as a synagogue or basilica,[26] while a mid-second century work, the *Apocalypse of St. Peter*, described heaven as a garden.[27] Other martyrs after Perpetua recorded their vision of heaven as a garden as well. Perpetua's companion, Saturus, also dreamed of a heavenly garden, "with rose bushes and all manner of flowers. The trees were as tall as cypresses, and their leaves were constantly falling."[28] Today's Christians more often than not envision heaven as an Eden-like garden rather than a divine city or church, and these images derive in large part from the dreams of martyrs. Christians in general believed these visions of heaven because they were given more credibility by having come through dreams of those who had been chosen by God.

Perpetua's second and third dreams also contributed a great deal to Christian images of the afterlife. These paired dreams concerned the fate of Perpetua's younger brother who had died of cancer of the face when he was seven years old. In the first dream, Perpetua saw her brother Dinocrates suffering in a shadowy place. "He was thirsty, pale and dirty," and he could not reach a nearby pond to slake his thirst. Perpetua awoke grieving for her suffering brother, and during her waking time she prayed and wept for him. Then she experienced her next dream. She saw the same place she had seen before, but now Dinocrates was "clean, well-dressed, and refreshed." His wound was healed, and he not only could drink from the pool but also could play in it as children do. She awoke and interpreted her dream: "I realized that he had been delivered from his suffering."[29]

In these dreams, Perpetua revealed an afterlife separate from the wonderful garden inhabited by white-clad martyrs. Here was a location where someone might continue to suffer, and perhaps, more important, a place where prayers of the living could alleviate the pain of the dead. This vision significantly shaped later ideas of purgatory as a location for souls to rest in varying degrees of comfort, and it contributed to the idea that the Christian community extended beyond the grave.[30] Many Christians believed Perpetua's dream diary foretold the geography of the afterlife.

While most of the confessors dreams foretold either their martyrdom or the future that awaited them after their death, a few dreams revealed a continued concern for the communities they left behind. These were instructive dreams, messages for the living sent through those about to die. Many martyrs were careful to warn their communities against internal quarrels and divisions that were more threatening to the young congregations than persecution was. (See chapter 8 for more information on the hazards of divisiveness.) In texts as early as the Epistles of Paul, we read of the threat of discord among Christians. In his great letters to the Corinthians, Paul wrote, "It has been reported to me . . . that there is quarreling among you" (1 Cor. 1:11). Almost a century later (ca. A.D. 96) Clement of Rome wrote a letter to the Corinthians urging them to put aside their quarrels and get along, and a decade after that, the confessor Ignatius of Antioch wrote to another congregation to beware of discord. Ignatius wrote, "Allow nothing whatever to exist among you that could give rise to any divisions."[31] With all these warnings from the respected leaders of the church, it is not surprising that as they faced martyrdom, confessors might be concerned with the harmony of their congregations. After all, Ignatius wrote his epistle as he was being led to his death. Other confessors revealed their concern in their dreams (that were taken as instruction from God).

In the account of the third-century martyrs, Montanus and Lucius, Montanus had a dream or vision that beautifully warned against disputes. Montanus had quarreled with a companion named Julian, and although they had made up, Montanus maintained "a certain coolness because of the quarrel." That night, Montanus had a dream, which he recounted to Lucius:

> I saw some centurions come to us and when they had conducted us a
> long distance, we came to a huge field, where we were joined by Cyprian
> and Leucius. Next we arrived at a very bright spot, and our garments
> began to glow, and our bodies became even more brilliant than our
> bright clothing. Indeed, our flesh became so bright that one's eyes could

see the secrets of the heart. Then, looking into my own bosom I saw
some stains, and then, in my vision, I awoke.[32]

This dream was prophetic in that it foretold Montanus's death when his
body would be transfigured into a spiritual, glowing body (see chapter
2), but it was also instructive. For when Montanus dreamed he awoke,
he further dreamed he interpreted the dream to Lucian, who had
appeared in his dream as a companion. Montanus dreamed he said,
"Those stains, you know, are there because I did not at once make up
with Julian." Notice that this dream interpretation within the dream fits
the new Christian paradigm that claimed that God would provide the
interpreter as well as the dream. When Montanus actually awoke, he further revised his interpretation of his dream to offer a lesson to others:
"Wherefore, dearest brothers, let us all cling to harmony, peace, and
unanimity in every virtue."[33] This dream with its interpretation became
an instructive letter for the Christian community Montanus left behind.

The prison dream of Perpetua's companion, Saturus, gave an even
more explicit message of congregational harmony. Saturus dreamed he
and Perpetua were entering a heavenly garden, and they were greeted by
a vision of two church leaders, a bishop and a priest, "each of them far
apart and in sorrow." The two church leaders "threw themselves at our
feet and said: 'Make peace between us. For you have gone away and left
us thus.'" As Saturus and Perpetua tried to reconcile the two, angels
appeared and told the priest and bishop, "Allow them [the martyrs] to
rest. Settle whatever quarrels you have among yourselves." The officials
were confused, but the angels said, "You must scold your flock. They
approach you as though they had come from the games, quarreling
about the different teams."[34] This dream once again shows the difficulties of congregations in strife, and it also reveals the limitations of the
martyrs' abilities to bring peace. As the angels showed, the martyrs
could now rest and the living had to reconcile. All the confessors could
do was record their prophetic dream-instruction for the faithful to read.

And read these dreams they did. Congregations read and reread the
oneiric accounts with great fervor, and even centuries after the martyrdom, people venerated their accounts almost as if they were scripture.
After all, they believed the dreams were sent by God, so they were valued as the word of God. Indeed, the ancient Christian who preserved

the dream records of Perpetua and Saturus added a preface that treated their visions as the revelations promised by John quoted at the beginning of this chapter. He paraphrased scripture, writing, "I will pour my Spirit, and the young men shall see visions and the old men shall dream dreams," and he claimed to have preserved these writings so that all would learn that the glory of the Holy Spirit continued to work through the dreams of the martyrs.[35]

What long-term effect did these martyrs' dreams have on Christian understandings of dreams and their meaning? The answer is full of ambiguities, because Christian leaders warned about dream interpretation as a form of pagan divination just as they venerated the martyrs' dreams. The situation is made more complicated because we all dream; it is a central part of the human condition, so we cannot ignore it or legislate it away. People want to make sense of their dreams. Was it enough to say that if God sent a prophetic dream, He would send its interpretation, and all other dreams were to be ignored?

AFTER THE MARTYRS

In spite of the value placed on martyrs' dreams, dreaming in general was not embraced by the church once the age of martyrdom had ended. By eliminating dream interpreters as remnants of pagan superstition, Christians also were left without any guideposts to indicate which dreams were true and which were deceiving. After all, Christian authorities had kept the three-part belief on the origin of dreams—some came from the body, others from demons, and only the occasional dream was sent from God—but the divine dream was very rare. The sixth-century encyclopedist, Isidore of Seville, wrote that extreme caution must be used in dealing with dreams, for even true dreams "must not be believed readily for they stem from various qualities of the imagination and attention is rarely paid to their origin. We must not believe easily in dreams lest Satan . . . deceive us."[36] Warnings about diabolic trickery, particularly at night when the soul was more accessible, led to fear of even delicious dreams.

Churchmen's concern with heresy also contributed to a fear of prophetic dreams, for false prophets seemed as ready as Satan to lead the faithful astray. As early as the middle of the second century, before the age of martyrs had ended, a movement known as the New Prophecy arose in a village in Phrygia (modern Turkey). This movement (known after the fourth century as Montanism, after its founder Montanus) grew from ecstatic visions of Montanus and his two followers Priscilla and Maximilla. This group saw a heavenly Jerusalem about to descend to earth in Phrygia, and their appeal lay largely in the passion with which they believed in their visions.[37] As the church condemned this movement, and others like it, they also condemned the dreams that seemed to lead so many astray. Dreams themselves fell further under suspicion.

Throughout the Middle Ages, dreams remained suspect. Churchmen admitted that God sometimes chose a worthy vessel for prophetic dreams, but these were sent to saints or other specially chosen individuals. They were not for everyone. Pope Innocent III in the late twelfth century best summarizes the fear of medieval dreams. In contrast to the joy with which martyrs received dreams, Innocent wrote, "The time conceded to rest is not necessarily conceded to be restful: dreams terrify, visions attack."[38] Dreams had become nightmares rather than consoling messages from the world beyond.

Such condemnations were not the end of the story, however. Old ideas do not die easily, and people continue to dream and long to understand their meanings. Some Christians sought divine dreams just as the pagan Aristides had done, sleeping next to tombs of saints to look for information on cures. For example, the sixth-century chronicler Gregory of Tours told of a paralyzed woman, Fedamia, who lay down at the entrance of Saint Julian's basilica. She fell asleep and a man appeared to her. She dreamed that she showed him her affliction, and he carried her to the tomb where she saw chains falling from her body. Upon waking, she discovered that she was cured, and the man she described turned out to be Saint Julian himself.[39] This was not an isolated case, for many churches and saints' shrines turned into places for dream incubation. Even a great sanctuary of Asclepius near Athens (similar to the one in Pergamum where Aristides spent so much time) was converted into a healing shrine of Saints Cosmas and Damian, who appeared to petitioners in dreams offering instructions for a cure.[40]

Christians even rediscovered the art of oneiromancy, translating and preserving old pagan dream manuals of Artemidorus and others. In the Byzantine Empire as well as in the Muslim lands dream books proliferated. Interpretations were added to the old pagan works to make them relevant to the faith of the new dreamers. For example, Achmet's Greek dream book written in the ninth century offers the following interpretation:

> If a Christian dreams that he became a Jew, . . . he will come into perdi-
> tion. . . . If someone dreams of becoming a Mohammedan, the same
> interpretations apply. If someone dreams that he was a *magus*, he will be
> a lover of riches and wealth; for magicians are worldly minded and think
> nothing of retribution in the hereafter.[41]

Perhaps consoled by such entries, medieval Christians could believe that the other entries that derived from ancient pagan times were also applicable to them. These dream books helped medieval men and women map the night travels of their souls.

And what about modern dreamers? Have we moved far beyond the dreams of ancient pagans and Christians? I began this chapter with the influential interpretation of Freud who claimed that all dreams originated in the mind—and in the past—of the dreamer. While Freud diminished the role of the divine in dreams, he restored the position of oneiromancer. A dream can be understood by a dreamer's free association on the dream, by group projection and discussion, or by direct interpretation by a sensitive counselor. All these methods share the assumption that the dream has something to tell, that it offers insights that will help or heal the dreamer.[42] This is not so far distant from Aristides, who shared his dreams with the priests and with his fellow dreamers to understand the messages of the night.

All modern dream theorists do not share Freud's insistence that dreams only reveal the past. Even Freud's successor, Carl Jung, established the possibility that dreams can reveal something more transcendent than the individual. By exploring archetypal images in dreams, Jung believed that dreams led individuals to truths larger than those that reveal one's own psyche. He even allowed for the possibility that some dreams point to the future—prophetic dreams reasserted themselves in the twentieth century.[43] Jung was not alone; many people in the twenty-first century believe that some dreams come from outside the dreamer and reveal truths beyond the dreamer's personal experience. A cursory browsing of bookstores (online and off) show the insatiable appetite of modern readers for dream books to help us understand the dark world of our dreams.

What impact did the martyrs have on our understandings of dreams? While this book in general reveals the deep impact the veneration of the martyrs' experience in so much of our lives, in this area their impact was mixed. They offered a brief moment when Christians excitedly believed that the dreaming soul could lift the veil that separated people from their God. But that moment was only brief. After that people again recoiled from the mysterious nightmares that arise in our sleep and sought wisdom in dream analysts from Artimedorus to Freud to the many others that line our bookshelves. When all is said and done, our night visions remain as frustratingly inscrutable as ever.

Stephen is stoned by the Jews as Paul watches, which made Stephen the first Christian martyr. His experience also became a connection between anti-Semitism and martyrdom. Fourteenth century. *Les Belles Heures of the Duke de Berry*. The Metropolitcan Museum of Art, The Cloisters Collection, 1954 (54.1.1 Folio 162).

MISPLACED ANGER
THE GROWTH OF ANTI-SEMITISM

According to the gospel of Matthew, after Pontius Pilate sentenced Jesus to be crucified, he washed his hands and said, "'I am innocent of this man's blood; see to it yourselves.' And all the people answered, 'His blood be on us and on our children!'" (Matt. 27:24–25). Through this account, the Jews—not the Romans—were given the responsibility for killing Jesus, and this narrative points to the growing split between Jews and the followers of the risen Jesus. In the second century, Bishop Melito of Sardis (in modern Turkey) first brought the explicit charge of deicide against Jews, and this charge was only lifted at the Second Vatican Council of 1965.[1] What has happened here? How could followers of the same One God become such bitter enemies that many Christians today forget that Jesus was a Jew. Part of this story comes from the violent political environment of the Holy Land during the century that followed Jesus' crucifixion, but the animosity was solidified in the accounts of the Christian martyrs.

DIVISIONS WITHIN JUDAISM

The Jews in Palestine during Jesus' lifetime were divided among various competing groups who differed on matters of belief and practice. The Sadducees, composed of members of priestly families, were religious conservatives who believed proper worship was centered at the Temple in Jerusalem. (This is the "Second Temple" that had been rebuilt in the sixth century B.C. and further expanded in 10 B.C.) The Sadducees produced the High Priest, who alone could enter the Holy of Holies—the sanctuary in the center of the Temple. These priests presided over ritual sacrifices of animals that formed the traditional core of worship, and they refused to allow any "new" ideas that were not explicitly written in the Torah (the first five books of the Bible). The Sadducees also were willing to compromise with the surrounding pagan government as long as the Temple cult remained secure.

Other groups, however, found the highly aristocratic, traditional beliefs of the Sadducees unsatisfying. The Pharisees drew their followers mostly from the countryside and the poor. Pharisees believed the heart of Jewish worship was not the Temple sacrifices but the private observances of Jews all over the Roman Empire. They remembered that it had been the observances of purity laws in households everywhere that had helped Judaism survive after the destruction of the first Temple, and this was where they centered worship. Since the Pharisees emphasized strictly following dietary rules and other rituals that separated Jews from their Roman neighbors, they refused any compromise with the ruling establishment. Their adherence to these purity laws, however, did not stop the Pharisees from accepting ideas that the Sadducees thought were outrageous innovations. For example, Pharisees believed in the existence of angels, and hoped for the resurrection of the just. They also supported interpretations of Torah that expanded the laws that had been written down.

Although the Pharisees believed strongly in separating themselves from the surrounding gentile (non-Jewish) world, they avoided political revolution. Another group in Palestine, the Zealots, took a different approach. The Zealots recalled the successful revolt of Judas Maccabeus in 166 B.C. against the Hellenistic ruler Antiochus IV. Antiochus tried to bring Jews into conformity with the rest of the kingdom by ordering an altar to Zeus to be erected in the Temple, and he ordered sacrifices to be offered to the Greek god in addition to Yahweh, the God of the Hebrews. Thus, many Jews believed the Temple had been horribly polluted, and they revolted against Antiochus's rule. The Maccabeans won the armed struggle, and in 164 B.C., Jewish priests rededicated the Temple. From then on, Jews celebrated this restoration of their sovereignty at the feast of Hanukkah. If Judas Maccabeus could lead a successful armed rebellion against the Hellenistic king, Zealots believed they too could throw off the Roman yoke and restore a political kingdom.

Despite their differences, all these groups struggled in some way with the same question: how to maintain a separate identity within the Roman world. A fourth group, the Essenes, tried to avoid the problem altogether by withdrawing from the social world of Jews mingling with gentiles. The Essenes moved to separate communities away from urban life—often in wilderness regions. An ancient historian, Josephus gave the fullest description of these communities in which people held everything in common and worked and studied with faith and piety. Josephus claimed that they strictly observed the religious laws; for example, he wrote they "abstain from seventh-day work more rigidly than any other Jews," claiming they even avoided bowel movements on the Sabbath. Josephus noted that they were "wonderfully devoted to the work of ancient writers, choosing mostly books that can help soul and body."[2]

This last characteristic of the Essenes seems to have contributed to one of the greatest finds in the study of biblical history: the Dead Sea Scrolls. In 1947 a shepherd boy discovered a deep cave containing ancient pottery jars holding hundreds of scrolls of texts dating from as early as 250 B.C. Most scholars believe these texts were produced by an Essene community in their mountain retreat in Qumran, some fifteen miles from Jerusalem, and hidden in the cave during the Roman invasions of about A.D. 70. The scrolls probably represent a large library of various Hebrew documents that reveal much about the diversity of the Jewish lands during the time of Jesus.

During this time of spiritual longing, many Jews believed that a savior—a Messiah—would come to liberate them. Some, especially the Zealots, believed he would be a political figure who would liberate Judea from the Roman yoke. Others, especially the Essenes, expected a spiritual savior who would rejuvenate Judaism. Some Essene texts write of a Teacher of Righteousness who may have actually been such a spiritual leader or who was a hoped-for savior. It was into this volatile religious time that Jesus was born in Bethlehem.

Most Jews probably viewed Jesus as a charismatic reformer of Judaism. Like the Pharisees, he appealed to the poor and focused his ministry primarily away from Jerusalem itself. Like the Essenes, he spent time in the desert and was baptized by John the Baptist, a man who most closely resembles a member of the Essenes's community.

In the course of his reform, Jesus offended or frightened a number of groups. He struck at the Sadducees when he entered Jerusalem riding on an ass surrounded by throngs of people cheering him. He went into the Temple, and as the gospel of Matthew describes, he "drove out all who sold and bought in the temple, and he overturned the tables of the money-changers and the seats of those who sold pigeons. He said to them, 'It is written, My house shall be called a house of prayer; but you make it a den of robbers'" (Matt. 21:12–13). There was actually nothing unusual about the presence of merchants in the court of the Temple: the heart of the Temple worship was sacrifice, so the faithful came to buy pigeons to offer. They were forbidden to buy sacrificial animals with gentile money, so money-changers were essential. However, Sadducees could not help but see Jesus' rage as directly undercutting their central role in Jewish worship.

The gospel of Matthew also reports that Jesus attacked the Pharisees and the scribes who carefully recorded the teachings of the Pharisees. "Woe to you, scribes and Pharisees, hypocrites! For you are like white-washed tombs, which outwardly appear beautiful, but within they are full of dead men's bones and all uncleanness. So you also outwardly appear righteous to men, but within you are full of hypocrisy and iniquity" (Matt. 23:27–28). Jesus' attacks on the Pharisees were what one might expect of a reformer claiming that previous sects were inadequate.

Romans, too, worried about a popular prophet in such a volatile region. They did not want anyone to serve as a rallying point for Zealots who were always prepared to rebel. Furthermore, Pontius Pilate, the governor of Judea, had a history of stirring up trouble in his province. The historical Pilate bears no resemblance to the mild-mannered official "washing his hands" of the crucifixion of a popular preacher. Contemporary non-Christian sources indicate that he disregarded traditional Roman respect for Jewish sensibilities in religious matters, for example, by bringing in a garrison that carried imperial figures on their standard, thus violating Jewish idolatry laws against venerating images. The contemporary Jewish writer, Philo, described Pilate as a man of "inflexible, stubborn, and cruel disposition" whose administration was characterized by "greed, violence, robbery, assault, abusive behavior, frequent executions without trial and endless savage ferocity."[3] Under Pilate's administration, rebellion lay very close to the surface, so Jesus' popularity (and the suspicion that he might be a politically minded Zealot) troubled the Romans.

In about 29, Pontius Pilate crucified Jesus–a cruel death reserved for many of Rome's enemies. Jesus' brief three-year ministry had come to an end. But after Jesus' resurrection three days later and his ascension into heaven, a new next stage of his ministry began. What shape would the movement take? Would followers of Jesus continue to be one of the groups of reform within Judaism? Since we know that was not what happened, it is hard to imagine a time when this resolution was unclear, but that time did exist.

The Book of Acts in the Bible tells how after Christ ascended into heaven the apostles gathered together under the leadership of Peter. They waited and prayed–perhaps uncertain what to do next–until Pentecost, when the Holy Spirit descended on the group. Now, the group was prepared to spread the account of the risen Jesus. At this beginning, Peter and the group began in Jerusalem, and by this choice, the Jesus movement remained connected to Judaism and to Jewish society. The apostles did not withdraw to the desert like the Essenes, nor did they go back to rural Galilee to challenge the Pharisees; they went to Jerusalem, and Peter and John immediately preached to the people at the Temple and were arrested (and later released) (Acts 4). These followers of the Jesus movement saw themselves as Jewish reformers.

There are many other signs that the early church was a Jewish one. As late as the early third century archaeological surveys show that it is often impossible to tell the difference between Jewish and Christian burial places.[4] The symbols of worship were often the same. For example, Jews touched their foreheads, breasts, and both shoulders as they prayed as a mark of the Hebrew letter beginning the word "Torah," and they only stopped using it when it became associated with Christian use of the sign to symbolize the cross.[5] Jews also used the symbol of the fish and other mosaic symbols that later became associated with Christians. The followers of Jesus did not yet use the cross as an overriding symbol (which would eventually mark their decisive departure from Judaic symbols), because in these early centuries they focused on the resurrection rather than the passion of Jesus. Thus, here at the beginning of the movement it still seemed a struggle for the soul of Judaism, and this battle became violent early on, for the earliest martyrs were killed by Jews, not by Romans.

The followers of Jesus began to attract many others in Jerusalem. As written in Acts, "And the word of God increased; and the number of the disciples multiplied greatly in Jerusalem, and a great many of the priests were obedient to the faith" (Acts 6:7). It is perhaps not surprising that exactly this success led to repression by those who were not converted, as they struggled to preserve older Jewish traditions. Their wrath first fell on Stephen, a Greek-speaking Jew who had been appointed by the apostles to distribute alms to the faithful (especially widows) and to help in the ministry of preaching. Stephen challenged the priests at the Temple and claimed that the old law had been superseded by Christ. Stephen ended by accusing his critics of killing Christ as their fathers had killed the prophets. The enraged Jews "cast him out of the city and stoned him" (Acts 7:58). Stephen died praying to Jesus, and he became the first martyr. This probably took place in about 35, six years after Jesus' crucifixion.

Nine years later, the first apostle was martyred. James the Greater (see chapter 3) was the brother of John and a highly respected witness to Jesus' mission and resurrection. James came to the attention of Herod Agrippa, puppet king of Judea, who was a zealous follower of traditional Jewish practice. (It may be that he wanted to prove to his Roman overlords that he could maintain peace in his lands, and he may have decided that the conservative Saducean party was the best way to do this.) The king made Jerusalem his capital, and he piously offered the prescribed sacrifices at the Temple every day.[6] It was perhaps inevitable that the dissenting Christians would come to his attention, and as Acts recounts, "Herod the king laid violent hands upon some who belonged to the church. He killed James the brother of John with the sword; and when he saw that it pleased the Jews, he proceeded to arrest Peter also"

(Acts 12:2–3). Peter escaped from jail, and Herod died before he could pursue the persecution.

With Herod's death, the brief persecution faded, and most of the apostles traveled spreading the word. James the Lesser was the undisputed ruler of the church in Jerusalem, and it appears that his aim was not to establish a separate Christian community but instead to make all Jews follow Jesus as well as the law of Moses. However, at the same time, the apostle Paul was spreading the Christian message to gentiles, which raised the possibility of Christianity splitting from its Jewish roots.

Paul (the Roman version of his Jewish name, Saul) had been a participant in the early persecution of the followers of Jesus. In fact, he had witnessed and supported the execution of Stephen (Acts 8:1). However, on the road to Damascus to arrest more Christians, Paul experienced a dramatic conversion. From this time on, he was the greatest missionary of Christianity rather than its persecutor. Paul wanted to make it easier for gentiles to follow Christ, and he persuaded Christian leaders that converts need not be circumcised as orthodox Jews and that baptism was sufficient. Paul's vision of a universal church was different from that of James, who seems to have wanted to locate the followers of Jesus within Judaism. Paul's missionary work was successful and many converted.[7]

There is no direct evidence that Paul intended to create a separate church. Before his conversion he lived as a pious, strict Jew. He defended himself on charges of impiety, saying "according to the strictest party of our religion I have lived as a pharisee" (Acts 26:5), and in the letter to the Romans, Paul said further, "Has God rejected his people? By no means! I myself am an Israelite. . . ." (Rom. 11:1). Thus, it appears that although he believed in converting gentiles, he was as certain as James that he was bringing about a renewed Judaism, not beginning a new religion.

The anonymous Letter to the Hebrews in the Bible (probably written sometime before 70) indicates the fluidity between followers of Jesus and other Jewish sects. The letter was written to a group of Jews who were on the point of giving up their Christian faith and returning to older Jewish beliefs, and the author wrote to convince them to remain in the Christian synagogue. This letter gives insight into the missionary work among the Jews and shows that even several generations after the death of Jesus there remained a thin almost imperceptible line between Christians and Jews: the author of the letter writes, "Let brotherly love continue" (Heb. 13:1), for Christians and Jews were indeed brothers.

The first real evidence of a split between the followers of Jesus and other Jews accompanied the first large-scale spilling of the blood of martyrs. When Nero initiated his search for scapegoats in 64 in response to the great fire that burned Rome (described in chapter 1), he turned to the large Jewish community in Rome. This community included synagogues who followed Christ as well as those who did not. Peter and Paul were probably preaching in Rome at this time, and the small congregations were growing. The Jews in general had been considered suspect in Rome since they did not worship the imperial cult, so why didn't Nero simply round up a large number of Jews?

Curiously, the Jews had a friend in high places: Nero's wife Poppaea Sabina was interested in Judaism and had even used her influence before to secure the release of Jews who had been sent under arrest to Judea. It is likely that Poppaea used her influence to save orthodox Jews from Nero's wrath, but she may have brought the Christians to Nero's attention as a group that was causing dissent within the Jewish community.[8] Ironically, an ambitious and cruel empress defined Christians as separate from Jews, allowing a vicious emperor to initiate the first martyrdom. This definition first separated the groups; the final split also took place in the midst of violence—the destruction of Jerusalem and the Temple.

THE JEWISH WARS

Violence accelerated in Judea in 66, where a succession of incompetent and cruel governors had stimulated a revolt. Revolutionaries, confident in their numbers, and led by a Sadducee, Eleazar, claimed they would no longer permit sacrifices to the emperor, an act that in effect proclaimed rebellion against Rome. The revolutionaries experienced early successes, and in Jerusalem an independent government was formed that even issued its own coins (the ancient world's mark of sovereignty).

Nero heard of the revolt and quickly intervened. He sent his general Vespasian with three legions to put down the rebellion. Josephus, the

Jewish-Roman historian, participated in the battle and was besieged by Vespasian. Josephus surrendered to the general and later wrote the detailed history of this war. (See chapter 10 for more details on the war and Josephus.) Vespasian became emperor while the war raged, so his son Titus took over command of the troops. Jerusalem fell in a brutal battle on 7 September 70, and the Temple was burned, leaving only the remnant of the wall today called the "wailing wall." A second rebellion in 130 led Rome once more to devastate Palestine, and this time they forced Jews to leave Jerusalem completely, ending any hope of a political revolution.

This horrifying destruction solved many of the questions of the competing Jewish sects. The communities of Essenes were decimated in the wars; fortunately for modern scholars, the Qumran group buried their precious scrolls before they were destroyed. Without a Temple, Sadducees no longer could preside over their sacrifices. Zealots were destroyed and with them the political aspirations of the Jews.

During the siege of Jerusalem an elderly Pharisee appealed to Vespasian and received permission to go to the coast at Mania and establish a settlement of refugees. Here they founded a distinguished school to study and interpret the Law. At this point Pharisees who taught in the academy began to be known as rabbis. The rabbis over the next century began the great work of writing down the Mishnah, which was the analysis and expansion of Hebrew scriptures. The future of Judaism rested in the hands of rabbis who preserved their religion through the Law, as it was taught in communities all over the Roman world and beyond.

Christians, too, were shocked by the destruction. The party of James that had planned to bring Jews in Jerusalem to follow Jesus was left without a space. The followers of Paul who spread the word to gentiles all over the empire seemed to have made the right decision, and as captives in the war were enslaved and taken from Judea, some followers of Jesus spread their beliefs to even further corners of the Roman Empire. Not surprisingly, everyone affected by the devastation searched for the cause.

Josephus blamed the Jews for the many factions within them that kept them from peace. Of course, the general had a stake in blaming the Jews, whom he had abandoned to Vespasian, but his narrative, nevertheless, captures the faction-filled land: "Every town was seething with turmoil and civil war, and as soon as the Romans gave them a breathing-space they turned their hands against each other." He further described the fighting that went on in Jerusalem, with citizens fighting against Zealots. Josephus said when Zealots were wounded by other Jews, they retreated into the Temple, "leaving bloodstains on the sacred floor. It might indeed be said that their blood alone polluted the Sanctuary."[9] By his narrative, Josephus blamed the Jews for violating the sacred Temple before the Romans got there.

What of the Jews who followed Jesus? They, too, were a faction within the divided Jewish world, even though Josephus did not mention them. Like the peaceful Pharisees who withdrew from the struggle to think and write, some Christians must have gathered to reflect on the horror that surrounded them and to consider what the traumatic event meant. They too began to write. It was only after the destruction of Jerusalem that the four gospels were written down. The earliest, the gospel of Mark, was written either right at the end of the First Jewish War or shortly after.[10] Matthew and Luke wrote some ten to twenty years later, and the gospel of John was written about 95. Mark's words, written in the shadow of war, shaped the subsequent accounts.

Mark wrote that the destruction of the Temple was in God's plan and predicted by Jesus: "Do you see these great buildings? There will not be left here one stone upon another, that will not be thrown down" (Mark 13:2). Furthermore, Mark claimed Jesus had predicted the wars and the dissension among the Jews that Josephus so abhorred. Mark recalled that Jesus warned that they would be beaten in synagogues and "brother will deliver up brother to death, and the father his child" (Mark 13:9, 12). Finally, Jesus warned his followers to run to the mountains when the war began (Mark 13:14). Did Jesus actually say these things, or did Mark's mind create these memories to help him come to terms with the violence he had witnessed? Historians cannot know for sure, but we can show how the account of Mark was profoundly influential.

While many Christians must have fought and died in the siege of Jerusalem, tradition following Mark consistently separates Christians from the carnage and distances them from the revolt against Rome. Eusebius, writing centuries later and drawing from Josephus and the Gospels, claimed that Christians did not participate in the war: "The

members of the Jerusalem church, by means of an oracle given by revelation to acceptable persons there, were ordered to leave the City before
the war began and settle in a town in Peraea called Pella."[11] To confirm
the separation, Eusebius explained the disaster in a way that finally separated Christians from Jews: he blamed the Jews for not following
Christ, writing "the judgement of God at last overtook them for their
abominable crimes against Christ and His apostles, completely blotting
out that wicked generation from among men."[12]

As the gospels told the story of Jesus' crucifixion, the accounts were
shaped by the belief that Jews were being punished for Jesus' death.
Thus, we read the version at the beginning of this chapter, in which
Pontius Pilate–by all non-Christian accounts a vicious Roman governor–appears reluctant to sentence an innocent man, literally washing
his hands of the murder.

All the gospels followed Mark–and drew from the violence of the
war–in blaming the Jews for their own destruction. Christian communities then cultivated the Romans to make sure that the Roman's wrath
did not wipe out their own people. Matthew makes the Pharisees Jesus'
primary antagonists, and Luke argues that God had intended to offer
salvation to everyone, thus separating the movement further from the
Jewish church that had spawned it. John, the latest gospel, was probably
written by a Jew whose Jewish community had expelled him and other
Christians from the synagogue, so he too blamed the Jews for their
intransigence.[13] The path was established: Christians and Jews would go
their own ways, and after 70, most of the converts were gentiles.

This moment in the development of the church has generated much
discussion, animosity, and pain. As Elaine Pagels noted, "And here, as
in most human situations, the more intimate the conflict, the more
intense and bitter it becomes."[14] As the narrative of the gospels shows,
in this instance the separation between these groups that had originally
been one became very bitter indeed, and the violence of the Romans
only served to heighten the hate. Does this mean that the gospel writers
falsified the situation? No, the situation is more complicated than that.
Until the account of Jesus' ministry was written down, it remained
memory, not history, and memories of any event are shaped and
reshaped by current experience. The writers of the gospels could not

help but remember Jesus' words and actions in the light of their times.[15] However, once the words were written, they became history, not memory, and they served to shape the ways Jews and Christians interacted in the future. The animosity that was written in the heat of the moment fed more animosity in the future.

A number of Christian writers in the next two centuries developed the same themes of separation between the two religions. A letter written about 130 by a Christian identified only as Barnabas circulated widely and was valued almost as highly as scripture. In it, Barnabas developed an allegorical interpretation of Hebrew Scripture and argued that there was never any link between Christians and Jews. Instead, he claimed that all the ceremonies of the old law—including the sacrifices in the Temple—had been intended by God simply as mystical pointers to Christ. The Jews had been led by an "evil angel" into regarding these laws literally, as a sufficient end in themselves.[16] Accordingly, Barnabas rejected in the strongest terms all the things that marked the Jewish communities: the Sabbath, sacrifices, dietary laws, and so forth. He even ridiculed circumcision by saying that Egyptians, Syrians, and Arabs practiced it, so it could be no real mark of a covenant.[17] Finally, he turned to the devastation of the Temple, justifying its destruction because he claimed the Jews mistakenly pinned "their hopes to the building itself, as if that were the home of God."[18]

Here, then, is an example of a text that was written in response to the horror of the violence in Jerusalem, and it was written by a Christian who wanted to reassure other Christians that the disaster to the Jews did not touch them. Texts like this may have been reassuring to those trying to hold on to hope, but they fueled a growing anti-Semitism.

It is important to note that this split was not all one sided. Many Jews were as vigorous in their rejection of their fellow Jews who followed Christ as the other way around. Jews had martyred Stephen and driven followers of Christ from their synagogues. Although the written information is fragmentary, it appears that during the Rabbinic age Jewish writings and synagogues explicitly reminded their followers that they were not Christian. In a text called the Eighteen Benedictions of the Jews, part of the synagogue liturgy includes a condemnation of followers of Jesus: "May the Nazarenes and the heretics be suddenly destroyed and removed from the Book of Life."[19] In about 190, some Jews compiled a book that was subsequently titled *Toledoth Yeshu*, which contained in considerable detail a purported life of Jesus that described him as a bastard son of a soldier, a sorcerer, and the "son of uncleanness." This work enjoyed an enormous circulation through the next centuries.[20]

These written texts alone were probably enough to ensure that these two peoples both claiming descent from the Jewish patriarchs would remain separate. However, there was more. The violence of the Jewish wars defined the differences, but the age of the martyrs solidified it. The Christians were brought to execution by Romans, but according to the texts, Jews came to cheer.

THE MARTYRDOMS

According to Christian Scriptures, the Jews were immediately involved in the first martyrdoms. According to Acts, when Herod the king killed James by decapitating him (see chapter 3), "he saw that it pleased the Jews . . ." (Acts 12:2). This account portrays what you might expect to happen between competing groups: one revels in the ill fortune of the other. This was not the last time that the accounts of martyrdoms included accounts of Jews enjoying the destruction of their rivals.

In the martyrdom of Polycarp (ca. 155), the author wove an account of Jewish anger into the story of Polycarp's death. The passion told how Polycarp boldly announced that he was a Christian, and then "the entire mob of pagans and Jews from Smyrna shouted out aloud in uncontrollable rage" and urged that he be thrown to the lions. Instead Polycarp was sentenced to be burned. The author wrote how the pagan residents of Smyrna "swiftly collected logs and brushwood from workshops and baths, and the Jews (as is their custom) zealously helped them with this."[21] The parenthetical addition served to heighten the animosity toward the Jews by claiming Jews *always* wanted to persecute Christians.

The author noted the participation of Jews even after Polycarp's death. The fire miraculously did not consume the martyr, so the Romans had to stab him to death. The Jews seemingly knew that the Christians would want to take his body to venerate the remains, and they fought with Christians over custody of the martyr's body. A

Roman centurion intervened in the struggle between Christians and Jews, took the body and cremated it, presumably thinking that would end the dispute. The Christians claimed the ashes "that were dearer to us than precious stones" and buried them suitably.[22]

A similar account is given in the martyrdom of Pionius, two hundred years later in about 350. As Pionius was arrested, also in Smyrna, a crowd gathered to watch, and the author listed "Greeks, Jews, and women" as spectators. When Pionius addressed the crowd, he directed his message to both Greeks and Jews, urging them not to laugh at those who were to be sacrificed for their beliefs. He told Greeks that Homer warned against gloating over those who were about to die, and he warned Jews against similar misplaced joy: "At whom then do the Jews laugh without sympathy? For even if, as they claim, we are their enemies, we are at any rate men, and men who have been treated unjustly."[23]

What was going on in these accounts? Were Jews actually celebrating the cruel murder of their rivals, or were Christian authors deliberately implicating Jews in the crime to attack *their* rivals? While it is hard to know for sure, I think it is perfectly plausible to think that Jews were pleased at the death of people who seemed to be destroying their traditional beliefs. Everyone in the ancient world was accustomed to witnessing public executions of criminals, so why wouldn't Jews come see the deaths of these condemned people? In the same way, Christians later would cheer at the destruction of Jewish synagogues and blame Jews for bringing about their own destruction in the Jewish wars. Unfortunately for the future relationship between Jews and Christians, the written accounts of behavior that was perfectly normal for the times served to cast Jews in the role of evil persecutors of Christians. This was even more true once pagans had disappeared so Jews were left as the only group who had cheered at the spilling of martyrs' blood.

The rivalry between the two extended beyond the confrontation in the arenas when Jews joined other Romans in celebrating the death of the empire's enemies. Tertullian wrote of a different confrontation between Jews and Christians in the arena when he described an incident that took place in the Colosseum at Rome. A Jew who had converted to paganism worked in the arena as a hunter and manager of the beasts who were brought to the games. This man used the arena to demean Christians, for he carried about a caricature supposedly representing Christians–it had an ass's ears, a cloven hoof, and wore a toga. This figure caused the audience to ridicule Christians, and Tertullian had heard of this incident far away in Carthage. He wrote, "And the crowd believed this infamous Jew. For what other set of men were in the seed-plot of all the calumny against us."[24] Here is an example of perfectly gratuitous ridicule. It seems likely that this converted Jew was trying to distance Jews from the newly visible Christians, and in doing so, he further drove a wedge between them.

Even beyond accounts of Jews ridiculing Christians and celebrating the suffering of the martyrs, the highly respected accounts of martyrdoms contributed to the separation of Jews and Christians in other ways. Many preserved tales of confessors carefully warning Christians to separate themselves from Jews, and these admonitions further split these groups that had grown from the same roots. For example, as early as 107, the confessor Ignatius of Antioch included in his letters to the faithful warnings to avoid Judaic practices. He wrote, "Never allow yourselves to be led astray by the teachings and the time-worn fables of another people [Jews]. Nothing of any use can be got from them. If we are still living in the practice of Judaism, it is an admission that we have failed to receive the gift of grace." He praised Jews who used to keep the Sabbath, and who now celebrate Sunday, the day Jesus died.[25] In another letter, Ignatius warned, "if anyone should . . . propound Judaism to you, do not listen to him."[26]

One hundred and fifty years later the same message of separation was preached by the confessor Pionius. In his words to the faithful before his martyrdom he said, "I understand also that the Jews have been inviting some of you to their synagogues. Beware. . . . Do not become with them rulers of Sodom and people of Gomorrha, whose hands are tainted with blood. We did not slay our prophets nor did we betray Christ and crucify him."[27] As you see from his rhetoric, by this time the warning to remain apart from the Jewish communities included accusations against the Jews that became all too common by the Middle Ages (and beyond). Pionius seems to have read or heard of the *Toledoth Yeshu*, the Jewish text that had been circulating by Pionius's time, because the confessor repeated (and dismissed) some of its claims against Jesus—that he was a criminal and a sorcerer.[28] In this battle of texts, people believed Pionius's death as a martyr gave proof to his claims against Jews. No longer was the difference between Christians and Jews one of disagreement, it was another battle between good and evil.[29]

All that was left to solidify this growing theology of anti-Semitism was to clarify the relationship between the Hebrew people and their Scriptures, and the Christians and theirs. After all, the Hebrew Scriptures (that are also venerated by the Christians) claimed the Jews as the Chosen People bound by the Law and God's love. As the Christians renounced Jews, where did they fit in this system? Christians slowly began to adopt the method proposed in the Epistle of Barnabas described previously and claimed that the Hebrew Scriptures—which they increasingly called the "Old Testament"—simply existed to predict the message of Christ. The "New Testament" now had replaced the "Old" and Christians were the new Chosen People.[30]

Like the other significant developments in the relationship between the two peoples, this position was given sanction by the blood of martyrs. In the middle of the second century, Justin Martyr included in his many writings (that were given greater status after his martyrdom) a "Dialogue with Trypho," a Jew (whom he identified as a "Hebrew of the circumcision") who had escaped from the final Jewish War against Rome in 130. Trypho ran from the devastation of the war that completely ended Jewish occupation of Jerusalem and was living in Greece. Justin engaged in this dialogue to persuade Trypho to convert to Christianity. Justin approached the Hebrew scriptures allegorically to prove they foretold the birth and death of Christ, and he continued the dialogue, arguing that keeping the old Law was useless. He further claimed that Christians had superceded Jews: "The prophetical gifts of the Jews were transferred to the Christians." He went on to argue that "Christians are the true Israel."[31]

The account of the martyrdom of Phileas, which took place under the persecution of Diocletian in the fourth century, drew on arguments like Justin's succinctly to state the relationship—the confessor claimed that Hebrew Scriptures existed only to foretell the coming of Christ. After recounting the miracles and death of Jesus, Phileas claimed, "For the sacred scriptures (which the Jews think they adhere to, but do not) had predicted all this. Anyone who wishes may go and examine them to see whether or not this is so."[32] Thus, at the end of the age of martyrdom, Phileas stated the position that would extend into the future: Christians had replaced Jews.

AFTER THE MARTYRS

The respect for the texts recounting the passion of the martyrs served to finalize the distance and anger between Christians and Jews. At that point, it was probably impossible to turn back, to reconcile the peoples who had been so split by violence and bloodshed. In any case, neither wanted to turn back. Church fathers for the next two centuries refined and elaborated this message. However, as the texts of the martyrs show, there were two main stands Christians took with regard to Jews. In some texts, Christians perceived Jews as having been replaced by the coming of Christ. In others texts, Christians claimed that Jews chose to reject the message of Christ and persecute his followers.

Tertullian, the second-century church father, emphasized the former position in his "Answer to the Jews." In the tradition of Barnabas and Justin Martyr, he wrote an elaborate, highly detailed, allegorical analysis of scripture to prove that the Old Testament foretold the New.[33] Presumably, he wrote to convince members of Carthage's Jewish community to convert to the new Law, but it is unlikely that his complex scriptural interpretation convinced many. However, the prolific church father likely further convinced his Christian readers that their Jewish neighbors were misguided.

The second Christian approach to Jews—blaming them for persecuting Christ and Christians—came to predominate in the fourth century with Emperor Constantine's acceptance of Christianity. Christians came to power as the age of martyrdom ended. With their victory over paganism, Christian attempts at converting Jews by arguments like Tertullian's ended. What was left was anger at Jews who had refused to believe in Christ. For example, when Eusebius, Constantine's biographer, quoted Justin Martyr's dialogue with Trypho, he eliminated all Justin's allegorical persuasion and quoted his attack on Jews:

> Not only did you feel no remorse for your crimes, but you [chose picked] men at that time and dispatched them from Jerusalem to all parts of the world, saying that a godless sect of Christians had appeared, and retailing all the accusations which those who do not know us invariably bring against us, so that you corrupt not only yourselves but the entire human race.[34]

This accusation is devastating. With this quotation, Eusebius brought the veneration of a martyr to bear in condemning Jews as enemies of the whole human race.

Now that they were in power, some Christians had the opportunity to act on this festering anger. In the late fourth century, a Christian mob rioted and destroyed a synagogue in Callinicum, a fortress town on the Euphrates frontier. Emperor Theodosius ordered the bishop to repair the synagogue and punish those guilty of the crime. However, Ambrose, the influential bishop of Milan in Italy, intervened. He wrote to the emperor in strongest terms forbidding this restoration of the synagogue. He claimed that Christian churches had not been restored when they had been destroyed by Jews. Even worse, Ambrose said any investigation of the crime would be impossible because the Jews would lie: "Into what calumnies will not men break out who are liars, even in things belonging to God?" The bishop continued his accusation, saying that Jews would testify against even innocent Christians so they could see them "beheaded, given over to the fire, delivered to the mines. . . ."[35] By this reference, Ambrose recalls the texts that claimed Jews cheered over the martyrdom of Christians and claims they would celebrate again.

Theodosius had to back down and the crime went unpunished. This incident is often quoted to note the growing power of the church by the late fourth century in which a bishop could dictate policy to an emperor. However, it also served a darker example—Jewish people and property were fair game for destruction. Fortunately for Jews in the ancient world, the most influential church father, Augustine, intervened on their behalf.

In the *City of God*, written at the beginning of the fifth century, Augustine (like Eusebius a century earlier) wrote down his understanding of God's plan. Within this monumental work, the bishop considered the role of Jews. He unveiled his view of history in which the Hebrew Scriptures foretold the Christian ones, but in his view, Jews continued to have a place in God's unfolding plan. In the last days, they would convert to follow Christ.[36] While this analysis offers a reason not to persecute Jews, nevertheless, it is not an argument for acceptance of religious pluralism. As James Carroll writes, Jews became the "permanent negative other" that helped define Christians by showing what they were not.[37] Augustine's view only put the fires of hate on simmer; it did not extinguish them.

It is hard to find a way to end this chapter that I find almost unutterably sad to write. Jews and Christians grew from the same rich tradition, for as the Lord said to the matriarch Rebecca when she was carrying the twins Jacob and Esau, "Two nations are in your womb, and two peoples born of you, shall be divided" (Gen. 25:23). Two great peoples were divided indeed. Could they have peacefully agreed to disagree and each go his own way? We will never know. The violence of the Jewish Wars and the blood of the martyrs spawned an animosity that long outlasted its cultural context and that would shed much more innocent blood.

Monica and Augustine. Monica is placed higher in the painting than the famous church father Augustine, which shows her importance. Due to her son's writings, she became the prototype for Christian mothers. Andre Thevet, *Les Prais Portaits et Vies Hommes Illustres*, 1543 edition. Special Collections Library, University of Michigan. www.earlychurch.org. uk/augustine.html

6

HOW MARTYRS BECAME
MOTHERS AND MOTHERS
BECAME MARTYRS

In today's Western vocabulary, the word *martyr* often has negative connotations, meaning someone who sacrifices their own needs excessively in support of another. (Notice that this usage has nothing to do with dying for one's faith.) Thus, in common usage, one person will tell another, "Don't be a martyr." An additional complexity of this usage is that it is often attributed to women, and particularly mothers. In our role as mothers, each of us struggles to walk the fine line between being a good mother and oversacrificing ourselves and becoming a "martyr." Was this struggle always so? In fact, there was a time when mothers were not martyrs.

During the golden age of martyrdom, men and women followed Jesus' command to leave behind their parents, spouses, and children in their quest for spiritual perfection. In this view, motherhood was a social tie which one renounced for religion, and thus it was incompatible with martyrdom. However, the story is not as simple as a choice between two opposites. In fact, as church writers struggled for metaphors to describe the sacrifice of martyrs they looked to maternity; martyrs took the role of mothers who cared for the faithful and, in turn, ideal mothers began to resemble martyrs in their self-sacrifice. In these formative centuries, our images of even motherhood changed as martyrs' blood was turned into mothers' milk.

The associations between martyrdom and maternity begin with the earliest example of martyrdom in the Judeo-Christian tradition–the account of the Maccabean martyrs in the Hebrew Scriptures. In this account of a Jewish mother and her seven sons, there was not a distinct choice between martyrdom or maternity. Instead, the roles were complementary. The Maccabean martyrs were tortured in the second century B.C. because they refused to break Jewish law and eat forbidden food. The longest account of this martyrdom is preserved in 4 Maccabees, written probably in the first century A.D. In this account (that influenced many subsequent Christian heroics)[1] an aged mother was brought to the authorities with her seven sons. The author of 4 Maccabees was careful to detail maternal love: "Observe how complex is a mother's love for her children, which draws everything toward an emotion felt in her inmost parts. . . . In seven pregnancies she had implanted in herself tender love toward them, and because of the many pains she suffered with each of them she had sympathy for them. . ." (4 Macc. 14:13, 15:6–7). Yet she did not try to save her sons; instead she "urged them on, each child singly and all together, to the death for the sake of religion," and "they obeyed her even to death in keeping the ordinance" (4 Macc. 15:10, 12). The mother too was martyred after watching her sons die.

While the author of 4 Maccabees found the mother exceptionally brave–"She fired her woman's reasoning with a man's courage" (2 Macc. 7:21)–he nevertheless seemed to find nothing structurally incongruous about a mother becoming a martyr. Judaism in the Hellenistic world was a community-centered religion. As we saw in chapter 5 the central tenet of Judaism was precisely to preserve a separate community intact in spite of the strength of a surrounding culture. One of the ways societies traditionally had marked community was by eating together, and indeed family and community meals were frequently guided by the women of the households, the mothers. So in this traditional structure, mothers drew the community together through control of the food that the group shared. Jewish dietary laws, while satisfying biblical injunctions of purity, served to mark the Jewish community and keep it separate from the surrounding society.

Presumably, before their arrest the Maccabean mother cared for the integrity of her Jewish household. As part of that care, she kept the dietary laws that marked her family as Jewish, and she made sure her sons kept the same laws. After their arrest, the mother fulfilled the same function: she urged her sons to keep the dietary laws that preserved the family as members of the Jewish community. This martyrdom was about family and about preserving family identity and piety in the face of oppression. This family role was appropriate to a mother, especially a pious mother raising dutiful sons. The author of the text called her the "mother of the nation, vindicator of the law and champion of religion . . ." (4 Macc. 15:29). Religion was joined with nationality and law, providing a complete picture of what traditionally constituted community, and mothers guarded the continuity of the Jewish people.

A century after 4 Maccabees was written, Christian martyrs looked back to this model of martyrdom, but the situation had changed. Christian martyrdom was not primarily about a besieged chosen people trying to preserve its traditions. It was about individuals breaking from tradition to create a new path. Motherhood with its emphasis on family, on continuity, and on creating and preserving future generations would seem to be incompatible with personal salvation gained through martyrdom.

The accounts of the martyrs tell us that some of the Christians arrested during the periods of persecution were mothers. Yet pagan Roman mothers fulfilled many of the same community functions that the Maccabean mother had done, so they had to confront the problem of resolving the incompatibility between their social obligations and spiritual desires.

The defining element of a mother is that she gives birth, which guarantees the continuity of the family (and indeed the community). Other functions with which we associate mothers tend to be more culture bound. In the modern United States, mothers nourish and nurture their children as part of their defining role (at least in the myth of U.S. motherhood). In imperial Rome, mothers were not necessarily expected to nourish their infants since wet nurses were customarily employed by the upper classes. Furthermore, Roman mothers were not expected to fulfill an affectionate nurturing role that we often attribute to mothers (as we inaccurately cite "maternal instinct" as an explanation for such affection).[2]

Roman mothers were supposed to preserve and transmit Roman values to their offspring, leaving affectionate nurturing to a slave nursemaid. She was to be a firm disciplinarian and thus instill traditional morality. The job of the ideal Roman mother seems to have been as single minded as that of the Maccabean mother. She was to preserve the culture's values in her children, just as the Jewish mother had done. A Roman mother was not to let affection for her children interfere with that goal, just as the Maccabean mother watched her sons be tortured and killed rather than sacrifice the purity of religious values and identity. The value of community preservation was perfectly linked with the one universally defining element of mothers—that of guaranteeing the continuation of society by bearing children. As mothers, women were to put cultural continuity over their own needs and indeed at times even over the needs of their children, as in the case of the Maccabean mother. This self-sacrificing quality of mothers of Judaism and Rome made a striking contrast with the goals of early Christian martyrs.

The goal of Christian martyrdom was to follow the example of Christ and not let considerations of family, society, or cultural continuity get in the way. The martyrs took seriously Jesus' call to leave worldly concerns behind. The second-century church father Tertullian, in his letter to imprisoned Christians, succinctly reminded the would-be martyrs of this point: "The Christian . . . even when he is outside the prison, has renounced the world. . . ."[3]

MOTHERS CANNOT BE MARTYRS

These general notions of motherhood and of martyrdom were current in early third-century Carthage, where there was a growing Christian community. These competing ideas of motherhood were expressed in the record of the martyrdom of Perpetua.[4] Perpetua was a catechumen who was in the position of violating an imperial edict against new converts to Christianity. Like so many families of the early Christian centuries, Perpetua's family was divided by religious aspirations, because although her father and one brother were pagans, another of her brothers was a catechumen like Perpetua. Her mother also may have had Christian sympathies, for Perpetua later says only her father grieved for her arrest and impending execution. Her mother may have been a Christian and joined her in rejoicing in an expected heavenly reward. In such a family, which lacked shared cultural goals, the position of mother (whether Perpetua's or the martyr herself) was not clear.

Perpetua represented much of what was valued in Roman family and social life. She was a favored daughter, who already had borne an infant son to carry on the family name. While most women hired wet nurses, Perpetua adhered to the highest of traditional ideals[5] and nursed her son herself. She was well educated and thus well placed to serve as a formative influence on her son in the best Roman tradition. Perpetua's family surely expected her to move smoothly from her role of dutiful daughter to diligent mother and fulfill her purpose of preserving family and Roman traditions. The narrator of the account of her passion gave a brief summary of her background that placed her firmly within this Roman social structure: "She came of a good family; she was well brought up and a respectably married woman. . . . At her breast she nursed an infant son and was herself about twenty-two years old."[6] Her conversion to Christianity threatened her fulfilling her traditional roles; her martyrdom prevented it.

In the course of the persecutions that were conducted in North Africa in the early third century, Perpetua was arrested with four friends (two of whom were slaves). (Later, Saturus, another member of the Christian community, voluntarily joined the small group in prison.) Much of the narrative of her experience is in her own words in a diary she kept while imprisoned, and this narrative was supplemented by an eyewitness to her passion. Her narrative is rich with the tensions between social ties and an individual's longing for Christian spiritual perfection.

When Perpetua was arrested, she had to break the filial ties that bound her to her father, who, as she wrote, "because of his affection for me wanted to talk me out of all this and overturn my resolve."[7] Tertullian recognized the strength of family bonds in his letter to imprisoned martyrs (quite likely to this group) to steel their resolve for the coming ordeal. He noted the difficulties of rupturing the social ties that might prevent their martyrdom. He warned of "attachments . . . [that] may have accompanied you to the prison gate; . . . your relative, too, may have escorted you."[8] Perpetua seemed to break the filial ties with her father somewhat easily, confirming the anti-Christian polemicist Celsius's opinion that Christians were "destroying the traditional authority of the pater-familias."[9] It seemed harder for her to renounce the maternal tie with her son. However, she would find that renouncing that tie was essential for her to pursue her spiritual goal of martyrdom.

She wrote of her concern for her infant son who was with her in prison: "And worst of all, I was torn with anxiety because of my baby." The group bribed someone to get better accommodations in prison so they could care for their needs more easily. Then Perpetua was more able to tend her son: "I nursed my baby, who was already faint with hunger." Even though imprisoned for her seemingly antisocial confession of Christianity (see chapter 1), Perpetua's maternity continued to link her to her family. As many young mothers did, Perpetua consulted with her own mother about the welfare of her child. She wrote that her anxiety for her child "caused me to speak to my mother about him. I consoled my brother and I entrusted the baby to them." After a few days without the child and in an agony of worry over him, she "worked things out so I could have my baby stay with me in prison. I right away grew stronger, relieved as I was of my worry and anxiety for the baby. All at once my prison seemed like a palace to me. I preferred being there to anywhere else."[10]

At this point, it seems that Perpetua at some level hoped to maintain both roles: mother and martyr. If she knew of the story of the Maccabean martyrs (which is likely), she may have been following the path of that mother-martyr. But being a Christian witness was more individual. She was not to have her son join her in martyrdom. Her final ties to her family were broken at her trial a few days later. Perpetua's father appealed to her maternity: "Perform the sacrifice—have pity on your infant." The governor also reminded her of her family ties: "Spare your father's white hair, spare the infancy of your boy! Perform the rite for the safety of the emperors." She replied, "I will not do it. . . . I am a Christian."[11]

Her self-definition as a Christian broke the social ties that had defined her as a daughter and mother of Rome. Her father took her son and would not send him back to Perpetua in prison when she asked for him. However, she saw God's blessing in the ending of her maternity: "As God willed, the baby no longer desired the breast, and my breasts were not inflamed either. So I did not suffer any vexation over the baby or any soreness in my breasts."[12] Her martyrdom was not the same as that of the Maccabean mother; she would seek salvation alone, leaving her son to find his own path.

The degree to which Perpetua rejected her maternal role to seek martyrdom was reinforced as the story of her passion was passed on through the Middle Ages. In the influential thirteenth-century compilation of saints' lives written by Jacobus de Voragine and known as the *Golden Legend*, the Franciscan shortens and summarizes Perpetua's story. In this account, Perpetua's anxiety for her child disappears:

> Then the father laid her child upon her neck, and he . . . said: "Be merciful to us, daughter, and live with us!" But she threw the child aside, and

repulsed her parents, saying: "Begone from me, enemies of God, for I know you not!"[13]

Perpetua's family, including her child, are portrayed as "enemies," and in her search for martyrdom, she throws them aside. This account highlights the implicit incompatibility between motherhood and martyrdom.

The need to reject motherhood to achieve martyrdom was reinforced in the original narrative of the passion by the account of Felicity, a slave who shared Perpetua's imprisonment. Felicity was pregnant when she was arrested, and Felicity's greatest worry was that her condition would keep her from sharing the struggle in the arena with her companions:

> She became greatly disquieted that the ordeal might be deferred because of her pregnancy, since it is against the law for pregnant women to be put to death.[14]

Felicity was right about the Roman law; Romans would not execute a pregnant woman even if she was a confessed Christian. Acts of the martyrs repeatedly show pregnant women exempt from execution. Another such example was that of Eutychia, arrested with several female companions. The others were executed, but the prefect said, "Since Eutychia is pregnant she shall be kept meanwhile in jail."[15]

Since Felicity was a slave, Rome had an interest in her child even if it no longer valued the mother, for after all, the child was property belonging to Felicity's owner. In accordance with the law and with the values of Rome, a pregnant Felicity would not be executed with her companions. However the group prayed together and the Lord answered their prayers by bringing on premature labor pains. Felicity bore her child and immediately gave up her infant daughter to be raised by her sister.[16] Just as God relieved Perpetua's maternal responsibilities so she could focus on her martyrdom, He freed Felicity's burden of motherhood.

In this account of two martyr-mothers, we can see the degree to which Christians were expected to break the social obligations of motherhood if they were to achieve martyrdom.[17] Both Perpetua and Felicity had to reject their maternal roles if they were to proceed to martyrdom. As significant as the social links that bound mothers were, motherhood represented a physiological state that seems to have been inconsistent with martyrdom. Mothers make milk, martyrs make blood.

Classical understandings of physiology linked blood with milk. Physicians (and the general populace) believed fetuses were nourished in the womb on menstrual blood, and after childbirth the mother's body transformed the blood into milk to nourish the infant.[18] Not only were the substances of blood and milk linked but, as Professor Atkinson has demonstrated, "menstruation, pregnancy, and lactation represented difference stages of one process and . . . a woman could or should not occupy more than one stage at a time."[19] Thus, women who were lactating should not bleed and vice versa. These deep-seated beliefs certainly must have affected people's attitudes toward mothers becoming martyrs. As we have seen, Rome did not execute pregnant women, and the *Passion of Perpetua* reveals there was some concern about lactating mothers.

God had readied Perpetua for martyrdom by drying up the milk in her breasts; she was prepared to shed blood. Felicity had given birth, and the narrator associated the blood of childbirth with the blood she would shed in the arena: "She had advanced from the midwife to the gladiators' nets, washed first in the blood of childbirth and ready to meet a new baptism of blood." The delivery of the child in her blood had become one part of the blood of martyrdom. However, that did not address the problem of lactation. When the martyrs were brought into the arena naked except for gladiator nets, the crowd was "horrified to see that one was a delicate young girl and the other a young woman who had just given birth, her breasts still leaking with milk."[20] They were sent back and clothed in unbelted tunics for their martyrdom.

Why was the crowd squeamish at this sight? It was not a sympathetic crowd. Before they saw the young mothers, the crowd had flown "into a fury" at the intransigence of the group and insisted that they be flogged "by a row of gladiatorial huntsmen" before being given to the beasts.[21] More than likely the spectators recognized what the martyrs had already discovered: motherhood and martyrdom were incompatible states. Mothers as guardians of social continuity were not the same as individuals' leaving behind social ties to seek their individual perfection. Perpetua and Felicity became martyrs as themselves, not as the nameless Maccabean mother who remained a mother during her martyrdom.

MARTYRS AS MOTHERS

Ironically, however, the story of martyrdom and maternity does not end here with the renunciation of motherhood to achieve martyrdom. This was the lesson of the *Passion of Perpetua*. However, as we have seen, the role of mothers is a critically important one for ensuring cultural continuity, and motherhood became an image that writers used as a shorthand to express the need for preserving community. Martyrs may have been individuals in expressing their faith, but Christianity was not a religion solely of individuals. In fact, from the earliest Christian years, people came together as communities. Early Christians gathered in homes and called each other "brother" and "sister" and "father." The communion meal served much of the same ritual function as the Jewish dietary laws: those who ate together formed a community distinct from the surrounding society. Just as the Maccabean mother presided over the Jewish community, maternal images expressed the need for Christians to come together. Consequently, images of maternity were often used to refer to martyrs. Mothers may not become martyrs, but martyrs serve as mothers.

The faithful believed that martyrs in the arena went happily not to their deaths but to their birth into eternal life. The images of birth pervade the accounts of the passions. Eusebius, for example, referred to Christ as a martyr and "Firstborn of the dead."[22] Subsequent martyrs were to follow Him in rebirth from the arena into eternal life. Eusebius continued the birth metaphor in his description of the martyrs in Gaul in the second century. He described some Christians who were too frightened to confess and accept imprisonment. Of these he said, "Some ten proved stillborn, causing us great distress. . . ." Yet he recognized the power of the confessors, who would become martyrs, for they had the power to forgive the lapsed, allowing the church to receive "her stillborn children back alive."[23] The martyrs in this case served as mothers giving rebirth to others in the community.

After birth, mothers care for their children. Irenaeus described the care confessors showed other Christians in maternal terms. He said the confessors "bestowed . . . motherly affection on those who lacked. . . . Shedding many tears on their behalf in supplication to the Father. . . ."[24] Perpetua and the other martyrs had to renounce their families and social ties to achieve martyrdom, but they joined new families. In these families, God was the Father and sometimes martyrs were the mothers.

A good example of the transformation of martyrs into mothers was the case of the martyr Blandina. Blandina was a slave apparently with no blood ties to the others in her group. She was described as physically ugly ("what appears to men as worthless and uncomely and despicable")[25] but her strength of character and God's grace gave her the fortitude to withstand extraordinary tortures. During her ordeal, the slave gave encouragement to her companions, and it was this role of stirring the courage of this surrogate family that caused Eusebius to cast her in the image of the Maccabean mother. The narrator described how the slave urged her young companion on to martyrdom: "Like a noble mother who had encouraged her children and sent them before her in triumph to the King, blessed Blandina herself passed through all the ordeals of her children and hastened to rejoin them. . . ."[26] The slave Blandina was not a mother; the confessor and martyr Blandina was.

Sometimes the images of maternity applied to the church itself. In that case, martyrs metaphorically became siblings cared for by a nurturing mother church. Romans believed that infants who shared the same milk formed family bonds. For example, the wife of the Elder Cato suckled slaves' children along with her son so they would have a natural affection for him,[27] and the Maccabean martyr brothers were bound together by sharing the same milk from their mother (4 Macc. 13:19). If maternal milk formed family bonds, then in that spirit the martyrs were made one family by the nurturing of their mother, the church. Tertullian makes this association explicit in his letter to the martyrs when he refers to the food sent to the confessors in prison purchased through church resources: "the nourishment for the body which our Lady Mother the Church [furnished] from her breast."[28] The abundance of maternal metaphors testifies to the strength of the images in discussing and establishing communities.

New Christian families were formed among Christian communities and in the arenas of martyrdom. When Tertullian spoke of the blood of martyrs as seed, the associations were rich. Martyrs' blood was like menstrual blood with which mothers bore and nourished new life and new communities. The martyrs' blood fed the Christian communities and brought forth a rebirth into eternal life. Martyrs served as mothers to the Christian communities.

Maternal metaphors for martyrs allow us to understand the accounts of some martyrdoms that certainly stretch the credulity of the modern audience. The *Golden Legend* has the account of several martyrs in which Jacobus brings the maternal metaphors vividly to life. Jacobus's work offers good insights particularly because he felt free to depart from the original texts. His transformations of the texts reveal precisely his perceptions about the "truth" underlying the events, including his views on motherhood and martyrdom. In one case, Jacobus recounts the martyrdom of Saint Sophia and her three daughters, Faith, Hope, and Charity. The three daughters were tortured for their profession of Christianity, and Jacobus's description of the torture of Faith was rich with symbolic association:

> Faith therefore first was beaten by thirty-six soldiers; then her breasts were torn off, and from her wounds milk gushed forth, but from her breasts flowed blood.[29]

By describing blood coming from the "maiden's" breast, Jacobus explicitly rejected any notion that the martyr was a mother. In this he is consistent with the same ideology that caused him to recast the Perpetua story so that she rejected her maternal role strongly as she sought martyrdom. Yet by having milk flow from the wounds of martyrdom, he was expressing the belief that martyrs served as nurturing mothers to the young church.

Jacobus expressed these same truths in his account of the martyrdom of Catherine of Alexandria. When she was beheaded, milk—not blood—flowed form her veins.[30] Like Faith, this martyr became a mother at her death to nourish future generations of believers. Perpetua had to renounce her physical maternity to become a martyr, but she joined the ranks of martyrs that future generations would see as mothers to a growing Christian community.

MOTHERS BECOME MARTYRS

The references to martyrs in terms of motherhood seems in turn to have shaped some of the descriptions of ideal Christian mothers—the best Christian mothers took on some of the qualities of martyrs. The story of famous Christian mothers begins with Helena, the mother of Constantine, the emperor who ended the age of martyrs. Constantine bestowed the title of empress on his mother and gave her the even more honorable title of "*nobilissima femina*," meaning "most honored and noble lady," and this influential woman was Christian and no doubt influenced Constantine's patronage of the church. In this way, subsequent Christians saw Helena as a nurturing mother of the church just as she was a treasured mother of the emperor.

In 326, Helena made a trip to Palestine to find the holy sites. During her trip, Helena lavished money on the poor and on the faithful soldiers of Rome. Her journey did more—it reinforced the Christian message and ensured a Christian victory over paganism. Helena reclaimed Jerusalem itself, for in 326 it remained a destroyed backwater city as it had been since the Jewish wars of 70 and 130 (as described in chapter 5). Now, Jerusalem would be a Christian center, and Helena located the sites that would draw pilgrims for the next millennia. In 335 Constantine traveled to Jerusalem to preside over the dedication of the Church of the Holy Sepulcher that his mother had begun.

By 395, a sermon by Ambrose, Bishop of Milan, links the story of Helena's visit to Jerusalem with an account of her discovery of the True Cross.[31] With Constantine, the Cross had become the definitive symbol of Christianity that separated it once and for all from Judaism, and Ambrose joins the finding of the Cross with anti-Semitism, for he claimed that the Cross had been hidden by Jews (see chapter 5).[32] For Ambrose, and centuries of Christians after him, the Cross was rescued from Jews by Helena, the perfect Christian mother. In the eyes of early Christians, Helena redeemed the Cross from Jewish perfidy, just as martyrs had preserved Christianity from Jewish persecution—the mother served the same role as martyr, without the need for witness until death.

Even more than Helena, Monica, mother of St. Augustine, was the most famous Christian mother. Monica was more influential not because of her own status but because of the writings of her prolific son; just as with martyrs, the texts were more influential than the deeds themselves. Augustine wrote after the age of martyrs was over, Christians no longer needed individuals who were willing to break social ties. Instead, they needed those who could care for and preserve the community and its members. Like the Maccabean mother who so many centuries earlier had served as such a model, Christian mothers began to be revered. When Augustine described his mother, it was in many of the same terms that had previously characterized the martyrs. Thus, images in the

Christian world were coming full circle—first martyrs became mothers; now mothers were becoming martyrs.

Augustine's mother Monica fulfilled many of the same roles as the martyrs who were described in such maternal terms. Her overwhelming characteristic was faith and spirituality that was never shaken. Furthermore, just like the martyrs that Eusebius described "praying for the stillborn," Monica prayed and wept repeatedly for the salvation of her son. Augustine wrote,

> My mother, your faithful servant, wept to you for me, shedding more tears for my spiritual death than other mothers shed for the bodily death of a son. . . . You heard her and did not despise the tears which streamed down and watered the earth in every place where she bowed her head in prayer.[33]

Like the intercession of the martyrs, Monica's prayers were effective. A local bishop told the distressed mother, "It cannot be that the son of those tears should be lost."[34] Augustine (and the fifth-century reader) accepted these words as prophetic foreknowledge of the salvation of her son through the mother's efforts.

As we saw in chapter 4, confessors had received prophetic dreams and visions as marks of their holiness. While imprisoned, Perpetua received four prophetic dreams. Two of the dreams concerned her dead brother Dinocrates. In the first dream, she saw he was suffering in the afterlife, deprived of comforting water. Perpetua did not despair of her brother: "I was sure that I would be able to help him in his affliction. . . . I prayed for my brother day and night, groaning and shedding tears that my prayer might be granted." These words could have been written by Monica, praying and crying for the salvation of her son, Augustine. Perpetua's prayers were rewarded by a vision in which she saw Dinocrates "clean and nicely dressed and refreshed." Perpetua was reassured, writing, "I awoke, recognizing that he had been released from his affliction."[35]

Monica also received a dream vision in which she was reassured of the efficacy of her prayers. In her dream, Monica said she was weeping for her son's soul, but a young man who appeared to her told her not to worry and showed her son standing in the same place as she. Monica interpreted this vision as prophetic of Augustine's future salvation,[36] just as Perpetua had received reassurance of Dinocrates's release from pain.

The popularity of Augustine's work guaranteed that his portrayal of Monica as the ideal mother influenced people's ideas of Christian motherhood. Christian mothers were to perform the same functions for their family members as martyrs had done for the early Christian communities that became surrogate families for Christians breaking away from pagan society. Christian mothers were not simply responsible for the physical well-being of their offspring, nor were they primarily charged with socializing their children into the culture of the community as their Roman counterparts had been. Instead, they cared for the spiritual health of their families. Augustine wrote of his mother, "In the flesh she brought me to birth in this world: in her heart she brought me to birth in your eternal light."[37] Monica may be seen as the prototype for the new Christian mothers who watched out for spiritual health by exhortation, prayers, and the shedding of many tears. All these actions were characteristic of the confessors preparing themselves for martyrdom.

In the same way that Jacobus rewrote tales of martyrs to express metaphorically the way martyrs fulfilled the function of mothers, he may also be used to show the final association of mothers as martyrs in the Christian consciousness. Jacobus wrote a brief account of the martyrdom of the "Seven Sons of Saint Felicitas" that purportedly took place in the year 110. There is little probability that this martyrdom actually occurred, but it seems a rewriting of the story of the Maccabean martyrs in a Christian context. Jacobus tells of the arrest of Felicitas with her seven sons. She urged the boys to stand firm in their testing, and like the Maccabean mother before her, watched her sons die before she herself was martyred. Then Jacobus wrote, "Felicitas [was] more than a martyr, for she suffered sevenfold in her seven sons, and an eight time in her own body."[38] In this account, we see Christian motherhood coming of age. Felicitas became a martyr not in spite of her maternity but strengthened through it, and like the Maccabean mother she was guarding the Christian community through her role as mother. This account would not have come from the age of martyrs in which families were divided in their faith. It came from centuries later when Christian mothers were charged with care for the salvation of their offspring, just as Monica had cared for that of Augustine. Felicitas, the perfect Christian mother, became a martyr, just as Monica the perfect Christian mother suffered as a martyr.

The changing perceptions of the associations between motherhood and martyrdom offer a number of insights into religion, society, and family. In the eyes of martyrs who were seeking salvation, early Christian martyrdom had nothing to do with maternity. Mothers were structurally and physically linked to family and society, precisely those things that held martyrs to this world instead of allowing them to seek the next. However, there is always a social component of religions, and this social component did provide for a role for people who served traditional functions of mothers. Before they died, martyrs were made holy by their confessions, and these confessors used their holiness in the service of the Christian community. In this role, they were referred to in terms previously reserved for mothers.

Finally, the associations are completed with the establishment of Christianity as the religion of the Roman empire in the fourth century. Then the age of martyrs was over, so confessors no longer fulfilled the maternal functions of holding together the surrogate families of the Christian congregations. Christian families once more became the central social unit. Mothers guided and preserved those families as they had during the pagan empire. However, they had acquired an additional role with the coming of Christianity. Christian mothers were responsible for the spiritual health of their families as well as their physical well-being. In this care, they used the same techniques and were referred to in the same terms as the Christian martyrs—mothers became martyrs. During these years, the stage was set for the later veneration of the Virgin Mary, the perfect Christian mother.

There is a relationship between martyrdom and maternity, but the relationship is not a firm and unchanging one. Martyrs and mothers both cared for their families (whether their physical or spiritual families). Sometimes that care took them into the arena with their children, whether their natural children as the Maccabean mother or their spiritual children like Blandina. Sometimes the care was in the world, whether confessors praying from their prison cells or Monica weeping for her wayward son. It seems that in the imagination and language of the West, the words and descriptions of maternity were the ones strong and descriptive enough to describe the role martyrs played for their communities. In doing so, Christian concepts of both martyrdom and motherhood were transformed, and many a mother today would not be surprised to know that part of her role as mother is to be a martyr.

Agatha, although a virgin, looks pregnant in this image of her torture. Such popular portrayals preserve the ideal of virgins as fertility symbols. Fourteenth century. *The Belles Heures of the Duke de Berry*, The Metropolitan Museum of Art, The Cloister Collection (54.1.1 folio 79 recto).

7

THE BLOOD
OF SACRIFICE

What is a martyr? In the previous chapter, I explored how mothers came to be considered like martyrs, and in this chapter I look even more closely at the transformation of the idea of martyr. The word *martyr* originally meant "witness," and people in the second and third centuries knew clearly what martyrs were: people who held fast to their faith and were killed for refusing to renounce their principles. Today the word has acquired an additional meaning, and it's not altogether a positive one. We often use the word to mean "long suffering" or sacrificing one's own pleasure or well-being for the sake of another. This is the role that too often becomes attached to mothers, but the attribution is not limited to a maternal function. When we say "Don't be a martyr," we mean "don't be self-sacrificing." What is going on here? How did the blood shed during martyrdom become the blood of sacrifice, and is sacrifice good or bad? As we look back at the age of martyrdom, we can see that pagan ideas of sacrifice entered Christian consciousness through the blood of martyrs, and as time passed, *martyr* no longer meant witness but instead meant a sacrificial victim, and in this form it retains its most insidious meaning in the twenty-first century. How did this happen?

THE IDEA OF SACRIFICE

The earliest relationship between people and their deities was one of a bargain. From time immemorial, people have offered sacrifices to the gods in the hope that if they renounce something valuable they would get something of value in return. In the ancient pagan world, people offered everything from a drop of wine, a bit of a sweet cake, a portion of meat, or a sacrificial animal. The animals varied in size, from a dove to a large ox, and the greater the sacrifice, the greater the blessing one asked in return. The idea of sacrifice lies within the worldview of ancient peoples (indeed of everyone before the industrial age) which says that all the goods of the world constitute a zero-sum game. Therefore, blessings in one realm come only at the cost of deprivation in another. In traditional villages, for example, this meant that if one person's crops were particularly abundant, one's neighbors were suspicious because such abundance came at the expense of someone else.[1] There was only a limited amount of good things in the world, so careful people had to find ritual ways to ensure their share of blessings.

In ways that seem a bit paradoxical to modern ears, this insurance against scarcity involved sacrifice–giving up what you hold dear. If people valued their food and wine, they gave up some of it to the gods to ensure more would be forthcoming. In a zero-sum game, you don't win by hoarding; you ensure continued prosperity by giving up what you value. The corollary to this idea is that the most valuable things you are willing to sacrifice, the greater the blessing that you hope to obtain.

The greatest sacrifice of all was life, and blood spilled on an altar represented the loss of life. Blood is seen as particularly valuable because in traditional societies (even today) blood is believed to be nonregenerative,[2] and thus the loss of blood is the highest sacrifice. This belief in the power of blood runs so deeply in human consciousness that we have forgotten its origins and indeed perhaps undervalue the degree to which it still retains its hold on us. (Notice how small children recoil in horror when they bleed from a small cut.)

Most blood sacrifices were of animals, and as the life drained away in the animals' blood, petitioners hoped their lives would be preserved. The age-old bargain was repeated: blood for blood, life for life, and this sacrificial tradition was at the heart of ancient worship from pagans to

Jews. In the Hebrew Scriptures, the eighth-century prophet Micah describes some offerings:

> With what shall I approach the Lord,
> Do homage to God on high?
> Shall I approach Him with burnt offerings,
> With calves a year old?
> Would the Lord be pleased with thousands of rams
> With myriads of streams of oil? (Mic. 6:6)

Thousands of rams offered on the altar would surely spill enough blood to bring blessings, but sometimes even this much blood did not seem valuable enough. If life is valued, why not spill human blood as the most valuable sacrifice? The prophet Micah escalated the offerings: "Shall I give my first-born for my transgression, The fruit of my body for my sins?" (Mic. 6:6-7). There were some cultures that offered human sacrifice in desperate times, and it appears that the ancient Hebrews, too, sometimes made this offering.[3] The Book of Exodus tells of God's command, "You shall give Me the first-born among your sons" (Exod. 22:28), and one of the most beloved passages of the Hebrew Scriptures tells of Abraham's deep faith as he was willing to place his favorite son Isaac on an altar to offer him as a burnt offering (Gen. 22:2-19). That Abraham's hand was stayed by an angel at the last moment does not change the fact that he was willing to give his son's blood. The patriarch's faith and the ram's blood that he shed instead of Isaac's was a sufficient sacrifice. In exchange for this willingness to sacrifice, God promised his blessings upon Abraham: "I will indeed bless you, and I will multiply your descendants as the stars of heaven and as the sand which is on the seashore" (Gen. 22:17). Here we can see the logic of the sacrifice in a world of limited resources: kill your descendent to gain more progeny–blood for blood, life for life.

The Bible tells us that many of the Hebrews' neighbors practiced human sacrifice. For example, a king of Moab who was losing a battle against Israel took his eldest son and "offered him for a burnt offering upon the wall." The sacrifice worked and Israel withdrew (2 Kings 3:26-27). Generally, scriptures describe people who "offer up their sons and daughters in fire to their gods" (Deut. 12:31). The Bible mentioned how the Phoenicians practiced human sacrifice in their earliest history, and the practice was preserved in the Phoenician colony of Carthage long after it had been abandoned elsewhere.

In the seventh century B.C., the Hebrew prophets began to oppose the sacrifice of eldest sons. The prophet Jeremiah vehemently separated the people of Israel from the Phoenician neighbors as he cried out against the practice of human sacrifice: "They have filled this place with the blood of innocents, and have built the high places of Baal to burn their sons in the fire as burnt offering to Baal" (Jer. 19:5–6). Jeremiah's words mark the end of human sacrifice for the ancient Hebrews, but they also describe the practice of blood offering in Carthage where for centuries people continued to kill their children.

Archaeologists of Carthage have excavated an ancient cemetery that contains only the ashes of sacrificial children and animals. This still-sad space vividly expresses the fears of ancient parents who responded to their deep anxiety about the future by sacrificing their children. What is perhaps most impressive about the site is the sheer number of urns buried there. Between 400 and 200 B.C., during the height of Carthaginian power, as many as twenty thousand urns may have been buried: an average of one hundred deposits a year. The excavations bear silent witness to written sources that accused the Carthaginians of sacrificing children. Plutarch, for example, described the sacrifice: "They themselves offered up their own children, and those who had no children would buy little ones from poor people and cut their throats as if they were so many lambs or young birds."[4]

While the Romans banned human sacrifice (or at least limited its expression to gladiators in the arena), Carthaginians continued the practice. Subsequent North African Christian writers continued to condemn the superstitious Carthaginians who spilled the blood of their children. The early third-century Christian writer, Tertullian, wrote that the practice continued into his own time.[5] In the fourth century, Augustine, Bishop of Hippo in North Africa, wrote that Carthaginians sacrificed their children because humans were the most valuable sacrifice of all.[6] Augustine's words do more than state the obvious; they show us how the need for sacrificial blood remained close to people's hearts, particularly in North Africa.

Sacrificial victims were supposed to volunteer for the sacrifice, or at least be willing participants. Wise priests made sure sacrificial animals were drugged so they followed docilely to the altar and the knife. For child sacrifice, compliant parents fondled their children to make them laugh at the moment of death, for if a single tear were shed, the good effect of the sacrifice was nullified.[7] It is perhaps not surprising in this context that many in the ancient world valued people who sacrificed themselves for political purpose.

The history of Carthage itself was punctuated at its turning points by a sacrificial suicide. The Carthaginian general Hamilcar Barca in 485 B.C. was fighting Greeks in Sicily. When the battle turned against the Carthaginians, he sacrificed himself for the cause. The ancient historian Herodotus described what happened: "Hamilcar remained in camp, sacrificing and offering for favorable results whole bodies of victims on a great pyre. But when he saw the rout of his troops happening and he was at that moment pouring the libations on the victims, he threw himself headlong into the pyre."[8] (As we shall see in chapter 8, the practice of self-immolation lasted a long time in this land of sacrificial suicide.)

Another legend added sacrificial blood to the building of the all-important aqueduct that brought water into Carthage: the story says that a Roman soldier fell in love with a native princess. She scorned his attentions and established what seemed to be an impossible condition to his winning her hand: she would not marry him until the waters of the Zaghouan River flowed into Carthage. The enterprising Roman built an impressive aqueduct and went to claim his bride. The princess killed herself rather than submit, throwing herself from the top of the newly built aqueduct.[9] By adding this legend to the founding of the aqueduct, the wary Carthaginians could rely on sacrificial blood of the princess to ensure the continuation of the water supply to the city. For Carthaginians, the opportunity to die for a cause was one that came back again and again.

CHRISTIAN SACRIFICE

As Christianity came to the ancient world it had to confront the tradition of blood sacrifice, and as they had been shaped by ancient culture, Christians shared the belief in the value of sacrificial blood. However, in the Christian tradition the blood of Christ was supposed to be the full and sufficient sacrifice. In biblical language, Jesus–God's beloved son–took the place of Isaac, Abraham's beloved son. While Abraham's hand was stayed and a ram sacrificed, God allowed his son's blood to be spilled as the soldier pierced his side with a spear. In this way, for Christians, Christ's blood was sacrificed for everyone's salvation.

The early Christian texts made these associations explicit to persuade new converts to renounce old forms of sacrifice and accept the value of Christ's blood. For example, the second-century letter of Barnabas (probably a converted Jew in Alexandria) directly addressed that there was no need for old offerings. Barnabas wrote, "The calf is Jesus and the sinners who offer it are those who dragged Him to the slaughter." Barnabas also links Jesus' sacrifice directly to Hebrew Scripture so there can be no doubt about the continuity in the ideas of the blood of sacrifice:

> Now, when the Lord resigned Himself to deliver His body to destruction, the aim He had in view was to sanctify us by the remission of our sins; which is effected by the sprinkling of His blood. For what Scripture says of Him (referring partly to Israel, but also partly to ourselves) is, *he was wounded on account of our transgressions, and bruised because of our sins, and by his scars we were healed. He was led to the slaughter like a sheep, and like a lamb that is dumb before its shearer.* (Isa. liii, 5, 7)

Barnabas concludes that the Lord no longer needs "sacrifices, burnt-offerings and oblations."[10] In the Christian tradition, the blood of sacrifice was satisfied once and for all by Jesus. As Tertullian succinctly put it, "Do you have desire for blood? You have the blood of Christ."[11]

The early Christian writers were certain that there was no longer any need for the blood of sacrifice to ensure the salvation of the community of the faithful. Each time they reenacted the Last Supper and recited Christ's words, "This is my blood which is shed for you," they were reassured that the necessity of blood for blood had been satisfied once and for all, and some of the texts of the martyrs reaffirm this position. For example, the Acts of Phileas from the second century includes (like many of the other texts) a dialogue between the Roman inquisitor and the confessor. The Roman asked, "What sort of sacrifices does God demand?" Phileas answered, "A pure heart, a spotless soul, and spiritual perceptions [which lead to] the deeds of piety and justice."[12] In this exchange, we can see the orthodox Christian position—God needs no more sacrifice; He requires us to live in the faith, not die for it.

However, the history of ideas does not proceed so neatly; one idea seldom thoroughly supplants another, and ideas of the power of sacrificial blood lay deeply within people's consciousness, whether they were aware of it or not. As soon as the age of martyrs dawned, the barely buried notion of the blood of sacrifice emerged again, and confessors could look in scriptures in the words of Paul for an expression of sacrificial blood. In his letter to the Philippians, Paul acknowledged that holding fast to faith might bring suffering, and the Apostle chose the words of sacrifice to express this affliction: "Even if I am to be poured as a libation upon the sacrificial offering of your faith, I am glad and rejoice with you all" (Phil. 2:17). In his second letter to Timothy, Paul is more explicit: "For I am already on the point of being sacrificed; the time of my departure has come" (2 Tim. 4:6). With these scriptural words widely circulating, it is not surprising that other confessors used the same sacrificial language on the eve of their martyrdoms.

One of the earliest accurate accounts of a Christian martyrdom tells of the death of Polycarp, bishop of Smyrna in the Roman province of Asia (modern Turkey). In about 155, a wave of persecution spread through the province and local pagans clamored for Polycarp's arrest. He withdrew to a house in the country, but was followed. One of his servants was tortured and betrayed his master's whereabouts; the Roman officials came and arrested the aged bishop. He, together with eleven other Christians, was sentenced to die in the arena for a festival in Smyrna. Soon after Polycarp's death, the congregation at Smyrna received a letter from members of the church at Philomelium (about two hundred miles to the east) asking for an account of the martyrdom. A man named Marcion, who had been one of the eyewitnesses to the martyrdom, wrote a vivid account of Polycarp's arrest and death, and this account was sent to the Philomelians with a suggestion that it be circulated to other churches. In this way, the account of Polycarp's martyrdom became widely distributed and formed the core of many subsequent ideas about martyrs. Polycarp's analysis of his experience, the words he used to describe the events all form a basis for our understanding of martyrs, and Polycarp defined his own martyrdom in terms of the blood of sacrifice.

Polycarp was sentenced to be burned alive, and in preparation for that his hands were bound behind him as he waited for the building of the wood pile that would become his funeral pyre. Marcion described the bishop: "Bound like that, with his hands behind him, he was like a noble ram taken out of some great flock for sacrifice: a goodly burnt-offering all ready for God." Here, Marcion evokes the traditional image of Isaac, bound by Abraham to become a sacrificial offering to God; he also evokes the beloved son, Jesus, who was sacrificed on the wood of the cross. The age-old images were made fresh and new in the account of martyrdom, and Polycarp, too, saw himself in this light, for in his final prayer, he called himself "a sacrifice, rich and acceptable."[13]

Polycarp was not alone in his belief that he was a sacrificial victim offered for the benefit of the community of the faithful. A few years earlier, an equally influential bishop, Ignatius of Antioch, was martyred. Like Polycarp, Ignatius saw himself as a sacrificial offering. In one of his letters, Ignatius expressed his fear that his many friends would intercede for him and rob him of his expected martyrdom. He urged his followers not to interfere: "This favor only I beg of you: suffer me to be a libation poured out to God, while there is still an altar ready for me."[14] For Ignatius and many other Christians, the arena in Rome had become not a place of pagan celebrations but an altar upon which the sacrificial blood of martyrs would be shed.

Through popular texts like these, one can readily see that even while Christians proclaimed that God asked for not sacrificial blood other than that of Jesus which had been shed for all humanity, the faithful saw continued sacrifice in the shedding of blood in the arenas of the empire. The idea of martyrdom as "witness" was rapidly broadening to include the concept of martyrdom as "sacrifice."

There was perhaps a clear logic in seeing martyrs imitating Jesus' sacrificial death, and thus becoming sacrifices as well, but in the fourth century when the age of martyrs ended, it seems equally logical that there would be no more need, nor occasion, for the shedding of sacrificial blood. However, it appears that humans were unwilling (or unable) to give up the powerful idea that blood shed unselfishly might be beneficial. In the accounts of the martyrs, then, the idea of sacrificial blood took on a broader, more symbolic meaning than simply the literal reality of martyrs sacrificed on God's altar for their faith. People began to think of other blood as sacrificial, and in this Christians also echoed other ancient beliefs. Through the accounts of martyr stories, the menstrual blood that virgins shed became perceived as sacrificial blood, an association that extended long after the age of martyrdom had ended.

FERTILE VIRGINS: A CONTINUING SACRIFICE

To understand the idea of virgin blood as sacrificial, I will start with the story of the martyr Eulalia of Merida, in Spain. While modern commentators wonder if Eulalia ever existed, Christians of the ancient world did not doubt it. Worship of her cult appears in the earliest lists of martyrs from Carthage and Rome, and church fathers and poets wrote of her martyrdom. These texts were so popular and influential that the memory of her martyrdom overwhelms any consideration of accuracy of the events. The following is the bare outline of the story.

In the fourth-century persecution of Diocletian, a young twelve-year-old Christian girl came to the attention of the authorities. As the inquisitor Decian required everyone to make a sacrifice to the gods and emperor, Eulalia's mother was afraid the pious girl would come to the attention of the authorities, so she tried to keep her home. However, Eulalia secretly escaped and took a torturous path to the Romans. She walked over brambles through the dark night for many miles toward the administrative center, and in the morning she arrived at the court and challenged the guards. She reproached them for persecuting Christians, and declared herself to be one.

The judge first tried to flatter and bribe her to recant, and finally tried to terrify her with tortures, but she withstood all pressure. The child was not frightened by his threats, and indeed she spit in the judge's face. He tried to persuade her to think of her parents and her future marriage, but she was intransigent. When persuasion did not work the Romans turned to torture. They tore her flesh with clawlike instruments until she bled, but she bravely withstood the torture. Her tormentors then threw her into a fire which consumed her. Her body was discarded outdoors where it was covered by snow until nearby Christians claimed it and buried the precious bones. Her body (and the oven that burned it) are preserved in Merida as her shrine.

Modern scholars question the veracity of the story, but there is no question that fourth-century Christians believed the tale. About a century after her death (and after the persecutions had ended), the Spanish poet Prudentius wrote a poem about the passion of Eulalia, and this is the earliest surviving text to preserve the story of her martyrdom. As we have seen, the account of the martyrdom is even more important than the death itself, for it is the story that shapes the memories, and in the account by Prudentius, the poet transformed the old image of the blood of sacrifice, giving it a new, richer meaning that outlasted the age of martyrdom.

Prudentius wrote a hymn that told of the young martyr's passion and urged the faithful to come to her shrine in Merida, where her relics were entombed. He wrote, "Boys and virgins come give gifts of wreaths . . . and thus we shall venerate her relics enshrined in this altar."[15] However, Prudentius offered more than a call for remembrance; he specifically told the faithful how her blood—her sacrificial blood—brought prosperity to the city: "A powerful city, wealthy people, but made more prosperous by the blood of the virginal tomb."[16]

There is a long tradition of associating blood with fertility that extends far beyond the age of martyrs. For example, the sixteenth-century French satirist, Rabelais, who brilliantly recorded age-old country legends in his works wrote that after "Abel's killing the earth absorbed his blood and became fertile,"[17] and this is exactly the principle that Prudentius expressed: Eulalia's blood that was sacrificed brought fertility to the land surrounding Merida.

Prudentius's poem was very popular and was probably read annually on the saint's day. This reading was institutionalized in the seventh century when the Fourth Council of Toledo that convened in Spain ordered that veneration of saints should be formally incorporated into the church worship. Several of Prudentius's hymns—including the praise of Eulalia—was included into the formal liturgy of the church services.[18] Therefore, for centuries after Eulalia's death, the praise of her sacrificial blood echoed in the voices and hearts of the faithful in Spain, North Africa, and Italy. The old idea of the gift of blood entered into Christian worship.

On the surface, Prudentius's poem praises the blood that was shed as the torture claw ripped Eulalia's flesh, but his choice of words yields a deeper, and older, symbolic meaning. When Prudentius wrote that the land was hallowed by the "virginal tomb," he surely intended his readers to think of the virgin's "womb" as well as "tomb." Ancient myths and folk tales have always linked women with death as well as birth, and women's wombs were described as a cave or a tomb. Deep within the woman's body a man's erection "dies" in the "little death" of orgasm. These associations between womb and tomb were so familiar to the ancient audiences that Prudentius's poem was readily understood to have two meanings: Eulalia's tomb blessed the city, and the blood from Eulalia's virgin womb was also a sacrifice that brought prosperity and fertility to the faithful. The blood of sacrifice became menstrual blood.

While all women were seen to embody both womb and tomb, people believed that a virgin's blood was a particularly efficacious sacrifice. Like the concept of sacrificial blood, the associations between menstrual blood and fertility are very old, probably dating back to prehistory, and they are not surprising. After all, a virgin signals her readiness to reproduce by shedding blood, and married women then become pregnant and stop bleeding, converting their blood to new life. Since a virgin sacrifices her own fertility by withdrawing from reproduction, she is thought to bring fertility to the community instead. In a zero-sum game, the absence of fertility in one body brings it to another.

Therefore, when Prudentius made the explicit association between Eulalia's sacrificed virgin blood and prosperity, he was expressing an old idea. The ancient Celts (many of whom had settled in northern Spain) had myths that linked a "water virgin" with fertility, and for their part, the Romans institutionalized the metaphoric associations in the religious college of Vestal Virgins. These women were to remain virgin and guard the sacred hearth of the state. In return for their sacrifice, the goddess Vesta ensured Rome's prosperity. If one of the Vestal Virgins betrayed her vows, the penalty was severe—she was to be sealed away and left to die of thirst and hunger. Her no-longer virginal womb was entombed; the sacrifice of her life replaced the sacrifice of her virgin blood, and the prosperity of Rome was again restored. Through the persecutions during the early centuries of martyrdom and the texts that told their tales, the old idea of the efficacy of virgin blood entered solidly into Christian consciousness.

Martyrs' accounts tell of many virgin saints during the persecutions; so many in fact that one wonders if only virgins held firm in their faith. More likely, in the telling, virginity was attributed to many female martyrs thus reinforcing the sacrificial virgin symbol that was so important. Eulalia was the archetype for these many virgin saints.

Perhaps the finest example of the inflation of sacrificial virgins may be seen in the legend of the martyr Ursula and her companions. Ursula and some fellow virgins were martyred in Cologne, Germany, during the fourth-century persecutions, and as was true with many (perhaps most) of the martyrs there was no written record of the circumstances of their deaths. All that remained was a Latin inscription carved in stone in about 400 that said the local church had been restored in honor of Ursula and some other virgin martyrs.

By the ninth century, local tradition had developed a story that said Ursula had come to Cologne from Britain where she was martyred with five (or eight or eleven) companions. In the tenth century, the number of her fellow virgins was fixed at eleven thousand! The influential thirteenth-century collection of saints' lives—the *Golden Legend*—recorded her legend in the form that remained hugely popular for centuries. The account is roughly as follows:

Ursula was the daughter of a British Christian king whose father betrothed her to a pagan prince. She delayed the marriage by claiming she needed a three-year delay during which she would take a sea voyage as a religious pilgrimage. She boarded a ship and was joined by 1,000 virgins. In addition, ten other noble daughters also accompanied her, each on her own ship and each joined by 1,000 more virgins. The flotilla with 11,000 virgins sailed into the mouth of the Rhine river and to Cologne. Eventually, Cologne was besieged by Huns. The virgins were captured, and Ursula refused to marry the Huns' leader who was captivated by her beauty. She was felled by an arrow and all her 11,000 virgins were martyred with her. The citizens of Cologne buried them and built a church to celebrate their cult.[19]

In spite of the elements of the legend that strain credulity (the resources needed to accommodate one thousand high-born ship-board virgins in each ship would require today's cruise ships rather than the ancient triremes), the story was popular and Ursula's cult was celebrated in Germany, the Low Countries, and other locations in Europe. Artists from the late Middle Ages through the sixteenth century loved to paint this legend, perhaps culminating with the lush portrayal by Rubens.

I suggest that the popularity of her cult came largely from the deep symbolic value of sacrificial virgin blood. If Eulalia's blood could ensure the prosperity of Merida, the blood of Ursula and her eleven thousand virgins could bathe all of Germany in blessings. The symbolic sacrificial blood mattered more than strict accuracy—at least until 1969 when the reform of the Roman church calendar of saints removed Ursula and her companions from veneration in the universal church. (Her cult is still permitted in some locations, like Cologne.)

We saw in chapter 6 how motherhood began to be perceived as incompatible with martyrdom, which offers the mirror image of this idea—only virgins shed sacrificial blood. The golden age of martyrs solidified the idea that virgin blood is efficacious as sacrifice, and this idea persisted long after the fourth century when the early martyrdoms ended. Virgins were the new martyrs who bled and brought prosperity to the faithful. As the fourth-century church father Jerome characteristically overstated, virgins were "simple, pure, unsullied, drawing no germ of life from without, but like God himself, fruitful in singleness"[20]—they were pregnant virgins, pregnant with spirituality.

Many of the illustrations of virgin martyrs that were created throughout the next few centuries portrayed virgins with bellies as if they were pregnant to reinforce this idea. The illustration of the virgin martyr Agatha that accompanies this chapter shows her torturer bracing his knee below her full belly as he tears her breasts off. In this powerfully important symbolic meaning, virgins were spiritually fertile, and these images move far beyond the initial meaning of their martyrdom—that of bearing witness.

To show how these ideas were expressed outside the arenas of martyrdom, I will describe two little-known letters from anonymous fourth-century Spanish virgins whose images capture beautifully the idea of the spiritual fecundity of their bleeding virgin wombs.[21] The first of the letters was written by a woman who had taken a vow of virginity. She likely did not live in a community of nuns but instead probably stayed quietly at home like many other early Christian virgins. She wrote to a dear friend and mentor in affectionate language and described the spiritual knowledge she had acquired by remaining virgin.

The images this anonymous virgin chose were most frequently those associated with fertility. In the short three-page letter, she used some form of the word *fertility* eight times, as well as including somewhat less-direct references to water, pregnancy, and the womb. The complex images may be summarized into one thought: by sacrificing sexual intercourse, a virgin receives God's spirit into her uterus from which she "gives birth" to spiritual knowledge. As she wrote, "Fruit pours forth from your womb; that you may carry your child [wisdom] about and show it . . . to us survivors of a darkened generation."[22]

At first glance, these images seem a little disturbing to our modern ears; we are not used to imagining God entering into one's uterus. Nor do we customarily think of the blood from a virgin's womb as "spiritual knowledge" that can benefit the community. Yet, in the context of the virgin martyrs like Eulalia, these images make complete sense. Blood that is shed voluntarily—since the virgin has chosen to remain virgin and continue to bleed—is sacrificial blood that brings salvation to the virgin and to the community.

The second anonymous letter shares the same themes, but it adds an additional dimension to the subject because the woman is writing to a married acquaintance. The author is urging her friend to withdraw from her family for a while to an isolated retreat where she can fast and pray for three weeks. This time was to be in imitation of the Virgin Mary's postpartum recuperation and was to be a restorative time. During this time, "with the box of your body in flood,"[23] she might receive a divine revelation.[24]

Once again, the positive images of menstrual blood are surprising, particularly in an age that believed that such blood was dangerous. Isidore of Seville, the great seventh-century Spanish encyclopedist who compiled much of then-current knowledge, expressed the dangers of menstrual blood, which caused "fruits not to germinate, wine to sour, plants to parch, trees to lose their fruit, iron to be corroded, bronze to turn black and dogs to become rabid if they eat anything that has come in contact with the blood."[25] The range of warnings Isidore includes about menstrual blood indicates the striking contrast between regular menstrual blood and the menstrual blood that had been converted to sacrificial blood by a martyr's death or a virgin's vow.

This discussion of the transformation of the age-old idea of the need for sacrificial blood into a Christian acceptance of the notion almost suggests that no deeply held idea is forgotten. But that is not so; the account of the experience of the martyrs preserved some ideas, but others were lost, and this contrast may be most readily seen in the ancient practice of ritual self-castration. The act of castration as a sacrifice to gain fertility has mythological roots as deep as those of the blood of sacrifice and respect for virgins' blood. Once again, it is fertility sacrificed to yield fertility—life for life.

In Greek mythology, Cronos, who was the youngest son of Heaven (Uranus) and Earth (Gaia), castrated his father with a flint sickle and took his place. Some myths claim that the goddess of love, Aphrodite, was born from Uranus's testicles that were thrown into the sea—an explicit association of castration with fertility.

From the ancient lands of Asia Minor (modern Turkey) came a similar myth that also had longer-standing popularity. This told of Attis, the companion of the fertility goddess Cybele. While there are various versions of the myth, in all of them Attis castrated himself, and in some he died from the self-inflicted wound. However, his sacrifice yielded fertility because flowers grew spontaneously from his grave. Attis's mutilation became part of the celebration of the worship of the goddess Cybele throughout the ancient world. The second-century writer Lucian of Samosata vividly described the continuing sacrificial castrations:

> For while the rest are playing flutes and performing the rites [of the goddess], frenzy comes upon many, and many who have come simply to watch subsequently perform this act. I will describe what they do. The youth for whom these things lie in store throws off his clothes, rushes to the center with a great shout and takes up a sword. . . . He grabs it and immediately castrates himself. Then he rushes through the city holding in his hands the parts he has cut off. He takes female clothing and women's adornment from whatever house he throws these parts into. This is what they do at the Castration.[26]

It was through this remarkable ritual that men became priests of the Great Goddess Cybele and participated in the mysteries that brought fertility and prosperity. They willingly sacrificed their own fertility just as virgins sacrificed theirs. Eunuchs did not necessarily renounce sexual activity, for a man who is castrated in adulthood can often continue to have sexual relations; he simply will not expel semen. In the ancient world, semen was considered to be vital spirit that fertilized women, yet debilitated a man who expended too much of it. Therefore, eunuchs were consciously preserving their own spirit and putting it to a religious purpose.[27] (Modern readers imbued with our scientific grounding might immediately object and say after the self-castration, the man no longer produced semen, so how could he be preserving this vital spirit? However, the ancients were not so literally physical. They believed testicles distilled a man's spirit and made it ready to expel, but the ancients did not locate the spirit that defined a man solely in his testicles.)

Could this ideal of sacrificial castration have entered Christian thought? Certainly some early gnostic Christians castrated themselves as a rejection of the flesh and a release of the spirit. This tradition was precisely consistent with the values of the old priests of Cybele. Furthermore, some orthodox Christians also believed the path to spirituality lay through the sacrifice of their fecundity. We have a document from second-century Alexandria (in Egypt) in which a Christian petitioned the Roman prefect for permission to have himself castrated for religious purposes. Without official permission, he and the physician could be prosecuted; in the ancient world one's sexuality was not fully one's own. The prefect turned him down, but the survival of the request testifies to the existence of this practice among early Christians.[28]

The most famous example of Christian self-castration was the early third-century church father Origen (whose influential ideas on resurrection of the body were discussed in chapter 2). As a young man, the devout Christian student read the passage in Matthew (19:12) "and there are eunuchs who have made themselves eunuchs for the sake of the kingdom of heaven," and he interpreted it literally. Origen castrated himself. Would Christians applaud his sacrifice? This was a critical question for the future. In the fourth century, the church historian Eusebius described Origen's "headstrong act," and yet, Eusebius admired Origen's "faith and self-mastery" and wrote that the bishop also approved of the young scholar's enthusiasm. It was only some years later when Origen had become more famous that jealousy changed the bishop's opinion. According to Eusebius, "For want of any other charge to bring against him, [the bishop] slandered him viciously for what he had done years before as a boy. . . ."[29] From this discussion, we can see that even by the fourth century, there was ambivalence about the sacrifice of self-castration.

I suggest that the definitive rejection of the practice took place in the arenas of martyrdom, not in discussions by theologians. When Christians spilled their blood bravely in their passion, surviving Christians embraced the blood as sacrifice. What if Christians had castrated themselves in the arena? The idea is not as improbable as it sounds; the church father Tertullian had watched condemned prisoners reenact Attis's death by self-castration,[30] and some Christians were made to engage in such reenactments to make their deaths more entertaining to the crowd. However, the fact that self-castration was so linked to pagan rituals made it unpalatable to Christians. If a Christian died through castration, it was seen less as a matter of pride than as a matter of sadness that he was forced to play the part in a pagan ritual. Martyrdom did not convert the sacrifice of castration to a Christian purpose, and as Origen discovered, that sacrifice was not acceptable to the Christian community. Only sacrificial blood was a worthy offering to God. The Council of Nicaea in 325 definitively banned the practice by forbidding anyone who had castrated himself from becoming a priest: "If anyone in good health has castrated himself, if he is enrolled among the clergy he should be suspended, and in future no such man should be promoted. . . ."[31]

The rejection of sacrificial castration shows how complex is the history of ideas. Some long-held ideas are lost, while others are retained and transformed to apply to new situations and ideas. The pagan idea of sacrificial blood entered the Christian consciousness through the blood of the martyrs, and it was preserved through the sacrificial blood of menstruating virgins. The definition of *martyrs* had been changed from "witness" to sacrificial victim and a sacrifice that could bring benefit to the community, as I detailed in the discussion of magic in chapter 3.

MODERN MARTYRS

The modern world has little opportunity for martyrs as witnesses to the strength of their conviction, but it has all-too-many chances for martyrs as sacrifices. For example, years ago in Spain I became friends with a woman who had entered a particularly strict monastery when she was eighteen years old. Years later she received a papal dispensation to leave the religious life. When I asked her why she had entered even though she knew she lacked a clear vocation, she said that she was distressed by the political situation in Spain and wanted to change it. She believed that her sacrifice of her public life would help her country–life for life. It was an age-old bargain.

In the twentieth and twenty-first centuries, the idea of sacrificial blood leaves the religious arena and enters politics in ways that are frankly disturbing. Periodically, political protestors have immolated themselves: Jan Palach, a Czech student, in 1969 doused himself with flammable liquid, set a match to his clothes and set himself aflame. He did this as a protest against the occupation of Czechoslovakia by Warsaw Pact forces. Twenty-six other students imitated his act. In the United States, we watched on television as Buddhists immolated themselves to stop the war in Vietnam, and in 1999 Kurds set themselves on fire to protest their treatment by the Turks.[32] These are only a few examples of such self-sacrificing protests. What ideas lie behind these acts?

First I should make clear that these protesters–while tragic and perhaps heroic–are not martyrs. Martyrs accept death rather than give up their beliefs; they are witnesses. In the political examples, we have people seeking death to force others to change their practices. Thus, these acts retain the old idea of blood sacrifice in which the sacrifice of that which is most precious–life–is given away in trade for some benefit for one's land or people. The saddest part of this sacrifice is that it does not work. Perhaps the ancient gods in Carthage listened to petitions that were sent on the blood of sacrificial victims, but modern politicians do not. Change is effected by the living, not by blood spilled. It is surely time to give up the old idea of the blood of sacrifice.

But the idea is so powerful it does not easily give up its hold on the imagination. Palestinian suicide bombers call themselves "self-martyrs" and they are hailed as martyrs who will go directly to heaven. They are not martyrs in the oldest sense of the word because they are not bearing witness to their faith, but they are martyrs in this newer sense of the word–they are willing to sacrifice themselves for a cause. During the U.S. bombing of Afghanistan in our war on terrorists, the Taliban leader Mullah Mohammed Omar said, "The Taliban will fight until there is no blood in Afghanistan left to be shed."[33] He did not just mean that they would fight to the last man–he meant their sacrificial blood would buy them victory. It did not.

The sacrificial blood of martyrs shed in the arenas of the old Roman Empire helped ensure the victory of Christianity. Tertullian's claim that the blood of martyrs is seed was accurate—people who remembered the brave deaths of martyrs were strengthened in their own faith. At the same time, the idea of sacrificial blood being efficacious continues to flow through our consciousness. While Christians believe that Jesus' death was a sufficient sacrifice, we continue to be in awe of those who shed their blood in a willing sacrifice. At the same time, we cringe at the accusation that we might be long-suffering sacrificial "martyrs." The ancient biblical tale of Abraham's willingness to kill his son Isaac still captivates—and repels—us.

It is not only the modern world that sees the danger in sacrificial martyrs. As early as the fourth century—virtually as soon as Christians declared the victory of good over evil in the battle for the soul of the Roman empire—Christian leaders saw the danger in the actions of sacrificial martyrs. Virgins could sacrifice their fertility for the good of the community and ascetics could pray and sacrifice their comfort for the faithful, but once the age of martyrs was over, the church soon took steps to regulate those who would sacrifice their lives for a cause.

CONTROLLING THE MARTYRS

This illustration from the Biblical Book of Revelations shows the struggle of good against evil as the evil dragon is confronted by the archers. In life, it began to seem harder to tell who is good and who is evil. Apocalypse Miniature: The Dragon Waging War, c. 1295. Anonymous. Founders Society Purchase with funds from Founders Junior Council and the Mr. and Mrs. Walter B. Ford II Fund. Photograph © 1983. The Detroit Institute of Arts.

REVOLUTIONARY MARTYRS
GOOD VERSUS EVIL AGAIN

ith the victory of Constantine, the age of the martyrs ended. For many, Constantine's 313 Edict of Toleration allowing Christians freedom to worship lifted the fear of persecution that had shrouded the Christian congregations like a deep fog. Constantine's historian Eusebius captured the joy that accompanied the lifting of that oppressive fog:

> Men had now lost all fear of their former oppressors; day after day they kept dazzling festival; light was everywhere, and men who once dared not look up greeted each other with smiling faces and shining eye. They danced and sang in city and country alike. . . .[1]

Many believed with Eusebius that the golden age of peace that had been promised by the book of Revelations, written at the beginning of the ordeal of martyrdom (see chapter 1), was now fulfilled with the reign of the tolerant emperor. Could anyone mourn the end of the hard times of persecution? Yes, many did.

When Christians lived under the fear of arrest, they experienced a passion and clarity in their faith. As we saw in the first chapter, they knew who was evil—the Roman empire—and who was good—the Christian congregations. They had their own heroes in the martyrs, and they could hope for their own certain path to heaven through their own sacrificial blood. Each meeting was invigorated by the possibility that some would be called to martyrdom before the next gathering. Heaven was imminent; the world irrelevant. Constantine, insisting on religious toleration, changed this with one signature.

Even before Constantine, in the quiet times between the fires of persecution, the congregations had relaxed their fervor. Origen, in the early third century, complained that services were being conducted in an atmosphere of "gossip and triviality."[2] Cyprian, too, noted that peace with the state led to laxness within the congregations. He wrote that people began to think of getting rich, and men trimmed their beards and women wore makeup, and both were consumed more with vanity than piety. Furthermore, the end of martyrdom caused congregations to split: "They maligned one another with an envenomed tongue; they quarreled with one another with stubborn hatred."[3]

Today, we take for granted this range of behavior and piety within our congregations, but for the ancient world emerging from the zeal of persecuted churches, this was shocking. For some, perhaps the most shocking contemplation was a church that was not besieged. Tertullian wrote with horror, "Yes, I should not be surprised if such people were not figuring out how they could abolish martyrdom. . . ."[4] Tertullian's fear came true—martyrdom had been abolished.

Eusebius's joy at Constantine's decree overlooked one other legacy from the age of martyrdom: anger. Many of the faithful had seen the range of reactions to the persecutions of Diocletian, from Christians who were tortured to Christians who rushed to please Rome and worship the emperor. Those who longed for a church with enough vigor to produce martyrs were in no hurry to forgive the lapsed, and those who looked for peace guided by a Christian emperor wanted the dissension to end. In North Africa, these two forces brought about a violent struggle that lasted more than a century in which both sides believed they saw a new struggle between good and evil, a battle that created new martyrs.

THE DONATIST SCHISM

This new struggle began in Carthage in 304, when the persecution of Diocletian swept through North Africa, even causing some bishops to bring sacred books to the pagan fires. Roman soldiers arrested a group of Christians in Abitina, a village near Carthage and brought them to Carthage for their trials. The account of their passion, written shortly after the event, tells in grim detail how the confessors were horribly tortured by the agents of Rome, whom the author describes as the "devil" in a "celestial battle" of good against evil.[5] So far, this account mirrors so many of the stories we have seen throughout this book. However, when the confessors, bleeding and torn, were returned to their prison cell the tale took a particularly odd turn.

It was customary for Christians to come to the prisons to bring food, drink, and comfort to the confessors, but this time they were impeded by the Christian bishop of Carthage himself. The bishop sent his deacon Caecilian and other supporters to drive away the faithful from the doors of the prison:

> People who came to nourish the martyrs were struck down right and left by Caecilian. The cups for the thirsty inside in chains were broken. At the entrance to the prison food was scattered only to be torn apart by the dogs. Before the doors of the prison the fathers of the martyrs fell and the most holy mothers [as well]. Shut out from the sight of their children, they kept their vigil day and night at the entrance of the prison. There was the dreadful weeping and the bitter lamentation by all who were there.[6]

What was this bishop and his deacon doing? Although the author does not mention it, there had been a recent Roman law issued forbidding people to bring food to prisoners, and the penalty for disobedience was death by starvation.[7] Perhaps the leaders were trying to keep the rest of their community from arrest, but the consequences of this act were monumental. The narrator identified Caecilian with the persecutors: "To keep the pious from the embrace of the martyrs and to keep Christians from a duty of piety, Caecilian was more ruthless than the tyrant, more bloody than the executioner."[8] Now, we have a Christian on the side of evil; the boundaries between good and evil were beginning to shift.

The persecution ended and the damaged congregations were left once more to pick up the pieces and heal the wounds. However, in 311 (a couple of years before Constantine would issue his decree of toleration), Caecilian, the loyal deacon and villain of the martyr account, was ordained bishop. Purists who remembered the blood shed by the martyrs, and perhaps family members who had been driven from the prison doors, objected. Many, including some bishops, believed Caecilian's actions disqualified him from the priesthood and his ordination was invalid. Furthermore, one of the bishops who ordained Caecilian had turned over sacred books during the Diocletian persecution. This made him a *traditore* in the minds of purists, and this term meant everything from a traitor to someone who turned over books to one who accommodated to the state. So, the purist bishops ordained another bishop named Donatus in Caecelian's place. The patronymic "Donatism" was given to the split in the African church caused by the rift between those who followed Caecilian and his successors and those who followed Donatus and his.

The Donatists had separate church buildings, a separate hierarchy, and separate congregations. They saw themselves in the tradition of rigorous North Africans like Tertullian, who believed a church should be one that was prepared for martyrdom. They believed they were a congregation of the chosen who could hope for imminent martyrdom by a world that was corrupt. But that world changed in 313 with the leadership of Constantine. If the emperor supported Christians, who was evil in a cosmic struggle? Unfortunately, this war would be between Christians.

In 313, the Donatists appealed to Constantine to determine the true bishop of Carthage—Donatus or Caecilian. This mattered because the emperor had decreed that imperial subsidies would go to the church, but which church would receive the funds in North Africa? Constantine appointed a commission of bishops which met in Rome in 313 and an appeals commission which met at Arles in 314. Both ruled in favor of Caecilian, so his party became the Catholic one and the Donatists were ordered to submit to his authority.

In traditional Roman fashion, Constantine sought to coerce the Donatists into obedience, and from 317 to 321, there was a period of repression and the creation of Donatist martyrs. The persecution was vigorous at certain points. For example, in one incident a whole congregation was killed inside a church in Carthage.[9] However, just as during the pagan empire, these persecutions only served to strengthen the resolve of Donatists who witnessed these new martyrdoms. In 321, Constantine suspended the laws against the Donatists, and from 321 to 346 the two churches existed side by side. Each church appointed its own bishops, held its own services, and looked with suspicion and often anger at the other party whom each accused of splitting the church. In 347, persecution began again under a new emperor (Constans), and more martyrs were created.

In the minds of the Donatists, these repressions confirmed that little had changed with the acceptance of Christianity by Constantine. The state was still a repressive entity that sought to interfere with the spiritual lives of the faithful. As Donatus wrote to Emperor Constans in 347, "What has the emperor to do with the Church?"[10] The accounts of the Donatist martyrs expressed this thought in language as strong as the Book of Revelations, which vilified the old Rome under Nero. The Passion of Marculus claimed the Catholics "were obeying the devil [who] chose the martyrs for the heavenly kingdom; and so the savagery of the traitors [*traditores*] who were serving the Antichrist sent them to heaven."[11] The Christian emperor was now the Antichrist, and his Catholic subjects were traitors who created new martyrs, the Donatists. This was now a war—perhaps the first holy war: "An accursed and detestable war was declared against the [Donatist] Church, so that the Christian people [Donatists] would be forced into unity with the traitors [Catholics], a unity effected by the unsheathed swords of soldiers . . . and by the shouts of crowds."[12]

By 392, Donatus was dead, but his movement continued to expand under the capable hands of his successor Parmenian. By now, Donatism had expanded and approached something of a regional church of North Africa, and it was a regional church that considered itself the only true church—one that preserved its identity within a hostile world. The Donatists viewed themselves as a Chosen People who had managed to avoid compromise with the impure of the world.[13] The Donatist Petilian, wrote eloquently, "Be ye not unequally yoked with unbelievers: for what fellowship hath righteousness with unrighteousness? And what communion hath light with darkness?"[14] The two sides were hardening in their attribution of "good" versus "evil."

Against Parmenian, the Catholics brought their own master theologian: the North African Augustine of Hippo. Augustine had returned to Africa from Milan, where he had converted to a Christianity imbued with Platonism that offered a transcendent universal appeal. In Africa, he found a church split over what he saw as local quarrels between bishops, and he was at first certain that his eloquence and rational arguments would resolve the issue. At Carthage in 411, he preached a sermon in praise of peace, and he recalled the Donatists into the unity of the Church. He called for patience and prayer rather than reproof. The bishop underestimated the depths of the passions that lay under the separation, and he forgot the Donatists' long memories of their own martyrs.

As early as 340, Donatists had acquired a radical fringe called the Circumcellions who drew their support from the rural provinces of Numidia. These men and women took the Donatist position to its logical conclusion, and included landowners, creditors, and property holders in their rejection of the state. In contrast, they saw themselves as a "Church of Saints," staying separate from the pollution of the surrounding society. In the hands of Circumcellions, Donatism became a revolutionary force that joined economic and social discontent with fierce religious conviction. They were the first Christian group to try openly to overthrow the existing social order, but they would not be the last, for their ideas resurfaced in the Peasants' Revolt in England in 1381, in the Peasant uprising in Germany in 1524, and in many other movements.[15]

Under their leaders Fasir and Axido called "Captains of the Saints," the Circumcellions terrified local property owners. As a contemporary witness wrote,

No man could rest secure in his possessions. . . . Very soon everyone lost what was owing to him—even to very large amounts, and held himself to have gained something in escaping from the violence of these men. Even journeys could not be made with perfect safety, for masters were often thrown out of their own chariots and forced to run, in servile fashion, in front of their own slaves, seated in their lord's place.[16]

At first glance, this description simply refers to angry brigands terrorizing their betters, but the Circumcellions linked this social revolution with the love of martyrdom and a separate church of the martyrs. This was their innovation; martyrdom justified terror, and this association resurfaces in modern headlines from the Middle East and elsewhere.

According to a Donatist writer, the revolutionaries drew their strength (and their supplies) from martyrs' tombs where they gathered. What was more shocking to Christians who took joy in the end of the persecutions was that Circumcellions actively sought martyrdom—sometimes by suicide. As Augustine wrote, "It was their daily sport to kill themselves, by throwing themselves over precipices, or into the water, or into the fire." He claimed that the would-be martyrs threatened travelers, forcing the Catholics to kill them out of self-defense, and if they "could not find anyone whom they could terrify into slaying them with his sword, they threw themselves over the rocks, or committed themselves to the fire or the eddying pool."[17]

The Catholic church, so recently a church that credited its victory to the blood shed by martyrs, was now confronted with a moral dilemma: How to condemn people who felt called to death by their faith? It raised a question that chillingly faces us today: What is the difference between martyrs and terrorists? Augustine and the property owners in North Africa believed the Circumcellions were terrorists, and Augustine defined a martyr as only one who suffered for the Catholic faith.[18] He dismissed Circumcellions as lunatics, "inflamed by wine and madness."[19] Thus, Augustine begins to restrict martyrdom (and indeed suicide, as we will see in chapter 10). The violence of the Circumcellions led the bishop to change his views on peaceful reconciliation.

In the violence of the terrorists, Augustine called for a just war against the self-styled martyrs. In developing his ideas of what might constitute a "just war," Augustine drew from two main sources: Roman ideas of a just defensive or retributive war and Old Testament examples of wars fought by God's will. Augustine's ideas were profoundly influential in establishing the notion of a just war for Christian leaders. For the church father, just wars had to meet several conditions. First, they must be led by someone in legitimate authority; that is, private persons may not call a just war. Second, hostilities must be motivated by charity; in this case, the desire to bring the Donatists back into the fold of the orthodox. Third, the cause must be just.[20] Even the casual reader will immediately see that this list will hardly eliminate any violence. In fact, the list could justify the original persecution of Christians: Roman emperors like Diocletian (who constituted a legitimate authority) believed their cause for persecuting Christians was just—they wanted a unified state. However, times had changed, and the legitimate authority was now Christian; Augustine was not worried about misplaced war.

Retreating from his ideals of peaceful reconciliation through logic, Augustine began to write that coercion was the kindest way to save Donatists from their errors. In one letter, he answered a critic saying, "You are of the opinion that no one should be compelled to follow righteousness. . . ." The bishop argued that God punishes those who go astray, so the state can do so as well, breaking "the bondage of custom . . . under the shock of this alarm."[21] Later, Augustine developed this idea in more detail, arguing that while it is better for someone to be persuaded to worship God by teaching, "many have found advantage . . . in being first compelled by fear or pain, so that they might afterwards be influenced by teaching. . . ."[22] This position articulated by such a respected church father would offer justification for religious persecution for centuries to come. It seems deeply sad to see the churchman justifying physical coercion so soon after the end of the age of martyrs. For the Donatists, of course, the age of martyrdom was still going on.

Augustine praised the "correction" offered by the lay authorities, saying "the rigor of their judges broke through the hardness of their most cruel hearts," but at the same time, he urged them to avoid imposing the death penalty. In part, this was to permit the Donatists to have time to repent their sins before death, but the bishop recognized the power of martyrs' blood, and he did not want heretics to be venerated as martyrs. Since many of the Donatists longed for martyrdom, just as many of the orthodox had done a century earlier, Augustine knew he could not withstand the force of self-sacrifice. He wanted to control those who were identified as martyrs and restrict the respect accorded them to those he considered orthodox: "The sufferings of the martyrs, which ought to shed bright glory on the Church, may not be tarnished by the blood of their enemies."[23]

Although Augustine himself considered his prohibition of the death penalty to be charitable, nevertheless, the penalties imposed on Donatists were severe and sadly reminiscent of the persecutions under Diocletian. Donatists were to be subject to heavy fines and their children were forbidden to inherit unless they converted to Catholicism. Donatist meetings were prohibited and houses in which they were conducted were confiscated. Even torture was applied, for bailiffs on estates where Donatist services were conducted were to be flogged with whips tipped in lead.[24]

The violence escalated on both sides. Donatists and Circumcellions rioted in the countryside, and Donatists were as harsh to their own who converted to Catholicism as the Catholics were against the Donatists. Newly converted Donatist clerics were seized and tortured by cutting out their tongues so they could no longer preach, or blinded with lime and vinegar. One priest was kidnaped, beaten, and left on view in a cage for twelve days until he was freed by a Donatist bishop.[25] Ultimately, the only thing that stanched the flow of blood between these two groups of North African Christians was greater violence—first by Vandals then Muslims.

After decades of violence, Donatists could no more make peace with Catholics who were supported by the now Christian Empire than the early Christians could have reconciled with Nero. Too much blood had been shed, and the Donatists believed themselves engaged in the continuing struggle between good and evil, and to them, the Catholics had joined the dark side. The Donatist Petilian wrote a series of letters to Augustine accusing the Catholics of behavior reminiscent of Rome. He wrote, "For you carry on war without license, against whom we may not fight in turn. For you desire to live when you have murdered us; but our victory is either to escape or to be slain." And furthermore, "Do you serve God in such wise that we should be murdered at your hand? You do err, you do err, if you are wretched enough to entertain such a belief as this. For God does not have butchers for His priests."[26] Like the pagan persecutors who had preceded them, the Christian emperor only succeeded in creating new martyrs and new accounts of their passion that were treasured and read for centuries. Just like the stories of the Catholic martyrs, these tales of resistance preserved the Donatist church itself.

The accounts of the Donatist martyrs contain all the elements we have seen appearing in the Catholic martyr tales. Donatists claimed their confessors withstood just as horrible tortures with God's help: "[Marculus] yearned for tortures more than he feared them and that someone could not feel the pains of torture in the body when the spirit embraces Christ. . . ."[27] They believed their blood was shed as a sacrifice "in imitation of the Lord's passion," they saw visions, and they believed their souls were honored after their sacrifice by a heavenly reward.[28] However, there was one tragic difference between the two accounts of martyrs: with the Donatists, in the struggle of good versus evil, Catholics, not pagan emperors, were evil.[29]

In the account of the earliest Donatist martyrs, the author casts the struggle in cosmic terms, giving "an account of celestial battles and struggles undertaken anew by the bravest soldiers of Christ. . . ." He cast this struggle as a "war," a "battle to be fought not so much against human beings as against the devil. . . ."[30] The rhetoric increased as the killings continued, until the later passions describe their struggle in terms as apocalyptic as that of Revelations: "The rage of the . . . [Catholics] who were obeying the devil chose the martyrs for the heavenly kingdom; and so the savagery of the traitors who were serving the Antichrist sent them to heaven." The emperor's generals were "two beasts sent to Africa" to declare "an accursed and detestable war" against the Donatist church.[31] Here, of course, is the final tragedy. Once the two groups of Christians had defined each other in terms of good against evil, there was no possibility of reconciliation.

The Donatists would rather die than join forces with the evil church that in their minds had sold out to the world and allied with the evil empire. And die they did. It was no doubt this struggle that in part stimulated Augustine to articulate his own vision of the relationship between the church and the world. The great bishop claimed that from Adam's fall, humans had been divided into two "cities"—one served

God and His angels and the other served the devil with his minions.[32] The early Christians and the Donatists agreed and were certain they could identify the two "cities"–the faithful with their martyrs were the city of God, and the Roman state led by the emperor, even the Christian emperor, was the city of the devil. Augustine explained that things were neither that simple, nor that clear. For him, the two cities were inextricably mixed on earth, even within an individual's heart, and the cities would only be separated on Judgment Day. At that time, the two cities, Babylon and Jerusalem, would appear, one on the left and the other on the right.[33] Then, and only then, would the inhabitants of the two cities separate; then, and only then, could there be a church of the pure.

In the meantime, for Augustine, Christians would live in a world that mingled good and bad. They should accommodate with the world (and the state) while longing for the heavenly city that would come in God's own time. Augustine's vision of the relationship between the church and the state has shaped the future of most Christian thought. However, there have always been groups like the Donatists who would rather reject society as evil and polluting.

CHURCHES OF THE PURE

There are some particular characteristics that define congregations who, like the Donatists, think of themselves as separate from the world. As I outline these traits, we can see that they were shared by the members of the early church–the church of martyrs–but these characteristics were no longer relevant in Augustine's world of the mixed cities. As we shall see next, these traits also characterize some modern movements.

At the most basic level, congregations of the pure kept themselves outside society–as an enclosed ark in the turbulent sea of the world from which they could watch the "drowning multitudes without."[34] Donatists had gone to war to avoid such contamination, and they believed they were being led to pollution by the swords of the emperor. We have seen throughout this volume that Christians before the age of Constantine had felt similarly besieged, as Cyprian (a North African martyr beloved by orthodox and Donatists alike) claimed the church was "a thing enclosed [that] cannot lie open to outsiders and profane men."[35]

On a practical level, it is hard for congregations to stay dramatically separate from all contact with a polluting society. Consequently, such congregations tend to believe in an imminent end of times. For them, the Last Judgment and the Second Coming of Christ will come soon. We have seen that the author of the Book of Revelations expected the Second Coming in the wake of Nero's persecutions, and Cyprian in the third century also consoled his besieged congregation that "these things have been predicted as about to come at the end of the world."[36] Donatists and the more radical Circumcellions also saw their times of troubles as forecasting the end.

With a focus on the end of the world, congregations of the pure concentrated on salvation. Unlike Augustine who wrote about how to live in this world, Donatists and other separatist churches concentrated on how to pass on successfully to the next. Augustine imagined each person struggled alone to reach the heavenly city. In contrast, Donatists shared with earlier congregations a belief that their salvation was collective, not individual. For Tertullian in the late second century, the church was a community of saints gathering together to await the end of the world. Cyprian, a century later, conceived of the church as a "brotherhood of the righteous," who also gathered to await salvation together.[37] The greatest danger to such congregations was for an individual to leave the group—salvation lay only within the fold of the faithful.

In the Catholic "Passion of Perpetua and Felicity," one can see this fear of separation from the group in the account of the pregnant slave Felicity. As we saw in chapter 6, Felicity was afraid she would not be able to die with her companions in the arena because of her pregnancy: "She became greatly distressed that her martyrdom would be postponed because of her pregnancy. . . ." She was not afraid that she would live, for she expected her execution simply to be postponed: "She might have to shed her holy, innocent blood afterwards along with others who were common criminals."[38] The source of her fear was her belief in the collective salvation of the group; she was less certain she would find heaven in the company of criminals. This was the underlying fear of the Donatists—they might lose salvation if their congregation was separated and mixed with an unsaved world. They did not want to die alone for that path to heaven was less certain.

Not surprisingly, Augustine rejected the idea of collective salvation. In *City of God*, he described groups of Christians (without naming them) who believed that since they had shared the Mass together, they had become one body in Christ's body. They then interpreted the resurrection of the body to be the resurrection of the body of believers—the community of the faithful. Augustine warned against this view, saying, "Those people who continue to the end of their lives in the fellowship of the Catholic church have no reason to feel secure, if their moral behavior is disreputable and deserving of condemnation."[39] Here again one can see the logical conclusion of Augustine's position on the relationship between church and state; in a mixed world, each is saved one by one and will join a saved community only at the resurrection.

Another characteristic of congregations trying to stay separate and pure is a longing for martyrdom. The presence of martyrs had marked the church from the beginning, and Constantine's declaration that the age of martyrdom was over did not change this perception. The Donatist Petilian threw this claim at Augustine to prove that indeed his church, not the Catholic one, was the pure one: "Blessed are they which are persecuted for righteousness' sake; for theirs is the kingdom of heaven. You are not blessed; but you make martyrs to be blessed, with whose souls the heavens are filled, and the earth has flourished with their memory."[40] Circumcellions insisted on martyrdom as a central feature of their salvation, and they linked this suicidal yearning for martyrdom to collective salvation, for many died together. Crowds flung themselves over precipices or leapt together into rivers to drown. Some burned themselves alive by jumping into great bonfires.[41] Modern readers join Augustine in recoiling from such acts of excess. Surely, preserving an age of martyrdom cannot be worth mass suicides.

The extreme acts of the Donatists can be only understood in the light of the final characteristic of separatist churches: they defined their struggle in terms of good versus evil. If the state is deeply and fundamentally evil, there can be no compromise, and any death is preferable to accommodation. The Donatist martyr accounts repeatedly cast the Catholics as agents of the devil, and Augustine responded by similarly identifying Donatists and Circumcellions as agents of darkness.[42] The lines were drawn and both claimed their warfare on the other was just warfare—after all, both sides believed they were fighting the forces of evil.

At the beginning of the fourth century, just as many Christians were rejoicing in the close of the age of martyrdom and the victory of the church, others rejected this vision and longed for a simpler time when the division between good and evil was clear and the communities gathered hoping for imminent salvation together and withstanding the pressure of martyrdom together. Augustine was the most articulate church father to explain why their position that seemed so natural a century earlier was no longer acceptable. Martyrdom had to end for peace in the church. It would be fine to be able to say that the drive for martyrdom was ended by Augustine's pen and the imperial forces. However, throughout history there have been other groups who have shared these characteristics of the besieged communities of the Donatists.

MODERN EXAMPLES

There is no space here to give a comprehensive overview of groups who, for one reason or another, decided to reject society in hopes of a collective salvation. Instead, I want to discuss just two examples that ended tragically, and see what light the story of the Donatists can shed on the twenty-first century.

In 1953, Jim Jones established a church in Indianapolis called the People's Temple as an interracial mission for the sick, homeless, and jobless. Interracial congregations were almost nonexistent in Indiana at that time, and Jones stimulated further suspicion by advocating communism during those cold war years. Feeling unwelcome in the community, Jones moved the congregation to California in 1965 and continued his mission to poor black families while developing political support for the communism of Cuba and the Soviet Union.

In the mid-seventies, events came together that led Jones to feel increasingly alienated, indeed persecuted, by the surrounding society. The magazine, the *New West*, wrote an article about the People's Temple, raising suspicions about their activities. At the same time, Jones reputedly was abusing prescription drugs, and some authors argue this fueled his paranoia. Either way, the congregation began to see itself as outside society and began to identify the surrounding society as evil and against their own virtue. As Jones claimed in his last speech, "They've robbed us of our land and they've taken us and driven us and we tried to find ourselves. . . . We've tried to find a new beginning but it's too late."[43] Just like the Donatists, the People's Temple felt there was no room for compromise when they felt their back was to the wall.

Jones decided to leave U.S. society, and with almost one thousand followers, he moved to Guyana, South America, where the People's Temple leased almost four thousand acres of jungle from the government. They established an agricultural cooperative there, called the "People's Temple Agricultural Project" (but better known as Jonestown) and raised animals and food plants. Reports of strange behavior and human rights abuses circulated in the United States, and there were relatives who were concerned about their family members living in Guyana, because the group included more than two hundred children. In 1978, Congressman Leo Ryan decided to visit Jonestown to see what was going on. The visit seemed innocuous at first, but when the congressman was ready to leave, a group from the People's Temple decided to return with him. At this point, the community seemed splintering— in a way threatening their looked-for communal salvation. At the airstrip, some heavily armed members of the group's security guards arrived and killed the congressman and three members of the press. The flight eventually did depart, but while it was in the air, one member of the People's Temple killed some passengers before being overpowered.

Back on the ground, the group decided (or Jones persuaded them) that it was better to die together rather than wait for the expected retribution for the killing of the congressman. More than nine hundred people died, including more than two hundred children. Some committed suicide by drinking poison-laced grape drink, others had needle tracks that made it appear they were victims of murder, and still others, including Jim Jones, were shot. A very few fled into the jungle and survived. There is a transcript of Jones's last speech, recorded as people were dying around him. In this horrifying document, it is apparent that he shared the same convictions that had led the Donatists to leap to their deaths in self-proclaimed martyrdom.

We have already seen that Jones saw his congregation as an island of good within an evil world. He also preached an imminent destruction of the world by nuclear war, for his retreat to Guyana was in part designed to look for a separate place to wait out the world's destruction. Just as martyrs who expected persecutions to preface a larger destruction, Jones warned his followers to expect persecution just as horrible as that experienced by the early Christians: "If these people land out here they'll torture our children, they'll torture some of our people here, they'll torture our seniors. We cannot have this."[44] Thus, for them, death together was preferable to martyrdom at the hand of someone else.

Finally, they shared the belief in collective salvation—the group would die together and go on to a new life together. Jones did not make it exactly clear where they'll be going—to another planet or to be reincarnated—but he did promise that the passage to death was easy. He claimed they can "step over quietly" and "death is not a fearful thing, it's living that's fearful." But the most important thing was that the group would remain together, and together with Jones. He said, "I'm standing with you people—you're part of me."[45]

Jim Jones did not use the word *martyr* as he spoke to his followers on the day of their death, but it is clear he thought of himself as one. For him, and we have to assume many of his followers agreed with him, his was a persecuted congregation who would rather die than be separated and forced to join the surrounding evil world. In his mind, all the deaths were a victory: "We win, we win when we go down, they don't have nobody else to hate. They've got nobody else to hate."[46] Hate and paranoia drove these deaths.

Fifteen years later, another religious group who felt themselves besieged faced a similar disastrous end, this time near Waco, Texas. On 28 February 1993, agents from the Bureau of Alcohol, Tobacco and Firearms confronted the religious community called the Branch Davidians at their compound called Mount Carmel; in the ensuing gunfire, people on both sides died. The leader David Koresh called the 911 operator asking for help, but a standoff had begun that quickly became viewed by both sides as a struggle between good and evil.

Within the complex, David Koresh (previously Vernon Wayne Howell) led a religious group that had broken away from the Seventh-

Day Adventists. Mount Carmel itself had been founded in 1935 and had experienced various leaders and changes in fortunes. Koresh, who had studied the Bible all his life, joined the group in 1981. In 1985, while traveling in Israel, Koresh experienced a transforming vision that led him to return to Mount Carmel and assume a leadership position. Koresh believed he had been chosen to explain the mysteries in the Book of Revelation and gather a chosen few to prepare for the last days. As Koresh wrote in his last statement while he was under siege, "What are the Seven Seals [described in Revelations]? And the answer remains—a Revelation of Jesus Christ which God gave unto Him to show unto His servants things which must shortly come to pass."[47]

Koresh and his followers believed the Seventh-Day Adventists had lost their previous rigorous stand as a separatist church that had remained pure in contrast to the world.[48] Although Koresh had probably never heard of them, he was echoing the Donatists who longed for a pure congregation uncorrupted by the world. Like the ancient Donatists, Koresh thought of the world, and the U.S. government, as "Babylon" that would seduce the faithful away from their pure stance.[49] For Koresh, those within his compound were good and those outside were evil.

In turn, those outside defined Koresh as evil. The press and the government reported Koresh as a crazy "cult" leader who brainwashed his followers. Furthermore, during the standoff, reporters drew parallels between Mount Carmel and Jonestown, building fears of mass suicide within.[50] Koresh surely accepted the idea of martyrdom, for he expected his group to become the martyrs described in the Book of Revelations,[51] but there was no indication that Koresh believed his moment of martyrdom was at hand. However, just as during the time of the revolutionary Circumcellions, established governments are suspicious of those who espouse martyrdom.

The mutual demonizing came to a head in April 1993. On April 14, Koresh issued a written promise that all eighty-four members of the Branch Davidians would surrender as soon as he finished his book explaining the Seven Seals in the Book of Revelations. However, on April 19, the FBI began an assault on the complex. As tanks crashed into the doors, fire broke out and most of the Davidians were trapped inside and died. The continuing controversy over the events demonstrates that many people believe the Davidians died as martyrs who refused to compromise their beliefs for the government.

Jonestown and Waco are but two examples of situations in which religious groups separated themselves from the surrounding society, believing that to be the way to achieve a collective salvation. I do not pretend to judge whether their leaders were paranoid or persecuted or whether the followers were misguided or faithful. I do know that when groups are demonized blood will be shed. Whether it is martyrs' blood depends on whom you ask.

Throughout this book we have seen that martyrdom is an influential phenomenon. People's willingness to die for a cause gives powerful impetus to that cause and is a strong force for change. All is well and good if we favor the change—the early Christians changed the Roman Empire from pagan to Christian. The situation is much trickier when one is on the other side; if we do not want change, then we do not want martyrs. This was Augustine's dilemma in the fourth century. With Eusebius, he gloried in the end of the persecutions and worked to build a peaceful church that had no more need of martyrs.

I sympathize with Augustine's desire for peace, and I can understand his frustration at the revolutionary martyrs of the Donatists. However, I disagree with his solution of calling for a just war to stop the deaths. Unfortunately, that course is too similar to modern desires to stop Palestinian suicide bombers—self-described "self-martyrs"—by violence. Killing those who want to die is no more an effective deterrent now than it was in the fourth century. How then to declare an end to the age of martyrdom?

Obviously, if the answer were easy, the brilliant mind of such as Augustine's would have seen it. However, I suggest that we need to recognize the forces that lead to martyrdom. When a group of people believes itself shut out of society, with no voice for change, things start to go wrong. When this group and the surrounding society begin to define each other as evil against good, things get worse. When these beliefs combine with an expectation that the world (or their world) will end, then people will die—either by their own hand, as in Jonestown, or by someone else's, as in Waco. At some point in this sequence, we have to stop the momentum.

Many will probably object to my characterizing all these groups as martyrs. Of course, it does not matter what I call them. What matters is how they view themselves. Augustine did not think the Donatists were martyrs, but the Circumcellions did. The only way to end an age of martyrdom is through tolerance; Augustine, and many who have come after him, think they can do it with force.

The corpse of St. Vincent cast out to the beasts, and a crow swoops down to protect the relics, implying that the martyr's body retained sacred power after his death. Fourteenth century. *Les Belles Heures of the Duke de Berry*. Metropolitan Museum of Art, The Cloisters Collection, 1954 (54.1.1 folio 163 recto).

9

CONTROLLING THE MESSAGE
ACCOUNTS OF VINCENT THE MARTYR

f force didn't end martyrdom, how about disinformation? Could changing texts control martyrs? In his struggles against the Donatists, Augustine discovered that martyrdom can be a powerful force against the social order, and thus he and others were ready for the age of martyrs to end. The church was victorious and thus had no more need of martyrs; it could simply celebrate those who already had died heroically for the faith. However, as we have seen throughout this book, the power of the martyrs lay not only in their deaths but also in the accounts by which people remembered their sacrifice. The texts, with their strong messages, were profoundly influential—we have seen how the texts shaped ideas as disparate as anti-Semitism and motherhood. As the church became organized and at peace, what would happen if a martyr's passion seemed to contradict the message of the church? Just as now, those in charge recognized the need to control important texts, and the accounts of the martyrs were no exception. Passions were often rewritten to be sure the message of the text conformed to contemporary values.

The accounts of martyrs' passions offer an immediate vivid snapshot of sanctity; martyrs' actions defined what was considered holiness. However, as we saw in the last chapter, ideas of holiness changed over time, and the deeds of all martyrs were filtered through the pen of a scribe who recorded them. As ideas of holiness changed over time, the very narrative of martyrs' acts changed as well. To show this process of controlling a martyr's message, I will discuss the changing story of one martyr and trace the differing views of sanctity presented by the different versions of the narrative. This will show that a narrative of holiness had more to do with standards of ideal Christian behavior in a particular time and place than with the manner in which a martyr earned his or her reputation.

In this chapter I shall analyze the different surviving versions of the passion of St. Vincent, martyr of Saragossa, to reveal the ways in which even the narrative of events was changed to conform to prevailing ideas of sanctity. Virtually from the beginning, Vincent's story belonged at least as much to the listeners' time as it did to the time of persecution during which he died. Vincent's passion was less a story of one man's heroism than a story of sanctity that was changed so it could speak to the values of different ages.

THE MARTYRDOM OF VINCENT

The persecutions begun by Diocletian affected Christians in all parts of the Roman Empire, including the province of Iberia (modern Spain and Portugal). There, a vigorous prosecutor arrested many men and women who had refused to comply with the edict that all must offer sacrifice to the emperor. In the course of this persecution, Vincent, deacon of the church of Saragossa, was martyred in 304.

The faithful in Spain celebrated the cult of St. Vincent shortly after his martyrdom, and his fame quickly spread to Gaul and Italy. Vincent was the only Spanish martyr whose passion was included in the liturgy of the universal church, so the text describing his martyrdom was highly influential.[1] A short account of Vincent's passion had been written by the mid-fourth century, but unfortunately this original narrative has been lost. There is a short passion known as the *Brevior* that probably is closest to the original. This text was read annually for centuries in churches for the saint's celebration, so we should first look at this influential account.

According to the *Brevior*, the Roman official Dacian vigorously implemented the persecution of Diocletian. He arrested Bishop Valerius of Saragossa and his deacon Vincent and ordered them to demonstrate their loyalty to Rome by worshiping at the imperial altar. With an appropriate sense of hierarchy, Dacian began to question Valerius: "What do you say, Valerius, you who under the name of religion go against the decrees of the Emperor?" Valerius began to give a "soft answer" to Dacian, but at that point, Vincent interrupted his bishop and reprimanded him for speaking timidly. Vincent proclaimed that one must cry out with a "free voice" to withstand tyranny against God's ministry. So far, this account is similar to so many we have seen: Christianity was victorious thanks to the heroic boldness of those who were uncompromising in the face of oppression.

This speech by Vincent was a crucial turning point, because the text makes it clear that at this moment Vincent received divine aid and power from God to withstand his ordeal. Dacian became enraged by Vincent's speech, ordered Valerius removed, and commanded that Vincent be tortured to break his rebellious spirit. His torturers whipped Vincent until they were exhausted, then they placed a heated iron plate with drops of molten lead on his chest to scorch his bruised and torn skin. Once again, the account echoes that of so many martyrs for whom torture was inconsequential.

Through all this, Vincent laughed at his torturers' efforts to weaken his resolve. Infuriated at the inability of his men to break Vincent's spirit, Dacian threw the deacon into a dark cell that had been strewn with bits of sharp pottery to further torment his torn body. According to the narrative, the cell was miraculously lit and the potsherds were transformed into soft straw. Vincent then was executed, dying victorious over Dacian's efforts to force him to sacrifice. This narrative shows Vincent as the prototypical early martyr: he had the strength of will to step forward to proclaim his faith, and his initiative was rewarded by an infusion of God's power to help him during his ordeal. Torture was ineffective and served only to prove that his very flesh was imbued with God's grace.

To reaffirm the importance of Vincent's bodily sanctity, the text does not end with the martyr's death. The author writes that Dacian tried to destroy Vincent's corpse because he could not destroy Vincent's spirit. The inquisitor threw the body into a field to be consumed by wild beasts, but a raven kept the predators away. Dacian then placed the body in a sack weighted with a heavy stone and had the body taken out to sea to be lost in the depths. However, body and stone floated back to shore, "guided by the hand of God." The account then ends with the saint's body having been delivered to the faithful for veneration.[2] The miraculous remains once more showed that Vincent had physically received God's power during his ordeal.

For all its brevity, this story presents a powerful picture of the church during the persecutions. It contains a villainous prosecutor, a miraculous intervention, and an heroic martyr. When Iberian bishops met at the Council of Elvira in 324 to reestablish order among the congregations shaken by the intensity of this persecution, at least one bishop who attended had an immediate knowledge of the power of Rome's inquisitors and had good reason to respect the strength of the martyrs: Bishop Valerius, who had spoken softly before Dacian and who had been released before Vincent was tortured, attended the Council of Elvira to represent his see of Saragossa. The strong anti-idolatry canons passed by the council become even more vivid when seen against the backdrop of experiences such as those faced by Valerius when he lost his deacon to martyrdom.

The council opened with a discussion of the problems posed by the persecution, and the first four canons dealt severely with Christians, priests, and catechumens (Christians who were not yet baptized) who succumbed to the pressure to worship idols[3] or who gave money to pagan temples to avoid having to worship idols directly.[4] As we saw in chapter 8, the persecutions had left the church with grave problems for its organization and development, but church leaders looked not only to conciliar authority and legislation to bring order to the troubled congregations. More important, they relied on the example and intercession of confessors who had not been martyred but who had proven their faith by withstanding interrogation and who could use their strength to benefit fellow Christians who had apostasized. The weak could be readmitted to the congregations on the strength of a letter from a confessor.[5] If confessors could intercede for their fellow Christians, how much more effective would be the intercession of martyrs who had died for their faith? The relics of the martyrs were seen to perform miracles virtually from the moment of martyrdom, and the example of the martyrs became important for the church as it attempted to reestablish order. The fourth-century Iberian church survived the persecutions and grew strong on the blood of the martyrs. The fortitude of heroic individuals compensated for weaker Christians and the stories of their brave martyrdom were powerful weapons in the church's battle against idolatry. All these results mirrored the experience of the many martyrs from all parts of the empire and helped the Christian church to become victorious.

AFTER THE AGE OF THE MARTYRS

As we have seen, in the late fourth and early fifth centuries, relations between church and state had happily changed. The age of martyrs was over (except in North Africa where the Donatists continued their battles), so the function of the texts of the martyrs was to remember and celebrate that great victory. However, now the message in the passions—one of stark uncompromising courage—seemed to need more nuance so the texts would still offer a story of sanctity even when the world had changed. The easiest way to control the message of the martyrs' passions was for priests, bishops, and even poets to surround the texts with analysis that refined the moral of the stories.

Two highly influential writers, Prudentius and Augustine, were inspired by Vincent's passion at the turn of the fifth century. The Iberian poet Prudentius composed a poetic account of Vincent's passion in about 399, and Augustine wrote several sermons between 410 and 413 that were to be delivered on the saint's feast day after the reading of the passion.[6] Both kept the significant elements of the story as related above, yet they highlighted and modified portions to make the account more immediately relevant for their audiences. As they increased the relevance, they subtly changed the message itself. Both commentators focused on the principal elements of the story: (1) Vincent's speech at the moment he received power from God, (2) God's help through his tortures, and (3) the salvation of the corpse and the martyr's intervention on behalf of the faithful.

However, both commentators made significant departures from the original text. Neither Prudentius nor Augustine referred to Valerius's presence at the beginning of the interrogation. Perhaps the timidity of the bishop during questioning was not quite the example that they wanted to present to Christian congregations. However, since Vincent's speech was central to the drama as the moment when the confessor received God's power, the commentators highlighted it. According to Prudentius, Vincent "cries out" his answer boldly in response to the interrogation[7] and Augustine simply but repeatedly praised Vincent's verbal prowess, saying he was "victorious in words," "composed in his words," and "tranquil in his voice."[8]

Both writers were unequivocal about the amount of divine help Vincent received from the moment of his speech, since, as we have seen throughout this book, the fortitude of martyrs was considered miraculous. As the *Decretum Gelasianum* articulated at the end of the fifth century, "For what Catholic can doubt that they suffered more than is possible for human beings to bear, and did not endure this by their own strength, but by the grace and help of God?"[9] Prudentius expressed this view poetically: "He [Vincent] was joyful, free of pain, with a serene light upon his face as he saw a vision of thee, Christ."[10]

Prudentius also enhanced the miraculous quality of Vincent's remaining constant during his ordeal by vividly describing the tortures, leaving no doubt that they would have been unendurable: "After this, strike blows that strip the flesh from his ribs so by deep wounds the throbbing liver may be laid bare."[11]

Since it would have been against the nature of the flesh to withstand cheerfully this kind of punishment, Vincent managed it not by his human efforts but by the power of God working through him, suspending the natural laws of pain and human weakness. Just as Prudentius changed the description of the torture to make it even more horrible, he also changed the narrative so that the comfort Vincent received was also more intense. The sharp bits of pottery were converted to fragrant flowers instead of soft straw, and an angel came to tend his wounds.[12] Thus God's grace was even more impressive.

Augustine argued even more strongly that Vincent received the power from God to endure his tortures, and there was an important intellectual reason for him to do so: the bishop was engaged in a theological controversy—against Pelagianism—that would shape Christian thought even more profoundly than did his Donatist attacks (discussed in chapter 8). Pelagianism was about salvation, whether one could be saved by one's own efforts (indeed, one's free will) or whether humans were incapable of refraining from sin without God's help.[13]

In 410, the British monk, Pelagius traveled through Augustine's home of Hippo, expressing his view that salvation could be obtained by free will. In accordance with this strong belief in free will, Pelagius believed that people had to strive to do good, because they could. Augustine adamantly opposed Pelagius's view, believing that humans did not have the strength to avoid sin. He knew from his own experience that he had been unable to abstain from sexual intercourse until God miraculously lifted desire from him.[14] Thus, the bishop believed that people from the time of Adam and Eve were fatally flawed with original sin, which made Pelagius's demand for human action impossible—sin explained human nature better than free will did. Augustine expressed his position in his many anti-Pelagian writings that he began in 411.

Since they were written in the few years after he began his attacks on Pelagianism, Augustine's sermons on St. Vincent were deeply influenced by the controversy.[15] For Augustine, Vincent's achievement could not have been the result of his free will and personal courage. Instead, the bishop stressed the miraculous power of God's grace: "If human endurance is considered in this passion, it begins to be incredible; if divine power is acknowledged, it ceases [to] be amazing."[16] He returned to this theme in his next sermon arguing, "How can corruptible dust endure against such enormous torment, unless God lives within him?"[17] Thus, by the beginning of the fifth century, the narrative of the martyr that had previously been used to combat idolatry was now brought by Augustine to combat a newly perceived threat to the church, Pelagianism.

Prudentius and Augustine also reinforced Vincent's importance to the local congregations by stressing that God's power remained in the martyr's relics to benefit the community. To make this point, both authors stressed the miraculous preservation of the corpse (shown in the illustration that begins this chapter). Augustine mentioned it repeatedly[18] and stated that the martyr died not only for himself but for the benefit of the community to "console the faithful."[19] Prudentius, too, elaborated on the original text to make more explicit the martyr's benefit for the community: "Many moisten linen cloths with dripping blood to save for posterity as sacred protection in their homes."[20] Prudentius concluded his poem with a plea for Vincent's intercession that recalls the spirit of the Council of Elvira, which looked to Christian heroes to help the faithful: "Have pity on our prayers that Christ may incline his ear to us and not blame us for our sins."[21]

The narration of the account has at this point come full circle. The congregations were captured and inspired by the account of Vincent's individual heroism and were guided to orthodox thought by commentaries on the themes implicit in the narrative. Finally, the faithful returned to their communities secure in the knowledge that Vincent's hard-won power was benefitting them. By the early fifth century, sanctity was represented by a strong individual who was seen to have received the miracle of God's grace and who had become a receptacle of God's power to benefit the community of the faithful. The main elements in the initial narrative of the *Passio* fulfilled these ideals, and the comments by Augustine and Prudentius did not change this message.

However, neither the early narrative nor Prudentius's or Augustine's elaborations dealt with a question that was central to both the text and the development of the early church. Exactly how did Vincent earn his power? The narrative made clear the moment he received his power—at the time of his brave speech. But in spite of God's miraculous intervention, Prudentius praised Vincent for creating his victory by his own efforts—"by yourself."[22] Even Augustine, who stressed God's grace at the expense of free will, did not really answer the question of whether Vincent received grace because of his individual boldness, and the strength of Vincent's speech in the early form of the tale suggests that this was the case. At most, these commentators leave the answer ambiguous. This was no real problem for the fourth-century church, which needed heroes—"soldiers of Christ"—who were willing to speak loudly for the faith.

REWRITING THE TEXT

By the seventh century, when the next versions of Vincent's passion were composed, the church had different needs, for it was no longer threatened by civil authority. In Spain, the Christian Visigothic kings in Spain worked closely with bishops to govern a Christian society, and council decisions of the late sixth and early seventh centuries make it clear that church leaders felt more threatened by diversity in practice within the church than by persecution. The spirit of the legislation and conciliar decrees calling for religious uniformity was summarized by the law in the Iberian Visigothic Code, which decreed that ". . . no man of whatever race or lineage . . . shall openly or silently, impugn the unity of the Catholic faith. . . ."[23]

As a concrete way to further this goal of religious uniformity, the Fourth Council of Toledo in 633 instituted a number of liturgical reforms designed to bring practices into conformity with one standard. The liturgical canons dealt with issues such as standardizing the forms of prayer and baptism,[24] calling for a uniform liturgy and providing a standardized missal to be used in all churches.[25]

Liturgical diversity was not the only perceived threat to the newly organized official church. Bishops had come to fear the popularity of wandering holy men whose veneration was outside the control of the hierarchical structure. From the mid-fourth century, when the age of the martyrs was past, popular veneration was increasingly being given to a new kind of holy man. People had begun to recognize holiness in ascetics who seemed to have received God's power through self-imposed mortification. These ascetics were venerated as martyrs who lived for the faith rather than dying for it. As early as the fifth century, while Augustine was condemning the Donatists martyrs, he had written, "There are two types of martyrs, one whose passion is apparent, another whose virtue is hidden in the soul. For they tolerate insidious enemies, and resist all carnal desires, because they glorify God in their heart. They exist during times of peace, when it is also possible to be a martyr."[26] This new kind of martyr—who would become the church's saints— offered a perfect outlet for people's longings for spiritual heroism once the age of martyrs was over.

Throughout the fifth and sixth centuries, there were many such ascetic holy men and women in Spain who were highly respected and contributed to the spread of Christianity to isolated areas. Many were also in the tradition of martyrs like Vincent—strong individuals who spoke out for the faith and seemed to have received God's grace and power. Yet by the seventh century, ascetic holy people, who were highly individualistic, were increasingly perceived as a threat to the organization of the church instead of as a principal vehicle for preserving it. The Fourth Council of Toledo ordered religious men to retire into monasteries and not wander about.[27] Furthermore, the council decreed that monks would all be under the authority of their bishop.[28] Thus, holy men—Augustine's martyrs of the soul—were brought under the control of the hierarchy. God's power could continue to work through them, but only through appropriate channels of hierarchy.

While living holy men were being controlled, church leaders encouraged the cult of dead saints as a way to guide the faithful toward appropriate worship. In the fifth century, Pope Vigilius had written to an Iberian bishop urging that the faithful venerate saints as examples of a Christian life,[29] and Martin of Braga, a sixth-century Iberian bishop, encouraged Christians to visit sites of saint veneration.[30] To permit an effective as well as controllable use of saints' lives as exemplars, the Fourth Council of Toledo enacted a canon permitting liturgical hymn singing about saints. While it was not uncommon in Spain by the fifth century for acts of martyrs to be read during the sacred office,[31] this canon formally permitted the inclusion of a number of Prudentius's hymns into the service and also created a demand for more saints' lives to be written to be included in the Mass. The mid-seventh century then enjoyed an upsurge in the composition of saints' lives, or hagiography.[32] As part of this liturgical stimulus to hagiography, Vincent's passion was rewritten, and in its revised form became the model for other martyrs' acts composed at this time.[33] Now the text of the passions themselves were transformed to become models for the new orthodoxy.

Since saints' lives were to be included in the Mass, hagiographers had to be certain that the narratives conformed strictly to ideals of sanctity established by conciliar decree designed to ensure uniformity of belief and worship. Therefore, even the popular text St. Vincent's passion was modified to conform. We have two main versions of the expanded modified passion, probably composed after the beginning of the seventh century. One is from a Vatican manuscript and is printed in the *Analecta Bollandiana*, a famous study of saints' lives. The other is a classic life edited by Ruinart, which is in the most comprehensive collection of saints' lives, the *Acta Sanctorum*. I shall refer to these as versions A and B, respectively. The versions are similar in most respects, so I shall discuss them jointly, indicating only when they differ.

Between the time of Vincent's death and the seventh century, some dramatic changes had taken place in the formulation of church doctrine, notably as church leaders met in councils to resolve theological disputes.

One of the most important councils was that of Nicaea, which convened in A.D. 325 to resolve differences about the understanding of the Trinity and the relationship between the Father and the Son, and this council resulted in the Nicaean Creed, which became one of the central confessions of faith for Christians. A second council, that of Chalcedon, met in 451 to refine further the understandings of the human and divine natures of Jesus. The decrees of both these councils spread throughout the Roman Empire. The Third Council of Toledo convened in Iberia in A.D. 589 to consider many issues confronting both church and state, and this council promised that all the faithful would adhere to the decisions of the Councils of Nicaea and Chalcedon.[34]

The hagiographers of the seventh-century versions of the passion of Vincent took into account these findings of the councils. When they recorded Vincent's deeds, they expanded one of his speeches to include a statement of faith that affirmed the decisions established at the Council of Nicaea.[35] The fourth-century deacon was portrayed commenting on religious controversies that had not yet been raised, resulting in an anachronism, or more precisely a manipulation of time that made the past conform to the seventh-century present. The authors of the passion were certain that a saint would have agreed with the findings of the councils if he had thought about them, so the authors believed it perfectly appropriate to insert these speeches.

Vincent's narrative was changed in other ways as well, and these modifications changed the fundamental perception of sanctity that was presented in the passion. Beyond the inclusion of the conciliar decisions, the key point of modification was Vincent's speech, which represented the all-important moment when he received God's power. At this pivotal point in the story, the two revised versions are different. Version A retains some of the same wording as the *Brevior* discussed previously,[36] but it modified the strong heroic individualism that marked the earlier version. In this version A, as in the original version, Dacian first questioned Valerius, believing that "if he could conquer the head of the church the rest would easily fall." Since this version was based on the original, which contained an account of Valerius's interrogation, the new hagiographer did not ignore Valerius's participation in the drama. Instead, he attempted to explain it. The narrative indicated that it was God's plan that the "lesser should be the greater" and that "he who had a minor office of the ministry would be victorious." Then, "heated by the spirit," the blessed Vincent rushed forward and reprimanded Valerius: "What? Under a murmur of mild words will you address the haughty?"[37] Valerius was then released and Vincent was tortured. This modification slightly reduced Vincent's role as a strong individual who by his free will chose the path to martyrdom. Since both Vincent and Valerius were merely fulfilling God's plan, Valerius could not be blamed for answering mildly, nor could Vincent be overly praised for speaking boldly. Vincent's words were still strong, however. Even if he was said to have been "heated by the Spirit" he still retained much of the quality of an heroic soldier of Christ that was present in the earlier version.

The final version, version B, changed the tone of this incident even more. This account explained Valerius's quiet response with even more detail: "He was of wonderful simplicity and innocent; learned, but he had a speech impediment." According to the hagiographer, Valerius recognized his physical inability to speak strongly to the inquisitor and spoke instead to Vincent: "I shall commit the care of the divine word to you. For the faith by which we stand, I commit the response." Thus, only after Vincent had appropriate authorization from his bishop did he speak: "Then Vincent, whose whole mind was now conscious of the crown, spoke to Dacian."[38] The message of this version is unambiguous. Holy power here was delegated and individualism was subsumed under hierarchy. The path to sanctity was to fulfill God's plan through channels, and bishops of the seventh century were striving to enforce this path, whether by forcing monks to place themselves under the jurisdiction of their bishop or by placing a martyr long dead under the jurisdiction of his bishop. The new ideal of sanctity and indeed the new Christian hero was one who was obedient to hierarchy.

This lesson was enhanced by the addition of a completely new section in both seventh-century versions: an account of Vincent's childhood. According to both versions, Vincent had been born of noble parents. This was perfectly consistent with the seventh century's preoccupation with hierarchy, in which even sanctity was expected to conform to social stratification.[39] According to the new texts, from boyhood the youth had given up secular literary studies after he had foreseen his future election to the church. He went to study under Valerius, the Bishop of Saragossa, where he became deacon. As a deacon, Vincent served his bishop well, even at times speaking for Valerius, who "was known to have a speech impediment."[40]

That the account of Vincent's childhood is the same in both version A and version B suggests a possible hypothesis for the changes in the narrative regarding Valerius's role in the drama. Version A mentioned Valerius's speech impediment in the initial discussion of Vincent's youth, but not during the moment of Vincent's speech to Dacian. The speech remained similar in language to the earlier *Brevior*. The speech impediment, however, provided a preview to God's plan to have the deacon speak for his bishop during questioning. In version B, the hagiographer, noting the speech impediment mentioned in the account of Vincent's youth, featured it in Vincent's crucial speech before his torture. Time was manipulated so that the past and present mirrored each other in a consistent narrative. The creation of Vincent's childhood–his past–based on his martyrdom–his future–was not as unusual (nor as expedient) as it might appear to modern eyes. We might consider this change a kind of "disinformation"–a manipulation of the truth to serve the needs of those in charge. The medieval audience, on the other hand, would have considered it a manipulation of *time* to *preserve* the truth.

WHAT IS TIME?

Scholars of saints have noted that veneration of cults in effect transcended time,[41] because the fundamental meaning of the veneration of a saint was that an event in the past (the martyrdom) was made immediate in the present and could indeed affect the future since power that had been gained in the past remained in the relics to benefit numberless subsequent generations. Time, however, was even manipulated within the passion of St. Vincent itself, so that not only the cult veneration transcended time but the narrative that formed the basis for the veneration also inverted time.

In a sense, it was not particularly miraculous that the narrative could invert expected time sequences–in this case by creating the child after the man–for medieval scholars believed time belonged to God, and He could do anything He wanted to with it.[42] In an influential analysis of time in the Middle Ages, Jacques LeGoff wrote,

Time is primarily theological time. It "begins with God" and is "dominated by Him." Consequently, divine action in its totality is so naturally connected with time that time cannot pose a problem; it is rather the necessary and natural condition of every "divine act."

The seventh-century versions of Vincent's passion make it clear that Vincent's pivotal speech was part of God's plan, therefore a "divine act," which then made irrelevant normal and expected patterns or sequences of time. In one of his sermons on the martyr, Augustine placed Vincent in divine time: Vincent's struggle was "not human, nor temporal, but divine and eternal,"[43] and this placement of Vincent outside human time paved the way for the manipulation of the text.

In Augustine's famous discussion of time, he defined it as "nothing more than an extension . . . ,"[44] by which he meant that time was an expansion of each present moment forward and backward in the mind, and in the mind of God. Furthermore, Augustine explained the relationship between past, present, and future: "The past is always driven on by the future, the future always follows on the heels of the past, and both the past and the future have their beginning and their end in the eternal present [that is, God]."[45] Augustine thus established the principles by which time could be inverted within the narrative of Vincent's passion and this perception of time profoundly shaped the medieval church and its hagiographers.

When the seventh-century hagiographers rewrote Vincent's story in a way that placed the martyrdom solidly within their perception of God's plan for an hierarchical structure, they drew on these principles to expand the narrative. Given the relationship between the past and the future and given the freedom of divine time from normal constraints, the seventh-century hagiographers could recreate Vincent's childhood from the present of his martyrdom. As the past was driven back by the future, it was possible to prophecy the past, and they did so. Furthermore, not surprisingly, Vincent's childhood foretold his future martyrdom, since as Augustine had argued, the future was consequent on the past. Within the narration of the passion, then, each moment—each present moment—provided an image of Vincent's future—his martyrdom—which then became timeless with the veneration of the cult. In the passion, time was inverted, God's plan was fulfilled; Vincent was reduced to a moment in God's time, and like a hologram represented all time.

The addition of Vincent's childhood completed the changes in the narrative of Vincent's martyrdom. The most familiar narrative, which I have called the seventh-century version B, provided an account of Vincent's martyrdom that was not threatening to the seventh-century church's requirement for conformity to hierarchical authority. Vincent gained his power by fulfilling God's plan to have it delegated from Vincent's ecclesiastical superior. Even a strong individualistic fourth-century martyr was brought under the control of the church in accordance with seventh-century conciliar decrees. In this form, the saint's passion was read to the faithful to provide an ideal of Christian sanctity. This reformed martyr continued to benefit the community that lived in proximity to his relics, and he helped the needy who did pilgrimage to his shrine. The power residing in the martyr was accessible to the community, but even more than that, the martyr belonged to the universal church in that his story articulated orthodox theology. To accomplish this, the hagiographers had to rewrite the history of the story of Vincent's acquisition of power—the church controlled the message of a martyr long dead.

Did the hagiographers intentionally falsify the "facts" of Vincent's death to make their point? While it is tempting to come to such a conclusion, it would be anachronistic to do so, because for the early church, manipulations in the narrative were secondary, indeed irrelevant, to the fundamental truth that martyrs were holy. With that as the basic premise, for a hagiographer to allow a narrative to stand that even hinted that the saint was less than holy by contemporary standards would have been the worst sort of falsification, so the narrative had to be changed as perceptions of sanctity changed. The saint's story could then point the way to holiness for the faithful, and in turn, permit historians to glimpse changing perceptions of holiness long past. Did Valerius have a speech impediment? No one cared about that truth; they were looking for a larger truth, one that said the martyrs always shed their blood in the service of orthodoxy.

Gaul and his wife. A defeated soldier kills himself after killing his wife to save them both from capture and enslavement. Such examples of "noble suicide" became linked to martyrdom and continue to exert an appeal. Late third century B.C. Alinari/Art Resource, NY. Museo Nazionale Romano delle Terme, Italy.

10

"YOU SHALL NOT KILL [YOURSELF]"

PROHIBITING SUICIDE

In a fourth-century confrontation between Roman authorities and a Christian woman named Agathonice, the crowd shouted angrily at the woman for her to burn a bit of meat as an offering to the emperor. In response, she said, "Let me do what I have come for!" and she flung off her cloak and threw herself joyfully on the fire that had been built for the sacrifice.[1] In another incident, a Christian named Euplus stood outside the Roman prefect's council chamber, shouting, "I want to die; I am a Christian!" So they obliged him, brought him in and killed him.[2] Did these two and many others like them commit suicide, or were they martyrs? Did martyrs commit suicide by stepping forward during times of persecution? If so, should they have done so? These questions have plagued ancient and modern writers, and the results of their deliberations have had an effect on our ideas about suicide long after the age of martyrdom has passed.

The answer to the first question is yes—some people did step forward and "volunteer" to be tested in the arenas of martyrdom, and in fact the persecutions before 250 were so sporadic, indeed idiosyncratic, that if one really wanted to avoid martyrdom it would not have been hard to do so. Therefore, we might argue that many martyrs chose to die, and many of the martyrs themselves would have agreed proudly with this assessment. Some martyrs (and many Christians) argued that Christ himself had committed suicide by allowing himself to be sacrificed,[3] so those who advocated voluntary martyrdom believed themselves in good company.

To answer the second question posed by the self-martyrdom of many—whether they should have done so—is more complex and it depends on culturally determined ideas about the legitimacy of self-killing. To begin to answer this question, we have to look at the ideas of the Roman and Jewish worlds in which they lived.

ANCIENT VIEWS ON SELF-KILLING

In the ancient world, there was no such word as *suicide*. This word was coined in the seventeenth century as a pejorative condemnation of the act of self-killing. This artificial word was built on Latin roots and literally means "self-murder." The use of "cide," or murder, causes listeners to associate the act with a crime, like *homicide* or *parricide*. Today, we use the word *suicide* to cover acts that range from youthful violence to end-of-life decisions to throwing oneself on a hand grenade to save one's companions. By tying such varied circumstances under one word we are hampered both in understanding suicide and in dealing with its consequences. The ancients (and some modern cultures such as the Japanese) saw more nuance in the act, and their vocabulary reflects their views.

In ancient Latin, there were many words to describe self-killing; indeed, scholars have identified more than three hundred that were used to describe the range of the practice.[4] The most common usage was *mors voluntaria*, "voluntary death," which unlike the word *suicide* offers a dramatically different impression. First, identifying it as "death" indicates that the victim is like the rest of us—we all die. Second, the phrase emphasizes choice—"voluntary"—which implies a freedom to choose one's own death. Indeed, the ancient Romans saw little to condemn in the practice of self-killing and much to admire.

As Romans found themselves less able to exert control over their political lives during the empire, noble Romans cherished their continued ability to choose their own moment and means of death. The philosopher Seneca eloquently reminded people that they always remained free:

> In whatever direction you may turn your eyes, there lies the means to end your woes. See you that precipice? Down that is the way to liberty.

See you that sea, that well? There sits liberty—at the bottom. See you that tree, stunted, blighted, and barren? Yet from its branches hangs liberty. See you that throat of yours, your gullet, your heart? They are ways of escape from servitude. Are the ways of egress I show you too toilsome, do they require too much courage and strength? Do you ask what is the highway to liberty? Any vein in your body.[5]

Many noble Romans shared Seneca's view. Some elderly, sickly men and women chose to stop eating to die. Others opened their veins to cheat a tyrannical emperor of their murder. The freedom and courage to choose one's own death was valued throughout the ancient Roman world. Perhaps the most extreme articulation of this value came from Pliny in the first century A.D. In his *Natural History* he wrote:

> The chief consolation for nature's imperfection in the case of man is that not even for God are all things possible—for he cannot, even if he wishes, kill himself, the supreme boon that nature has bestowed on man among all the penalties of life.[6]

Surely, few believed that the ability to choose their own death placed humans above the gods, but the extreme position frames the ideas of the ancients on the freedom implicit in voluntary death.

Many Jews who lived in the empire shared these views. The most vivid chronicler of ancient Jews who suicidally clung to freedom was Josephus, a Jewish general who described the violent war between Romans and Jews that culminated in the destruction of Jerusalem in A.D. 70 (described in chapter 1). Throughout the narrative, Josephus wrote of many Jews who chose a voluntary death over conquest by invading armies. For example, he claimed that during the invasions of Pompey some years before, some people "beyond number threw themselves over the precipices; some maddened by their hopeless position, fired the buildings round the wall and perished in the flames." In different incidents, fathers killed their wives and children before falling on their swords, and others leaped over cliffs.[7]

The most famous incident at the end of this Jewish war was the siege of Masada, a hilltop fortress that was the last outpost of the Jews after the destruction of Jerusalem. As Roman siege technology relentlessly built an access to the fortress, it was clear to the trapped that they would be over-run. Their leader Eleazar gave a long compassionate speech urging the Jews to deny the Romans a victory by exerting their right to take their own lives. Josephus recorded this speech that was purportedly recalled by the only survivors—an old woman who hid with five children as the carnage proceeded. Eleazar's words mark the fullest expression in the ancient, or modern, worlds of the praise of this voluntary death—of this martyrdom.

Eleazar first reminded his followers that this was a religious battle: "Long ago we resolved to serve neither the Romans nor anyone else but only God, who alone is the true and righteous Lord of men: now the time has come that bids us prove our determination by our deeds." He claimed that they had the right to "die nobly and as free men," a right that even the mighty Romans could not take from them. He reminded them that death was no disaster: "Death gives freedom to our souls and lets them depart to their own pure home. . . ," and he continued to extol the virtues of those who in the past had refused to submit to tyranny. Finally, he concluded with the final claim of freedom that proponents of voluntary death had always affirmed:

> While our hands are free and can hold a sword, let them do a noble serv-ice! Let us die unenslaved by our enemies, and leave this world as free men in company with our wives and children. That is what the Law ordains, that is what our wives and children demand of us, the necessity God has laid on us, the opposite of what the Romans wish. . . .[8]

In the tragedy that continues to capture our imagination, husbands killed their wives, children, and then each other, leaving the last man to die by his own hand.

Eleazar's speech offers disconcerting parallels to Jim Jones's final speech to his followers in Jonestown before they committed mass sui-cide (see chapter 8). Periodically throughout history, some groups have resorted to suicide when they felt their religious community was threat-ened, and Josephus's record of Eleazar's words summarizes their posi-tion. Leaving aside modern examples that remain too close for historical objectivity, were the Masada victims martyrs seeking religious freedom from Roman tyranny? It depends on whom you ask. Josephus himself was unsure.

While Josephus exhibited some compassion for the bravery of these people, he criticized a similar suicidal desire of those who made a last stand during the siege of Jerusalem. In his criticism, he took for granted the association of voluntary death with freedom, but in this case he found it misplaced: "If it indeed was right to fight for freedom, they should have done so at the start; once they had been crushed, and had submitted for many years, to try then to shake off the yoke was to show, not a love of freedom, but a morbid desire for death."[9] Josephus likely had a personal reason for rejecting the martyrdom of his compatriots. When he led the defenses of the besieged Jewish city of Jotapata, he chose to surrender to the Romans instead of fighting to the end, but he did so with a great deal of self-reflection. Just as he carefully recorded the arguments *for* the self-martyrdom of the defenders of Masada, he just as meticulously wrote his own arguments *against* his own self-killing.

Josephus argued that it is illogical and pointless to kill oneself to escape having the Romans kill one—the end result is the same. Furthermore, he argued that natural law, created by God, impels all things to want to live. Animals do not kill themselves, so people also should not. He also claimed that people are really not free to kill themselves; God gave them bodies, and it is for God to take the soul back from it. "It is from Him we have received our being, and it is to Him we must leave the right to take it away." Indeed, he called self-murder "impiety towards our Creator."[10] Josephus did not persuade his listeners; they turned on him and tried to attack him for his disloyalty. However, he found his own argument persuasive, and he surrendered to the Romans. He lived, and even prospered under their rule, and had the leisure to write his history of the Jewish wars.

After the destruction of Jerusalem (and at the same time Josephus was writing his self-justifying history), rabbis gathered at new centers of learning in Palestine and developed a body of scripture interpretation that produced a compilation of laws that remained profoundly influential in subsequent Hebrew tradition. It was within this collection, the Mishnah, that Jews first recorded a systematic prohibition of suicide. Even though they allowed for mitigating circumstances (e.g., if a child committed suicide as a result of his father's severity, the child was absolved),[11] the overwhelming conclusion of the rabbis was that self-murder was forbidden. One rabbi's summary that the commandment "Thou shalt not kill" included self-murder became central to the Jewish tradition.[12] The rabbis' analysis that people's lives are not their own to dispose of at will is one that will have a long history in the Mediterranean world.

THE AGE OF MARTYRS

Early Christians, then, had a good deal of precedent to draw on as they faced persecution. The Jewish tradition—from the Maccabean martyrs to the martyrs at Masada—offered praise for those who chose death over impiety, and the significant word here is *chose*. Christians also shared the long Roman tradition that praised people's right to die at the time and in the way of their own choosing. It is not surprising that some chose martyrdom instead of waiting for martyrdom to select them, and thus the borders between martyrdom and suicide were blurred. The fourth-century church father Ambrose wrote of a fifteen-year-old virgin named Pelagia who lived in Antioch and who chose suicide over letting herself be taken by a violent anti-Christian mob. Ambrose relayed a speech that Pelagia supposedly spoke while she wrestled with her decision: "Let us die if we are allowed, or if they will not allow it, still let us die. God is not offended by a remedy against evil, and faith permits the act."[13] Here Ambrose offered a succinct expression of the ideal of voluntary martyrdom: Pelagia's death was in her own control. The mob could choose neither the time nor the method of her martyrdom.

The example of Pelagia was very popular and her story was often repeated, but it was certainly not the only case of voluntary martyrdom. The influential martyr Ignatius of Antioch traveled eagerly to his martyrdom urging his supporters to do nothing to save him, and many others imitated him and hurried to Rome's amphitheaters to put themselves forward for martyrdom. For example, Perpetua's companion Saturus voluntarily joined a group in prison so that he could share their martyrdom. In fact, studies of martyrs indicate that more people were martyred because they volunteered than because they were arrested.[14] This vigor (or fanaticism) bothered many Roman authorities who did not want to be involved in what appeared to be outrageous behavior. For example, in 185 a group of Christians approached the stern but upright Proconsul of Asia carrying halters around their necks and demanding execution. He refused, telling them if they wanted to commit suicide they could find a cliff to jump off.[15] In some ways this dilemma paralleled that described by Josephus: should people die for their faith or live for their beliefs? In the late second and early third centuries, Christian writers were not unanimous in their answer to this question.

Some praised martyrdom as the highest goal; indeed the only certain hope for salvation. The most vigorous orthodox proponent of this view was Tertullian, the influential early third-century church father who lived and wrote in Carthage, North Africa. As we saw in chapter 7, North Africa long valued sacrificial suicide, and Tertullian brought that sensibility to his writings, urging the faithful to martyrdom. The North African was a prolific writer and articulated many of the ideas that shaped Western Christianity. He was also noted for his adamant view that Christians should never compromise with the pagan world when it came to matters of conscience. It was this view that led him to posit an increasingly firm advocacy of martyrdom.

In his early writings, Tertullian sought to firm up the resolve of those who had been arrested so that they could be strong under the threat of violence. In his tract "To the Martyrs," probably written in 203 to a group of Christians in prison, he reminded them of people who had died bravely before and assured them that heaven would be theirs at the end of their ordeal.[16] This group of Christians became martyrs, but Tertullian became more frustrated with other Christians who were not so strong. As time passed and the membership of the church grew, Tertullian saw people who were willing to make more compromises with the pagan world, and this infuriated him.

Tertullian then was drawn to a movement known as the New Prophecy that had arisen in Phrygia (modern Turkey). This movement was founded by a man named Montanus who had ecstatic experiences and spoke prophesies. He and two women followers, Priscilla and Maximilla, claimed that the Holy Spirit spoke through them, and they advocated the rigor of a besieged church and of preparation for martyrdom. These ideas (that came to be called Montanism) spread to North Africa, and after 207, Tertullian's works show a strong affinity to the movement. Tertullian was probably drawn to their prophecies, since like the Montanists, he too wanted to urge communities not to depart from the rigor and passion of the early Christian communities during the times of martyrdom.

In Tertullian's Montanist period, he wrote tracts in which he was even less willing to compromise with civil authorities. In one example, "The Chaplet," Tertullian told of a soldier in the Roman army who refused to wear a celebratory laurel crown as was customary. The soldier believed that act was inconsistent with his Christian beliefs. He was arrested, and he prepared himself for martyrdom. Tertullian was stimulated to write his tract not by pagans who arrested the soldier but by Christians who condemned the man for calling so much attention to himself over such a "trivial" matter as wearing a crown of leaves. Tertullian wrote, "Yes, I should not be surprised if such people were not figuring out how they could abolish martyrdom in the same way as they rejected the prophecies of the Holy Spirit."[17] In this incident, we see the beginnings of the ideas that would bathe North Africa in blood a century later during the Donatist crisis (described in chapter 8). Actually, Tertullian was certainly right that most Christians would like to see the end of the persecutions and to be permitted to live within the empire instead of in opposition to it.

The persecutions were not over in 211 when Tertullian wrote "The Chaplet," and he followed that work with a letter considering how Christians should respond to secular pressure. It is not surprising that in "Flight in the Time of Persecution," the North African took a firm stand in favor of martyrdom. He argued that God was the author of persecution, using it as a way to create His beloved martyrs. Therefore, Christians should neither flee nor bribe officials to avoid being arrested. Instead, they were to embrace the opportunity to die for the faith, even if it meant "volunteering":

> Indeed, . . . almost all are advised to offer themselves for martyrdom, never to flee from it. . . . Do not then ask to die on bridal beds, or in miscarriages, or from gentle fevers; rather seek to die a martyr that He may be glorified who suffered for you.[18]

In Tertullian's works, some Christians found a justification for even suicidal martyrdom. Like the Jews at Masada, these Christians would bode no compromise with a world that seemed at heart incompatible with their Christian beliefs. Tertullian himself was never selected for martyrdom (probably much to his disappointment), and his view of a rigorously separate Christian community was not the only model of Christian behavior that emerged in second-century North Africa.

While Carthaginian North Africa produced men and women like Tertullian with the rigorous zeal for martyrdom, Egyptian North Africa brought forth Christians with different ideas. Alexandria, in the Egyptian Delta, was a magnificent cosmopolitan city rich with a tradition of learning and which housed the greatest library of the ancient world. By the second century, Alexandria had a substantial Christian population, with thinkers that brought the traditions of Greek philosophy to the Christian message. One of the most influential of these Alexandrian church fathers was Clement, a contemporary of Tertullian.

Unlike Tertullian, Clement did not see the pagan world as a great evil to combat to the death. Instead, in his writings paganism emerges as an archaic, simple religion that can be treated with disdain. His tract "Exhortation to the Heathen" was written to urge pagans to abandon their "impious mysteries" in favor of the more sophisticated and satisfying Christianity.[19] He also wrote three books called "The Instructor" (*Paedagogus)* in which he described how Romans were to live a Christian life. These instructions contain detailed comments on daily life; for example, women were not to wear earrings, but men could wear gold seal rings since they had a practical use.[20] In Clement's eyes, Christians live quite comfortably in the world. They did not have to withdraw with a besieged mentality of would-be martyrs, but instead they should marry, work, and bask in the love of God.

It is in this context that Clement wrote about martyrdom, and his view departed dramatically from that of Tertullian's. Clement said that martyrdom meant living a Christian life—"a witness by life and word"—not simply dying for the faith. In fact, he condemned those who "rush" to martyrdom and thus commit voluntary death. He wrote, if someone "presents himself before the judgment seat" he is guilty of his own death, as an "accomplice in the crime of the persecutor." Clement goes on to say that it is right to flee from persecution, not because one is afraid to die but simply because one would not want to participate in the evil of persecution. He goes even further, arguing that someone who provokes the authorities is "wholly guilty" of seeking martyrdom.[21] This is quite a different view of what is required of a Christian from that proffered by Tertullian.

Clement wrote these tracts before 202, when the Emperor Septimius Severus began his persecution of Christians. During this persecution, Perpetua and her companions were martyred in Carthage spurred on by Tertullian's letter urging them to be strong and die for their faith. When this persecution approached Alexandria, Clement left town. He was true to his belief that a good Christian should not participate in the evil of martyrdom, and he traveled to Jerusalem and Antioch to wait out the storm of persecution.

Many others in Egypt (and elsewhere) shared Clement's views on the value of escaping rather than seeking martyrdom, and when persecutions broke out in 250 then again in 303, many Christians left the cities to seek safety and spirituality in the adjoining desert. These Christians began a movement—first of hermits then of monks and nuns—that would profoundly influence Western Christianity, including its views on suicide. The holy men and women who lived outside society were greatly revered, and consequently their opinions on various matters were carefully recorded and disproportionally influential relative to their numbers. It was within this body of work that appears the first direct Christian punishment of suicide.

AFTER THE MARTYRS

By about 330—the age of martyrdom had ended some fifteen years earlier—the Egyptian monk Pachomius had established a large community of monks who guided the spiritual lives of a community of nuns on the other side of the Nile. The early fifth-century text, the *Lausiac History*, recorded many of the words and actions of the Pachomian community, and this account tells of Pachomius's ruling on a double suicide: within the community of nuns, two began to quarrel, and one accused the other of inappropriate interaction with a wandering tailor who came plying his services to the convent. The accused nun was so distressed that she threw herself into the river and drowned. The second nun was so full of remorse that she hanged herself. When a priest was summoned from the monastery on the other side of the Nile, he declared that "for neither of the two was an offering to be made."[22] This statement was the first Christian record of people who committed suicide being forbidden a full Christian burial.

Why did Pachomius rule in this fashion? In part, he probably was drawing from a local pre-Christian Egyptian repugnance of people who died violently by their own hand. In part, he reflected the monastic belief in the value of community over one's own desires.[23] However, he was probably also drawing from the very tradition that had driven Christians into the desert to begin with: similar to Clement, he believed that people should live with their faith, not choose death or martyrdom to solve their problems. However, as we shall see in the following text, his ruling preserved in a tale of horror from the desert directly influenced church law, but first more centuries of struggle in North Africa would take place.

Tertullian, and Clement and Pachomius represent the two poles of opinions regarding martyrdom (and suicide). Their positions represented more than just possibilities for personal choice when faced with danger; instead, their arguments lay at the heart of Christian identity. Is the best Christian one who dies for the faith or who lives for it? However, the question of whether one should seek martyrdom was decided not in words circulated on scrolls but in the new violence that created many new martyrs in North Africa throughout the fourth and fifth centuries.

As we saw in chapter 8, the persecutions of Diocletian had set the stage for a conflict between those who believed that true Christians rigorously refused to compromise, and those who believed it acceptable to sway a bit in these changing winds so that the church as a whole could survive until a calmer day. This was essentially an implementation of the differing ideas of Tertullian and Clement—die or leave town. As we have seen, the Donatists that caused new bloodshed in North Africa spurred church leaders to end martyrdom. Perhaps it is not surprising that this desire to stop martyrs led church leaders also to condemn voluntary death. In reaction to the Donatist zeal, a church council met in Carthage in 348 and condemned self-killing, which marked a significant change in the classic Roman endorsement of suicide as a noble death.

The violence of the Donatists had frustrated the influential church father Augustine and led him to declare a just war of good against evil against the Christian Donatists. However, Augustine did more: in writing a detailed and philosophic explanation of the council's condemnation of suicide, Augustine established the roots of our society's current repugnance of suicide and voluntary martyrdom. Augustine condemned the intransigent Donatists who insisted that the heart of Christian freedom and salvation lay in martyrdom, and their voluntary pursuit of dramatic death. It was the very violence of this struggle that created the vigorous condemnation of martyrdom, and suicide, that persists to this day.

Augustine contrasted this suicidal search for martyrdom with a picture of new Christian communities living in harmony with the world:

> If you were to see the effects of the peace of Christ: the joyful throngs, their eagerness to hear and sing hymns and to receive the word of God, the well-attended, happy meetings . . . you would say that it [was] . . . not to be compared by any standard of judgment to that unnumbered throng, [who believe they] should destroy themselves in flames kindled by themselves.[24]

This indeed was the contrast between intense religious feelings expressed in martyrdom and a calmer, more content Christianity sought by believers who lacked the strength to withstand the rigors of a church besieged. This contrast was not new: it was the same one Tertullian had confronted with such anger, and it was the same one that shaped Josephus's discussion on suicide. Should one compromise with the world or refuse and die?

For his argument, Augustine first equated voluntary martyrdom with self-killing so he could prohibit both. This was a little tricky since there were plenty of voluntary martyrs like Pelagia who had the love and veneration of the faithful. Augustine acknowledged that those were special cases because they were acting in response to a call from God. He wrote in his influential book, *City of God*, "It may be that they acted on divine instruction and not through a human mistake—not in error, but in obedience. . . . When God orders, and shows without ambiguity that he orders, no one will bring an accusation against obedience. Who will lay a charge against a loyal compliance?"[25]

For Augustine, freedom was not only illusory, it was more often than not an occasion for sin; human pride can only be counterbalanced by obedience to higher authorities. To prove his point, Augustine pointed out that all homicide is not forbidden; those who kill under the command of God or of the state are not guilty of murder for they did not follow their own will but that of their superiors.[26] When he applied this principle to suicide, Augustine echoed the Jewish chronicler Josephus who wrote of the martyrs at Masada. Augustine claimed one's body and one's life were not one's own; they belonged to God, to the state, and to one's master. Just as in ancient Rome, slaves or soldiers did not have the freedom to choose death since their lives were not their own, for Augustine everyone was slave to someone else. Suicide and voluntary martyrdom were forbidden as part of his general suspicion of free will and his trust in hierarchy (see chapter 9).

However, with such a long Roman tradition of praise of voluntary death, Augustine had to marshal more arguments against the practice. The church father first looked to scriptures. He focused on the commandment, "You shall not kill" to argue that this meant that Christians were not to kill themselves. He said that since the commandment was not qualified in any way–that is, it does not say "You shall not kill your neighbor"–it included the prohibition of suicide.[27] This uncompromising prohibition of voluntary death probably came in large part from Augustine's rejection of the Donatists, but it also represented a departure from the ancient Roman respect for suicide, so the church father had to address his arguments to Romans, who might not be persuaded just on the basis of scripture.

Probably the most famous of the Roman suicides was that of Lucretia, who in the semilegendary history of Rome had been raped by the Etruscan king's son. Lucretia killed herself to save herself and her family from the indignity of the rape. Throughout Roman history, she had been praised as a heroine–indeed a martyr to feminine virtue and family honor. Augustine, however, said that she was wrong to choose death, and in fact he even went so far to suggest that the crime of her self-murder derived from a hidden guilt on her part. Augustine wrote that she must have enjoyed the rape and thus was not innocent: "In killing herself it was no innocent which she killed, but one conscious of guilt."[28] This almost shocking rewriting of the story of Lucretia is testimony to how far Augustine went in condemning suicide; he recast the history of Rome to prohibit people's freedom to choose death even if in doing so he attacked a Roman woman long remembered for virtuous chastity.

LEGAL PROHIBITIONS

With Augustine the great age of martyrdom ends. The church was no longer one besieged by a hostile power depending on the courage, and indeed freedom, of individuals such as Vincent or Pelagia or all the other martyrs discussed in this book to stand up and choose to die for their faith. Instead, the church itself had conquered the Roman Empire and now depended on the obedience of the faithful to carry it forward. Augustine's prohibition of voluntary martyrdom turned into an abhorrence of suicide that continues into modern times. However, Augustine's influential writings offered guidelines and principles; they were not yet formulated into laws against suicide. That happened a century and a half later in the Iberian Peninsula.

Early church law was formulated at meetings of bishops where they debated current issues and recorded their rulings. One such council took place in Braga (modern-day Portugal). This First Council of Braga (held in 561) was attended, and possibly conducted, by Martin of Braga, an influential, well-traveled churchman who shaped the ideas of the sixth-century Iberian church. The Braga council issued a canon that offered penalties against people who committed suicide: "Those who put themselves to death whether by an iron blade, or by poison, or jumping from a height, or hanging, or violently by any means, no commemoration should be made for them at Mass, nor should their bodies be taken to burial with psalms. . . ."[29] This influential canon was widely quoted and throughout the Middle Ages became the standard written justification for denying normal funeral rites for people who committed suicide.

Where did Martin get this idea that he turned into church law? He knew the writings of Augustine, so there was no lack of precedent for forbidding self-murder, but his real influence lay further afield, in the desert of Egypt. Martin was not originally from Spain; he hailed from Pannonia (roughly a portion of modern-day Hungary). Martin traveled widely in the east as a spiritual tourist going to the "holy places." It is likely that he visited the great monasteries in Egypt during his travels, but even if he did not, he was enamored of the monastic life. When he came to Spain, he set up a monastery along the lines of Pachomius's in Egypt. Furthermore, he set one of his monks to translate *The Sayings of the Egyptian Fathers*, which preserved the wise words of the Egyptian monks. Here we can see the influence of Pachomius across time and across the vast spaces of the Mediterranean. The anecdote of the two suicidal nuns came to Spain in the hands of Martin of Braga,[30] whose administrative genius turned it into church law.

Late in the Middle Ages as kings began to claim legal jurisdiction over their subjects, they incorporated much of church law into secular law. Thus, many prohibitions that had been matters of morality became issues of law, and prohibitions of suicide were no different. By late in the Middle Ages, suicide was no longer just immoral, it was illegal. The stage was set for our modern prohibitions.

There are moments in the history of Christianity when martyrs were again created: beginning in the sixteenth century, as missionaries left Europe and confronted new unbelievers, a number were killed and quickly hailed as martyrs. But no longer would Christians praise those who step forward to die; in modern times we are to live with oppression, not die in protest of it. However, our cultural memory includes praise of martyrs who lived in an age when choosing the moment of one's death was a noble, indeed sacred, deed, and this memory leads some to volunteer to die for a cause they believe in—whether it is self-immolation to protest the Vietnam War or the suicide bombers in the Middle East.

Was this prohibition of self-killing a good thing? Our modern ideas are as ambivalent as those of the ancients. As we saw in chapter 8, the same impulses that led the Donatists to preserve the ideal of martyrdom at the center of Christian identity led to horrible modern tragedies of religious groups like the Branch Davidians at Waco or Jim Jones's People's Temple in Guyana. It is the same belief in martyrdom as a powerful force that motivates the suicide bombers in the Middle East, who call themselves self-martyrs in recollection of people who step forward in voluntary death. I think most can agree with Augustine that it is time to end the age of martyrdom and create a world where people can live peacefully with their beliefs instead of dying for them. On the other hand, many of us sympathize with people at the end of their lives who want a comfortable voluntary death with dignity. Should the same prohibitions that condemn Jim Jones jail those who assist people who want a death with dignity? Should we remain bound by the prohibition of self-murder that was made in an age anxious to end the shedding of the blood of martyrs?

CONCLUSION

I began this book because I was surprised at the long-term unintended consequences of the age of martyrdom. Early Christians thought they were dying to keep from denying their faith and to secure heaven; they gave little thought to a world they believed would disappear soon anyway. Their motives and their experiences were deeply personal. Contemporary witnesses credited the martyrs with another result of their strength—Christianity won the battle for the soul of the Roman Empire, and the Roman Catholic Church was founded. They believed that martyrs' blood ensured the prosperity of the nascent church. Most historians since have considered this the end of the story.

I have tried to show that the violence that so captured the attention of the age and the imagination of subsequent generations had an impact on ideas that had nothing to do with the initial struggle over the religion of the Roman Empire. The CIA is right: blowback (or unintended consequences) appear in unforseen places. In some areas, the blood of martyrs served as a transition to bring very old ideas into a new age—traditional ideas of magic, sacrifice, and dreams became comfortably housed in the Christian churches. In other areas, the struggle transformed old ideas and gave new shape to theology and society—people expected their flesh to be resurrected and their mothers to be self-sacrificing, and suicide was banned. Finally and sadly, the violence spawned long-standing violence of its own—casting the world as a battle between good and evil and placing Jews on the side of evil for centuries.

Seeing the power of martyrdom, I have to agree with Augustine and others who decided it was time to put an end to the deaths. Of course, I completely disagree with using violence or even disinformation to change minds; such methods do not work in predictable ways. Even if we believe a cause is worthy of dying for, we cannot be sure of the actual results of violence. We do not want to "make martyrs" of people like bin Laden and others who want to claim the mantle of martyrdom to be sure their impact is great. There are better ways to achieve humane ends. I wrote this book because I believe in reason over blood, and that the pen is mightier than the sword—or as the Prophet Mohammed reputedly said, "The scholar's ink is more sacred than the blood of martyrs."[31]

CHART OF MARTYRS
MARTYRS MENTIONED IN THIS BOOK

Emperor and Dates of Rule	Martyr	Location
Tiberius 14–37	Stephen	Jerusalem
Nero 54–68	James the Elder	Jerusalem
Nero 54–68	Peter, Paul, and many others	Rome
Domitian 81–96	Many "eminent men"	Rome
Trajan 98–117	Symeon	Jerusalem
Trajan 98–117	Ignatius, Rufus, Zosimus	Rome
Trajan 98–117	Many others	Throughout the empire
Antoninus Pius 138–61	Telesphorus	Rome
Antoninus Pius 138–61	Germanicus, Polycarp, Metrodorus, Pionius, Thraseas	Smyrna
Antoninus Pius 138–61	Carpus, Papylas, Agathonice	Pergamum

Emperor and Dates of Rule	Martyr	Location
Marcus Aurelius 161–80	Justin, Ptolemy, Lucius	Rome
Marcus Aurelius 161–80	Publius	Athens
Marcus Aurelius 161–80	Sagaris	Laodicea
Marcus Aurelius 161–80	Vettius Epagathus, Sanctus, Maturus, Attalus, Blandina, Biblis, Pothinus, Alexander, Ponticus, Alcibiades, and others	Lyons and Vienne
Commodus 180–92	Gaius, Alexander	Apamea
Commodus 180–92	Apollonius	Rome
Septimius Severus 193–211	Leonides, Plutarch, Serenus, Heraclides, Hero, Herais, Potamiaena, Basilides, Marcella	Alexandria
Septimius Severus 193–211	*Perpetua, Felicity, Saturus, Saturninus, Revocatus*	Carthage
Decius 249–51	Fabian	Rome
Decius 249–51	Metras, Quinta, Apollonia, Serapion, Junian, Cronion, Besas, Macar, Epimachus, Alexander, Ammonarion, Mercuria, Dionysia, Hero, Ater, Isidore, Nemesion,	Alexandria

Emperor and Dates of Rule	Martyr	Location
	Ammon, Zeus, Ptolemy, Ingenuus, Theophilus	
Decius 249–51	Ischyrion	Egypt
Decius 258	*Cyprian*	Carthage
Valerian 253–59	Priscus, Malchus, Alexander	Caesarea
Gallienus 259–68	Marinus	Caesarea
Gallienus	Marcellinus	Rome
Diocletian 284–305 and Galerius 305–31	Euethius, Peter, Anthimus, Dorotheus, Gorgonius, and many others	Nicomedia
Diocletian 284–305 and Galerius 305–31	Five Egyptians	Tyre
Diocletian 284–305 and Galerius 305–31	Philoromus, Phileas, Hesychius, Pachymius, Theodore, and "immense numbers" of others	Egypt and Thebais
Diocletian 284–305	*Agatha*[a]	Sicily
Diocletian 303	*Felix, Bishop (Donatist martyr)*	Thibiuca, North Africa
Diocletian 304	*Maxima, Donatilla, Secunda (Donatist martyrs)*	Carthage
Diocletian 304	*Vincent*	Saragossa, Spain
Diocletian 284–305 and Galerius 305–31	"Countless numbers"	North Africa

Emperor and Dates of Rule	Martyr	Location
Maximin 286–308	Adauctus, and a whole village	Phrygia
Maximin 286–308	Large numbers	Arabia, Cappadocia, Mesopotamia
Maximin 286–308	Large numbers	Pontus
Maximin 286–308	Woman and daughters, two sisters, Tyrannion, Zenobius	Antioch
Maximin 286–308	Silvanus of Gaza and thirty-nine others, Peleus, Nilus	Phaeno
Maximin 286–308	Peter and many bishops	Alexandria
Maximin 286–308	Lucian	Nicomedia
Maximin 286–308	*Ursula*[a]	Cologne
Constantine–313	**Edict of Toleration ending persecution of Christians**	
Constantius II 341	*Tarbo*	Persia, near Baghdad
Constans 347	*Maximian and Isaac, Marculus (Donatist martyrs)*	Carthage and North Africa

Note. Martyrs not mentioned by Eusebius are shown in italics.
[a] Martyrs mentioned in this book whose legends are unreliable.

NOTES

INTRODUCTION

1. See Rodney Stark, *The Rise of Christianity: A Sociologist Reconsiders History* (Princeton: Princeton University Press, 1996), for a brilliant, albeit controversial, look at the growth of the Church. See also J. E. Salisbury, *Perpetua's Passion* (New York: Routledge, 1997).

2. M. Staniforth, trans., "The Epistles of Ignatius," in *Early Christian Writings: The Apostolic Fathers* (New York: Dorset, 1968), 61–125.

3. Herbert Musurillo, *Acts of the Christian Martyrs* (Oxford: Clarendon, 1972), 20–21.

4. Ibid., 62–86.

5. W. H. C. Frend, *Martyrdom and Persecution in the Early Church* (Grand Rapids, Mich.: Baker Book House, 1981), xi.

6. A. Gallanio, *Tortures and Torments of the Christian Martyrs* (Paris: Fortune, 1903), vi, vii.

CHAPTER 1

1. This full description of the fire is taken from Tacitus, "The Annals," in *The Complete Works of Tacitus*, trans. A. J. Church (New York: Random House, 1942), 377–78.

2. Ibid., 378.

3. Ibid., 380.

4. Ibid., 380.

5. Ibid., 381.

6. Minucius Felix, "Octavius," in *Tertullian: Apologetical Works and Minucius Felix*, trans. R. Arbesmann (New York: Fathers of the Church, 1950), 334–39.

7. Tertullian, "Ad Nationes," in *Latin Christianity: Its Founder, Tertullian*, vol. 3 of *Ante-Nicene Fathers* (Peabody, Mass.: Hendrickson, 1995), 115.

8. Herbert Musurillo, *Acts of the Christian Martyrs* (Oxford: Clarendon, 1982), 79.

9. Ibid., 41.

10. Pliny, *Letters*, ed. E. G. Hardy (Oxford: Oxford University Press, 1889), 210–17.

11. Eusebius, *The History of the Church*, trans. G. A. Williamson (Harmondsworth: Penguin, 1984), 144.

12. Tertullian, "Apology," in *Tertullian*, 10–12.

13. Musurillo, 89.

14. Eusebius, 162.

15. Ibid., 194.

16. Ibid., 200.

17. Cicero, *De Natura Deorum*, trans. H. Rackham (Cambridge: Harvard University Press, 1967), 131.

18. Musurillo, 87.

19. Tacitus, "Histories" in *The Complete Works of Tacitus*, 659.

20. Tertullian, "To Scapula," in *Tertullian*, 157.

21. Thomas Wiedemann, *Emperors and Gladiators* (New York: Routledge, 1992), 107.

22. Salisbury, 125–34.

23. Eusebius, 195.

24. Salisbury, 138.

25. Eusebius, 202.

26. Salisbury, 138.

27. W. H. C. Frend, *The Rise of Christianity* (Philadelphia: Fortress, 1984), 313.

28. Eusebius, 277.

29. Cyprian, "The Lapsed," in *Saint Cyprian: Treatises*, ed. Roy J. Deferrari (New York: Fathers of the Church, 1958), 63–64.

30. W. H. C. Frend. *Martyrdom and Persecution in the Early Church* (Grand Rapids, Mich.: Baker Book House, 1981), 455.

31. Eusebius, 328.

32. Lactantius, "Of the Manner in Which the Persecutors Died," in *Ante-Nicene Fathers*, vol. 7, ed. A. Roberts (Peabody, Mass.: Hendrickson, 1995), 305.

33. Eusebius, 329.

34. Ibid., 335.

35. Ibid., 344.

36. Ibid., 335.

37. Edward Peters, *Torture* (Oxford: Basil Blackwell, 1985), 1.

38. Eusebius, 196.

39. Ibid., 196.

40. Peters, 33.

41. Eusebius, 335.

42. Ibid., 333.

43. Ibid., 337.

44. Elaine Scarry, *The Body in Pain* (New York: Oxford University Press, 1985), 30–37.

45. Ibid., 37.

46. Musurillo, 235.

47. Ibid., 297–98.

48. Eusebius, 343.

49. Ibid., 340.

50. Ibid., 382.

51. Augustine, *Confessions*, trans. R. S. Pine-Coffin (New York: Penguin, 1980), 276–77.

CHAPTER 2

1. Josephus, *The Jewish War*, trans. G. A. Williamson (Baltimore: Penguin, 1959), 374.

2. Ibid., 375.

3. Caroline Walker Bynum, *The Resurrection of the Body in Western Christianity, 200–1336* (New York: Columbia University Press, 1995), 13.

4. Ibid., 13.

5. Eusebius, *The History of the Church from Christ to Constantine*, trans. G. A. Williamson (Harmondworth: Penguin, 1985), 272.

6. Elaine Pagels, *The Gnostic Gospels* (New York: Vintage Books, 1981) remains the clearest account of the gnostics as revealed through the Nag Hammadi find.

7. This hierarchy is most fully described in Irenaeus, "Against Heresies," in *Ante-Nicene Fathers,* vol. 1, ed. A. Roberts and J. Donaldson (Peabody, Mass.: Hendrickson, 1995), 316–26.

8. Pagels, 173.

9. Ibid., 115.

10. Tertullian, "On the Resurrection of the Flesh," in *Ante-Nicene Fathers*, vol. 3, ed. A. Roberts and J. Donaldson (Peabody, Mass.: Hendrickson, 1995), 550.

11. Pagels, 87.

12. Ibid., 111.

13. Tertullian, "On the Resurrection of the Flesh," 558.

14. Pagels, 155–56.

15. M. Staniforth, trans., "The Epistles of Ignatius," in *Early Christian Writings: The Apostolic Fathers* (New York: Dorset, 1968), 97.

16. Plato, "Phaedo," in *Great Dialogues of Plato*, trans. W. H. D. Rouse (New York: Mentor, 1956), 511.

17. Joseph Wilson Trigg, *Origen: The Bible and Philosophy in the Third-Century Church* (Atlanta: John Knox, 1983), 108–15.

18. Origen, "Against Celsus," in Collected Works in *Ante-Nicene Fathers*, vol. 4, ed. A. Roberts and J. Donaldson (Peabody, Mass.: Hendrickson, 1995), 623.

19. Origen, "De Principiis," in *Collected Works*, 294.

20. Bynum, 67.

21. "The Anathematisms of the Emperor Justinian against Origen," in *Nicene and Post-Nicene Fathers,* vol 14. ed. A. Roberts and J. Donaldson (Peabody, Mass.: Hendrickson, 1995), 320.

22. Bynum, 81.

23. Ibid., 82–83.

24. Ibid., 79.

25. Ibid., 88.

26. Herbert Musurillo, *Acts of the Christian Martyrs*, vol. II (Oxford: Clarendon, 1972), 163.

27. Ibid., 201.

28. Ibid., 333.

29. Tertullian, "The Chaplet," in *Disciplinary, Moral and Ascetical Works*, trans. R. Arbesmann (New York: Fathers of the Church, 1959), 233.

30. Tertullian, "A Treatise on the Soul," in *Ante-Nicene Fathers*, vol. 3, 187.

31. Ibid., 189.

32. Ibid., 188.

33. Ibid., 228.

34. Ibid., 231.

35. Ibid., 235.

36. Tertullian, "On the Resurrection of the Flesh," 555–57.

37. Ibid., 555.

38. Ibid., 555.

39. Ibid., 589.

40. Ibid., 592.

41. Ibid., 589.

42. Ibid., 593.
43. Ibid., 548.
44. Ibid., 549.
45. Ibid., 551.
46. Ibid., 551.
47. Bynum, 41.
48. Tertullian, "On the Resurrection of the Flesh," 548.
49. Joyce E. Salisbury, *The Beast Within: Animals in the Middle Ages* (New York: Routledge, 1994), 70.
50. Piero Camporesi, *The Incorruptible Flesh: Bodily Mutation and Mortification in Religion and Folklore*, trans. T. Croft-Murray and H. Elson (Cambridge: Cambridge University Press, 1988), 106–30.
51. M. Staniforth, trans., "Epistles of Ignatius," 105.
52. Tertullian, "On the Resurrection of the Flesh," 553.
53. See Bynum, *Resurrection of the Body*, for the fullest development of this idea of resurrecting the very flesh that dissolved at death.
54. Augustine, *City of God*, trans. D. Knowles (Harmondsworth: Penguin, 1972), 1062.
55. Peter Brown, *The Cult of the Saints: Its Rise and Function in Latin Christianity* (Chicago: University of Chicago Press, 1981), 6.
56. Celsus, *On the True Doctrine*, trans. R. J. Hoffman (Oxford: Oxford University Press, 1987), 86.
57. Musurillo, 165.
58. Ibid., 213.
59. Joyce E. Salisbury, *Perpetua's Passion* (New York: Routledge, 1997), 168.
60. Ibid., 169.
61. Musurillo, 183.
62. Ibid., 81.
63. Ibid., 171.
64. Brown, 7.
65. Salisbury, *Perpetua's Passion*, 168.
66. Augustine, 1047.
67. Ibid., 1048.

CHAPTER 3

1. Plutarch, "Isis and Osiris," in *Moralia*, trans. F. C. Babbitt (Cambridge: Harvard University Press, 1962), 9. See also J. E. Salisbury, *Perpetua's Passion* (New York: Routledge, 1997), 22–32.
2. Valerie I. J. Flint, *The Rise of Magic in Early Medieval Europe* (Princeton: Princeton University Press, 1991), 3–13.
3. Eusebius, *The History of the Church*, trans. G. A. Williamson (Harmondsworth: Penguin, 1984), 210.
4. Salisbury, *Perpetua*, 64–66.
5. "Acts of the Holy Apostles Peter and Paul," in *Ante-Nicene Fathers*, vol. 8, edited by A. Roberts and J. Donaldson (Peabody, Mass.: Hendrickson, 1993), 480–84.
6. Flint, 341.
7. Irenaeus, "Against Heresies," in *Ante-Nicene Fathers*, vol. 1, ed. A. Roberts and J. Donaldson (Peabody, Mass.: Hendrickson, 1995), 347–48.
8. Flint, 13–22.
9. Celsus, *On the True Doctrine*, trans. R. J. Hoffman (Oxford: Oxford University Press, 1987), 98.

10. Ignatius of Antioch, in *Early Christian Writings: The Apostolic Fathers*, trans. M. Staniforth (New York: Dorset, 1968), 81.

11. Maureen A. Tilley, *Donatist Martyr Stories: The Church in Conflict in Roman North Africa* (Liverpool: Liverpool University Press, 1996), 19.

12. Ibid., 20.

13. Ibid., 4–5.

14. Salisbury, *Perpetua*, 145.

15. S. P. Brock and S. A. Harvey, trans., *Holy Women of the Syrian Orient* (Berkeley: University of California Press, 1987) offers a fascinating translation and commentary on some of the accounts of these martyrs.

16. The following account may be found in Brock and Harvey, 73–76.

17. CBS National news 17 January 2002.

18. Joyce E. Salisbury, *Iberian Popular Religion* (Lewiston, N.Y.: Edwin Mellon, 1985), 165.

19. "Epistola Vigilii Papae ad Profuturum Episcopum" sec. IV, J. P. Migne, *Patologiae Cursus Completus, Series Latina* 84:832.

20. Salisbury, *Iberian*, 166.

21. Augustine, Sermon 319, 6.6., in Peter Brown, *The Cult of the Saints: Its Rise and Function in Latin Christianity* (Chicago: University of Chicago Press, 1981), 91.

22. Ibid., 92.

23. Braulio of Saragossa, in *The Fathers of the Church: Iberian Fathers*, vol. 2, ed. Claude W. Barlow (Washington: Fathers of the Church, 1969), 27–28.

24. Brown, 82.

25. Isidore of Seville, "Etymology" VI, c. XI, J. P. Migne, *Patologiae Cursus Completus, Series Latina* 82:290.

26. Salisbury, *Iberian*, 139.

27. Jerome, "Ep. 103" in *Letters and Select Works in Nicene and Post-Nicene Fathers*, vol. 6, ed. P. Schaff and H. Wace (Peabody, Mass.: Hendrickson, 1995), 13.

28. Salisbury, *Iberian*, 146.

29. S. P. Scott, trans., *The Visigothic Code*, (Boston: Boston Book Company, 1910), Book VI, title II, ch. III, 204.

30. Flint, 271–73.

31. Ibid., 271.

32. Gregory of Tours, *History of the Franks*, trans. E. Brehaut (New York: Norton, 1969), 182. See also Elizabeth Key Fowden, *The Barbarian Plain: Saint Sergius between Rome and Iran* (Berkeley: University of California Press, 1999), 129.

33. Jacobus de Voragine, *The Golden Legend* (New York: Arno, 1969), 369.

34. See David Van Brima, "The Brother of Jesus," trans. G. Ryan, *Time*, 4 November 2002, 70–73.

35. Linda Kay Davidson and Maryjane Dunn-Wood (*Pilgrimage in the Middle Ages: A Research Guide* [New York: Garland, 1993], 159) offers a good discussion of the possible derivations of the name. This work also provides an excellent entryway into the extensive bibliography of Santiago de Compostela.

36. This account is drawn from Jacobus de Voragine, 371–73. Other medieval accounts vary in some of the particulars, but Jacobus recorded the most well-known version.

37. Sulpicius Severus, "Sacred History," in *Nicene and Post-Nicene Fathers*, vol. 11, ed. P. Schaff and H. Wace (Peabody, Mass.: Hendrickson, 1995), 119.

38. Ibid., 122.

39. Salisbury, *Iberian*, 209–15.

40. Henry Chadwick, *Priscillian of Avila* (Oxford: Clarendon, 1976), 233.

41. Rafael Heliodor Valle, *Santiago en América* (Mexico: Santiago, 1946).

42. Barbara Tedlock, *Time and the Highland Maya* (Albuquerque: University of New Mexico Press, 1982), 21.

CHAPTER 4

1. Sigmund Freud, *Interpretation of Dreams*, trans. J. Strachey (New York: Avon Books, 1965), 659–60.

2. Timothy Roche, "A Short Course in Miracles," *Time*, 29 July 2002, 32.

3. C. A. Behr, *Aelius Aristides and the Sacred Tales* (Chicago: Argonaut, 1967), 25.

4. Ibid., 35.

5. Ibid., 207.

6. Ibid., 205, 292.

7. Virgil, *Aeneid*, trans. A. Mandelbaum (New York: Bantam Books, 1981), 162.

8. Jacques Le Goff, "Christianity and Dreams (Second to Seventh Century)," in *The Medieval Imagination*, trans. A. Goldhammer (Chicago: University of Chicago Press, 1985), 197–98.

9. Behr, 173.

10. S. R. F. Price, "The Future of Dreams: From Freud to Artemidorus," in *Before Sexuality: The Construction of Erotic Experience in the Ancient Greek World*, ed. D. M. Halperin, F. Zeitlin, J. J. Winkler (Princeton: Princeton University Press, 1990), 377.

11. Behr, 185.

12. Tertullian, "A Treatise on the Soul," in *Ante-Nicene Fathers*, vol. 3, ed. A. Roberts and J. Donaldson (Peabody, Mass.: Hendrickson, 1995), 222.

13. Ibid., 225–26.

14. Ibid., 226.

15. Le Goff, "Christianity and Dreams," 217.

16. Ibid., 223.

17. Ibid., 211.

18. *2 Esdras* in *New Oxford Annotated Bible* (New York: Oxford University Press, 1977).

19. F. X. Glimm, trans., "Shepherd of Hermas," in *The Apostolic Fathers* (New York: Christian Heritage, 1948), 230.

20. Herbert Musurillo, "Of Marian and James," in *Acts of the Christian Martyrs* (Oxford: Clarendon, 1972), 205.

21. Ibid., 217.

22. M. Staniforth, trans., "Martyrdom of Polycarp," in *Early Christian Writings: Apostolic Fathers* (New York: Dorset, 1968), 157.

23. J. E. Salisbury, *Perpetua's Passion* (New York: Routledge, 1997), 107–8.

24. Ibid., 112. See pages 108–12 for an analysis of the images within Perpetua's dream.

25. Ibid., 99.

26. C. McDannell and B. Lang, *Heaven: A History* (New Haven: Yale University Press, 1988), 40–42.

27. Salisbury, 102.

28. Ibid., 112.

29. Ibid., 105–6.

30. Jacques Le Goff, *The Birth of Purgatory*, trans. A. Goldhammer (Chicago: University of Chicago Press, 1984), 50–51.

31. Clement, "First Epistle to the Corinthians," in *Apostolic Fathers*, 51, and Ignatius of Antioch, "Epistle to the Magnesians," in *Apostolic Fathers*, 88.

32. Musurillo, "Of Montanus and Lucius," in *Acts of the Christian Martyrs* (Oxford: Clarendon, 1972), 223–25.

33. Ibid., 225.

34. Salisbury, 113.

35. Ibid., 70–71.

36. Le Goff, "Christianity and Dreams," 225.

37. See Ronald J. Heine, *Montanist Oracles and Testimonia*, North American Patristic Society, vol. 14 (Macon, Ga.: Mercer University Press, 1989).

38. Le Goff, "Christianity and Dreams," 228.

39. Ibid., 222.

40. Steven M. Oberhelman, *The Oneirocriticon of Achmet* (Lubbock: Texas Tech University Press, 1991), 52.

41. Ibid., 12.

42. Salisbury, 95.

43. Ibid., 93.

CHAPTER 5

1. James Carroll, *Constantine's Sword: The Church and the Jews* (New York: Houghton Mifflin, 2001), 7. This book gives a full and insightful analysis of the split between Christians and Jews throughout history.

2. Josephus, *The Jewish War*, trans. G. A. Williamson (Baltimore: Penguin, 1959), 372–74.

3. Elaine Pagels, *The Origin of Satan* (New York: Random House, 1995), 30.

4. Carroll, 144–45.

5. Ibid., 58.

6. W. H. C. Frend, *Martyrdom and Persecution in the Early Church* (Grand Rapids, Mich.: Baker Book House, 1981), 155.

7. See W. H. C. Frend, *The Rise of Christianity* (Philadelphia: Fortress, 1984), 91–110, and Alan N. Segal, *Rebecca's Children: Judaism and Christianity in the Roman World* (Cambridge: Harvard University Press, 1986), 96–117, for summaries of Paul's influence.

8. Frend, *Martyrdom*, 164–65.

9. Josephus, 223, 229.

10. See, Pagels, 3–34 for an excellent analysis of the relationship between the gospel of Mark and the Jewish war.

11. Eusebius, *The History of the Church* (Harmondsworth: Penguin, 1984), 111.

12. Ibid., 111.

13. Pagels develops this thesis in much detail. For this specific information, see 82, 89, 98.

14. Ibid., 15.

15. Carroll, 147.

16. Maxwell Staniforth, *Early Christian Writings* (New York: Dorset, 1968), 189.

17. Ibid., 205.

18. Ibid., 215.

19. Michael Grant, *The Jews in the Roman World* (New York: Scribner, 1973), 227.

20. Ibid., 266.

21. Musurillo, "Of Polycarp," in *Acts of the Christian Martyrs*, vol. II (Oxford: Clarendon, 1972), 11, 13.

22. Ibid., 17.

23. Musurillo, "Of Pionius," in *Acts of the Christian Martyrs*, vol. II (Oxford: Clarendon, 1972), 139.

24. Tertullian, "Ad Nationes," in *Ante-Nicene Fathers*, vol. 3, ed. A. Roberts and J. Donaldson (Peabody, Mass.: Hendrickson, 1995), 123.

25. Staniforth, 89.

26. Ibid., 111.

27. Musurillo, "Of Pionius," 153.

28. Ibid., 153–54.

29. See Pagels for the fullest development of this argument.

30. Carroll, 232.

31. Justin Martyr, "Dialogue with Trypho," in *Ante-Nicene Fathers*, vol. 1, ed. A. Roberts and J. Donaldson (Peabody, Mass.: Hendrickson, 1995), 240, 261.

32. Musurillo, "Of Phileas," 349.

33. Tertullian, "An Answer to the Jews," in *Ante-Nicene Fathers*, vol. 3, 151–75.

34. Eusebius, 179–80.

35. Ambrose, "Letter XL," in *Nicene and Post-Nicene Fathers*, vol. 10, P. Schaff and H. Wace (Peabody, Mass.: Hendrickson, 1995), 443.

36. Augustine, *City of God*, trans. David Knowles (Hammondsworth: Penguin, 1972), 957–58.

37. Carroll, 233.

CHAPTER 6

1. See W. H. C. Frend, *Martyrdom and Persecution in the Early Church: A Study of Conflict from the Maccabees to Donatus* (Grand Rapids, Mich.: Baker Book House, 1981) for a convincing demonstration of the influence of this text.

2. See S. Dixon, *The Roman Mother* (Norman: University of Oklahoma Press, 1988) for a fine explanation of the nonaffectionate role of Roman mothers. See also E. Cantarella, *Pandora's Daughters: The Role and Status of Women in Greek and Roman Antiquity* (Baltimore: Johns Hopkins University Press, 1987), 134.

3. Tertullian, "To the Martyrs," in *Disciplinary, Moral, and Ascetical Works*, trans. R. Arbesmann (New York: Fathers of the Church, 1959), 20.

4. See J. Salisbury, *Perpetua's Passion* (New York: Routledge, 1997) for the complete account of this martyr.

5. See Tacitus in *Dialogue on Oratory* in which he praises former times when citizens' sons were raised and nursed by their mothers instead of by hired nurses. Tacitus, *The Complete Works of Tacitus*, trans. A. J. Church (New York: Random House, 1942), 757.

6. Salisbury, 72.

7. Ibid., 82.

8. Tertullian, 19.

9. Origen, "Contra Celsum," in *Collected Works* in *Anti-Nicene Fathers*, vol. 4, ed. A . Roberts and J. Donaldson (Peabody, Mass.: Hendrickson, 1995), 486. In W. H. C. Frend, "Blandina and Perpetua: Two Early Christian Heroines," in *Women in Early Christianity*, ed. D. M. Scholer (New York: Garland, 1993), 89.

10. Salisbury, 85, 87.

11. Ibid., 90.

12. Ibid., 91.

13. Jacobus de Voragine, *The Golden Legend*, trans. G. Ryan (New York: Arno, 1969), 736.

14. Salisbury, 115.

15. H. Musurillo, *Acts of the Christian Martyrs* (Oxford: Clarendon, 1972), 22.

16. Salisbury, 116.

17. See Francine Cardman, "Acts of the Women Martyrs," in *Women in Early Christianity*, 150: "In both the maternal and the social body, the demands of mothering exert a pull away from martyrdom, and so must be denied in order for women to enact their final confession of faith."

18. See Clarissa W. Atkinson, *The Oldest Vocation: Christian Motherhood in the Middle Ages* (Ithaca, N.Y.: Cornell University Press, 1991), 58, and Danielle Jacquart and Claude Thomasset, *Sexuality and Medicine in the Middle Ages* (Princeton: Princeton University Press, 1988), 72.

19. Atkinson, 59.

20. Salisbury, 138, 142.

21. Ibid., 139.

22. Eusebius, *The History of the Church*, trans. G. A. Williamson (Harmondworth: Penguin, 1984), 204.

23. Ibid., 195, 200.

24. Ibid., 204.

25. Ibid., 202.

26. Ibid., 202.

27. O. Kiefer, *Sexual Life in Ancient Rome* (New York: Dorset, 1993), 23.

28. Tertullian, 17.

29. Jacobus, 592.

30. Ibid., 715.

31. See James Carroll, *Constantine's Sword: The Church and the Jews* (New York: Mariner Books, 2002), 195–205, for a full description of the impact of Helena's discovery.

32. Ibid., 201.

33. Augustine, *Confessions*, trans. R. S. Pine-Coffin (New York: Penguin, 1980), 68.

34. Ibid., 70.

35. Salisbury, 106.

36. Augustine, 68–69.

37. Ibid., 192.

38. Jacobus, 347.

CHAPTER 7

1. George Foster, "Peasant Society and the Image of Limited Good," in *Peasant Society: A Reader*, ed. Jack M. Potter, May N. Diaz, and George M. Foster (Boston: Little, Brown, 1967), 300–23.

2. Ibid., 309.

3. See Jon D. Levenson, *The Death and Resurrection of the Beloved Son: The Transformation of Child Sacrifice in Judaism and Christianity* (New Haven: Yale University Press, 1993).

4. Plutarch, *Moralia*, trans. F. C. Babbitt (Cambridge: Harvard University Press, 1962), 493.

5. Tertullian, "Apology," in *Apologetical Works*, trans. R. Arbesmann (New York: Fathers of the Church, 1950), 30.

6. Augustine, *City of God*, trans. D. Knowles (Hammondsworth: Penguin, 1972), 277.

7. Tertullian, "Apology," 29, 31; Plutarch, 493.

8. Herodotus, *The History*, trans. D. Grene (Chicago: University of Chicago Press, 1987), 528.

9. J. E. Salisbury, *Perpetua's Passion* (New York: Routledge, 1997), 55.

10. M. Staniforth, trans., "The Epistle of Barnabas," in *Early Christian Writings: The Apostolic Fathers* (New York: Dorset, 1968), 194, 198, 204.

11. Tertullian, "Spectacles," in *Disciplinary, Moral and Ascetical Works*, trans. R. Arbesmann (New York: Fathers of the Church, 1959), 104.

12. "Acts of Phileas," in *Acts of the Christian Martyrs* vol. II, ed. Herbert Musurillo (Oxford: Clarendon, 1972), 331.

13. "The Martyrdom of Polycarp," in *Early Christian Writings*, 160–61.

14. Ignatius of Antioch, "Epistle to the Romans," in *Early Christian Writings*, 104.

15. Prudentius, *"Hymnus in Honorem Passionis Eulaliae, Beatissimae Martyris,"* available 2003 http://harvest.rutgers.edu/latintexts/prudentius/crowns3.html, 9. The translation is mine.

16. Ibid., 1.

17. Mikhail Bakhtin, *Rabelais and His World*, trans. H. Iswolsky (Cambridge, Mass.: MIT Press, 1965), 279.

18. Joyce E. Salisbury, *Iberian Popular Religion* (Lewiston, N.Y.: Edwin Mellon, 1985), 162.

19. Jacobus de Voragine, *The Golden Legend* (New York: Arno, 1969), 627–31.

20. Jerome, "Letter XXII, xix, To Eustochium," in *A Select Library of Nicene and Post-Nicene Fathers, V. VI.*, ed. P. Schaff and H. Wace (New York: Christian Literature, 1893).

21. G. Morin, "Deux lettres mytiques d'une ascete espagnola," *Revue Benedictine* 40 (1928): 289–318.

22. Ibid., 294.

23. Ibid., 298.

24. Ibid., 301.

25. Isidore, *Etimologias*, ed. J. Oroz Reta and M. Marcos Casquero (Madrid: Biblioteca de Autores Cristianos, 1982), xi, 1, 37–39, 141.

26. Lucian of Samosata, "De Dea Syria," in *The Ancient Mysteries: A Sourcebook*, ed. Marvin W. Meyer (New York: HarperCollins, 1986), 139.

27. Aline Rousselle, *Porneia: On Desire and the Body in Antiquity* (New York: Basil Blackwell, 1988), 121–28.

28. Joseph Wilson Trigg, *Origen: The Bible and Philosophy in the Third-Century Church* (Atlanta: John Knox, 1983), 20.

29. Eusebius, *The History of the Church from Christ to Constantine*, trans. G. A. Williamson (Harmondworth: Penguin, 1985), 247–48.

30. Tertullian, "Apology," 48.

31. Jacqueline Murray, "Mystical Castration: Some Reflection on Peter Abelard, Hugh of Lincoln and Sexual Control," in *Conflicted Identities and Multiple Masculinities: Men in the Medieval West* (New York: Garland, 1999), 74.

32. For Jan Palach, see http://archiv.radio.cz/palach99/eng/, and for the report on the Kurds, see Robin Young, "Martyrs who fanned the flames of protest," www.hr-action.org/archiv/990216tmsl.html.

33. Johanna McGeary, "The Taliban Troubles," *Time*, 1 October 2001.

CHAPTER 8

1. Eusebius, *The History of the Church from Christ to Constantine*, trans. G. A. Williamson (Harmondsworth: Penguin, 1985), 413.

2. W. H. C. Frend, *Martyrdom and Persecution in the Early Church* (Grand Rapids, Mich.: Baker Book House, 1981), 399.

3. Cyprian, "The Lapsed," in *Saint Cyprian: Treatises*, ed. Roy J. Deferrari (New York: Fathers of the Church, 1958), 61.

4. Tertullian, "The Chaplet," in *Disciplinary, Moral and Ascetical Works* (New York: Fathers of the Church, 1959), 233.

5. Maureen A. Tilley, *Donatist Martyr Stories: The Church in Conflict in Roman North Africa* (Liverpool: Liverpool University Press, 1996), 27–28.

6. Ibid., 45.

7. Ibid., 26.

8. Ibid., 45–46.

9. Ibid., xvi

10. W. H. C. Frend, *Saints and Sinners in the Early Church* (London: Darton, Longman and Todd, 1985), 106.

11. Tilley, 78.

12. Ibid., 79.

13. Peter Brown, *Augustine of Hippo* (Berkeley: University of California Press, 1969), 219.

14. Augustine, "The Letters of Petilian," in *The Writings against the Manichaens, and against the Donatists. Nicene and Post-Nicene Fathers*, vol. 4 (Peabody, Mass.: Hendrickson, 1995), 556.

15. W. H. C. Frend, *The Rise of Christianity* (Philadelphia: Fortress, 1984), 573.

16. Ibid., 573.

17. Augustine, "The Correction of the Donatists," in *The Writings against the Manichaens*, 637.

18. Augustine, *The Writings against the Manichaens*, 390.

19. Augustine, "The Letters of Petilian," 537.

20. Frederick H. Russell, *The Just War in the Middle Ages* (Cambridge: Cambridge University Press, 1975), 16–26.

21. Augustine, "Letter XCIII," in Augustine, *Letters of Augustine: Nicene and Post-Nicene Fathers*, vol. 1 (Peabody, Mass.: Hendrickson, 1995), 382, 383.

22. Augustine, "The Correction of the Donatists," 641.

23. Augustine, "Letter CXXXIX," in *Letters of Augustine*, 489.

24. W. H. C. Frend, *The Donatist Church* (Oxford: Clarendon, 2000), 262–63.

25. Ibid., 257–58.

26. Augustine, "The Letters of Petilian," 539.

27. Tilley, 81.

28. Ibid., 56, 82, 85.

29. See Elaine Pagels, *The Origin of Satan* (New York: Random House, 1995) for a fine discussion on how Catholics grew to demonize heretics. Here the reverse occurs, and the heretics demonized Catholics.

30. Tilley, 27–28.

31. Ibid., 78–79

32. Brown, 314.

33. Ibid., 314.

34. Cyprian, *Saint Cyprian Letters,* trans. Sister Rose Bernard Donna (Washington, DC: Catholic University of America Press, 1964), 305.

35. Joyce E. Salisbury, "'The Bond of a Common Mind': A Study of Collective Salvation from Cyprian to Augustine," *Journal of Religious History* (June 1985), 237.

36. Salisbury, "Common Mind," 237.

37. Frend, *Donatist Church*, 119, 140. Salisbury, "Common Mind," develops this theme in detail.

38. Joyce E. Salisbury, *Perpetua's Passion* (New York: Routledge, 1997), 115.

39. Augustine, *City of God*, trans. David Knowles (Harmondsworth: Penguin, 1972), 998, 1008.

40. Augustine, "The Letters of Petilian," vol. 4, 567.

41. Frend, *Donatist Church*, 175.

42. Augustine, "The Letters of Petilian," 555.

43. Jim Jones, *The Jonestown Massacre* (Brighton, U.K.: Temple Press, 1993), 23.

44. Ibid., 18.

45. Ibid., 12–13.

46. Ibid., 15.

47. James D. Tabor and Eugene V. Gallagher, *Why Waco? Cults and the Battle for Religious Freedom in America* (Berkeley: University of California Press, 1995), 196.

48. Ibid., 26.

49. Ibid., 51.

50. Ibid., 158–66.

51. Ibid., 25.

CHAPTER 9

1. Genvieve Aliette and Marqui de Maille, *Vincent D'Agen et Saint Vincent de Saragosse: Étude de la "Passio S. Vincentii Martyris"* (Melun: Libraire D'Argences, 1949), for the spread of Vincent's cult to Gaul and its subsequent association with Vincent of Agen. For the development of the cult in Spain, see Carmen Garcia Rodriguez, *El culto de los santos in la España romana y visigoda* (Madrid: C.S.I.C., 1966).

2. "Acta S. Vincentii Martyris," *Analecta Bollandiana* 1 (1882): 260–62. All the translations presented in this chapter are my own.

3. *Concilium Eliveritanum* 1, 2, and 4 in J. P. Migne, *Patrologia Cursus Completus, Series Latina* 84.301–02; hereafter cited as *PL*.

4. Ibid., 3 *PL* 84.302.

5. Ibid., 25 *PL* 84.305.

6. For an analysis of the sermons, see B. de Gaiffier, "Sermons latins en honneur de S. Vincent antèrior aux X siècle," *Analecta Bollandiana* 67 (1949): 267–86.

7. Prudentius,"Passio Sancti Vincenti Martyris," http://harvest.rutgers.edu/latintexts/prudentius, 2. The translations are mine.

8. Augustine, *Sermo 74, PL* 38.1252, *Sermo 75, PL* 38.1254, *Sermo 76, PL* 38.1256.

9. Peter Brown, trans., "Decretum Gelasianum," in *The Cult of the Saints: Its Rise and Function in Latin Christianity* (Chicago: University of Chicago Press, 1981), 79.

10. Prudentius, 6.

11. Ibid., 5.

12. Ibid., 14.

13. See Elaine Pagels, *Adam, Eve, and the Serpent* (New York: Random House, 1988) for a clear explanation of this controversy and of the resulting weight of original sin that descended on the West.

14. Augustine, *Confessions* (New York: Penguin, 1961), 177–78.

15. Gaiffier, "Sermons," 269.

16. Augustine, *Sermo 76, PL* 38.1256.

17. Ibid., *Sermo 77, PL* 38.1256.

18. For examples, see ibid., *Sermo 74, PL* 38.1252 and *Sermo 76, PL* 38.1257.

19. Ibid., *Sermo 77, PL* 38.1257.

20. Prudentius, 5.

21. Ibid., 24.

22. Ibid., 23.

23. S. P. Scott, trans., *The Visigothic Code (Forum judicum)*, (Boston: Boston Book Company, 1910), 365.

24. *Concilia Hispaniae: Toletanum* 4:4, *PL* 84:366 and 6, *PL* 84:367.

25. Ibid., 4:2, *PL* 84:365 and 25, *PL* 84.374.

26. Augustine, *Eymology 7: De martyribus* 4, *PL* 82.290.

27. *Toletanum* 4:52 and 53, *PL* 84:378–79.

28. Ibid., 4:51, *PL* 84:378.

29. Vigilius, *Epistola episcopi Profuturi, PL* 84.832.

30. Martin of Braga, *De correctione rusticorum* 18 in *Martini episcopi Bracarensis opera omnia*, ed. Claude W. Barlow (New Haven: Yale University Press, 1950), 202.

31. B. de Gaiffier, "La lecture des actes des martyrs dans la priere liturgique en occident," *Analecta Bollandiana* 72 (1954): 143.

32. de Gaiffier, "Lecture," 162. See also Angel Fabrega Grau, "Pasionario Hispanico," *Monumenta Hispaniae sacra*, Series liturgica, no. 6 (Madrid, 1953), 261.

33. Garcia-Rodriguez, 259.

34. *Toletanum* 3, *PL* 84:345.

35. "De S. Vincentio Martyre," *Acta Sanctorum* (January): 2.395. For a discussion of the influence of the Council of Nicaea, see L. de Lacger, "Saint Vincent de Saragosse," *Revue d'histoire de l'église de France* 13 (192), 322.

36. Lacger, 327.

37. "Acta S. Vincentii," 264.

38. "De S. Vincentio," 394.

39. See Donald Weinstein and Rudolf M. Bell, *Saints and Society: The Two Worlds of Western Christendom, 1000–1700* (Chicago: University of Chicago Press, 1982), 194–96, for the preponderant association of sanctity with nobility.

40. "Acta S. Vincentii," 263; "De S. Vincentio," 394.

41. Brown, 81.

42. Jacques Le Goff, *Time, Work and Culture in the Middle Ages,* trans. Arthur Goldhammer (Chicago: University of Chicago Press, 1980), 30.

43. Augustine, *Sermo* 74, *PL* 38.1252.

44. Augustine, *Confessions*, 274.

45. Ibid., 262.

CHAPTER 10

1. Herbert Musurillo, *Acts of the Christian Martyrs* (Oxford: Clarendon, 1972), 29.

2. Ibid., 311.

3. Ibid., 153.

4. Anton J. L. van Hooff, *From Autothanasia to Suicide: Self-Killing in Classical Antiquity* (New York: Routledge, 1990) contains a full appendix that lists the Latin and Greek words.

5. Seneca, *De Ira* 3,15,4, in van Hooff, 41.

6. van Hooff, xii.

7. Josephus, *The Jewish War*, trans. G. A. Williamson (Baltimore: Penguin, 1967), 41, 63, 157, 219.

8. Ibid., 358–65.

9. Ibid., 284.

10. Ibid., 200–201.

11. Alexander Murray, *Suicide in the Middle Ages: The Curse on Self-Murder* (Oxford: Oxford University Press, 2000), 520.

12. Murray, 523. See also Sidney Goldstein, *Suicide in Rabbinic Literature* (Hoboken, N.J.: KTAV Publishing House, 1989), 51.

13. Ambrose, "Concerning Virgins," in *Ambrose: Select Works and Letters. Nicene and Post-Nicene Fathers*, 2d ser., vol. 10, ed. P. Schaff and H. Wace (Peabody, Mass.: Hendrickson, 1995), 386.

14. W. H. C. Frend, *Martyrdom and Persecution in the Early Church* (Grand Rapids, Mich.: Book House, 1981), 289. Joyce E. Salisbury, *Perpetua's Passion* (New York: Routledge, 1997), 80.

15. Frend, 293.

16. Tertullian, "To the Martyrs," in *Disciplinary, Moral and Ascetical Works* (New York: Fathers of the Church, 1959), 13–32.

17. Salisbury, *Perpetua*, 157.

18. Tertullian, "Flight in Time of Persecution," in *Disciplinary, Moral and Ascetical Works*, 294–95.

19. Clement, "Exhortation to the Heathens," in *Fathers of the Second Century. Ante-Nicene Fathers*, vol. 2 (Peabody, Mass.: Hendrickson, 1995), 171–206.

20. Clement, "The Instructor," in *Fathers of the Second Century*, 285–86.

21. Clement, "Stromata," in *Fathers of the Second Century*, 413, 423.

22. Murray, 576–77.

23. Ibid., 581–89.

24. Augustine, "Letter 185," in *Letters*, vol. 4, trans. W. Parsons (New York: Fathers of the Church, 1955), 173. The information on the Donatists here is generally drawn from Salisbury, *Perpetua*, 162–66.

25. Augustine, *City of God*, trans. D. Knowles (Harmondsworth: Penguin, 1972), 37.

26. Ibid., 32.

27. Ibid., 31. See also George Minois, *History of Suicide: Voluntary Death in Western Culture*, trans. Lydia Cochrane (Baltimore: Johns Hopkins University Press, 1995), 27–28.

28. Augustine, *City of God*, 29.

29. Murray, 183. For the influence of Martin of Braga, see Joyce E. Salisbury, *Iberian Popular Religion* (Lewiston, N.Y.: Edwin Mellon, 1985), 51–55.

30. Murray, 591.

31. www.angelfire.com/tx4/quixotic/hadith.htm, 2003.

BIBLIOGRAPHY

PRIMARY SOURCES

"Acta S. Vincentii Martyris." *Analecta Bollandiana* 1 (1882): 260–62.

"Acts of the Holy Apostles Peter and Paul." In *Ante-Nicene Fathers*, Vol. 8, edited by A. Roberts and J. Donaldson. Peabody, Mass.: Hendrickson, 1993.

Ambrose. *Ambrose: Select Works and Letters*. In *Nicene and Post-Nicene Fathers*, 2d ser., vol. 10, P. Schaff and H. Wace. Peabody, Mass.: Hendrickson, 1995.

"Anathematisms of the Emperor Justinian Against Origen." In *Nicene and Post-Nicene Fathers*. Vol. 14, edited by P. Schaff and H. Wace. Peabody, Mass.: Hendrickson, 1995.

Artemidorus. *The Interpretation of Dreams*. Trans. R. J. White. Park Ridge, N.J.: Noyes Press, 1975.

Augustine. *City of God*. Trans. David Knowles. Harmondsworth: Penguin, 1972.

Augustine. *Confessions*. Trans. R. S. Pine-Coffin. New York, 1980.

Augustine. *Letters*. Vol. 4, 165–203, Trans. W. Parsons. New York: Fathers of the Church, 1955.

Augustine. *Letters of Augustine: Nicene and Post-Nicene Fathers*. Vol. 1, edited by P. Schaff and H. Wace. Peabody, Mass.: Hendrickson, 1995.

Augustine. *The Writings against the Manichaeans, and against the Donatists. Nicene and Post-Nicene Fathers*. Vol. 4, edited by P. Schaff and H. Wace. Peabody, Mass.: Hendrickson, 1995.

Aurelius Prudentius Clemens. *The Poems of Prudentius*. Trans. Sister M. Clement Eagan. Washington, DC: Fathers of the Church, 1962.

Behr, C. A. *Aelius Aristides and the Sacred Tales*. Chicago: Argonaut, 1967.

Bettenson, Henry, ed. *Documents of the Christian Church*. London: Oxford University Press, 1963.

Braulio of Saragossa, in *The Fathers of the Church: Iberian Fathers*, vol. 2, edited by Claude W. Barlow. Washington: Fathers of the Church, 1969.

Brock, S. P., and S. A. Harvey, trans. "Martyrdom of Tarbo." In *Holy Women of the Syrian Orient*. Berkeley: University of California Press, 1987.

Celsus. *On the True Doctrine*. Trans. R. J. Hoffman. Oxford: Oxford University Press, 1987.

Cicero. *De Natura Deorum*. Trans. H. Rackham. Cambridge: Harvard University Press, 1967.

Clement. *Fathers of the Second Century. Ante-Nicene Fathers.* Vol. 2, edited by A. Roberts and J. Donaldson. Peabody, Mass.: Hendrickson, 1995.

*Concilia Hispaniae: Toletanum 4:*4 J. P. Migne, *Patrologiae Cursus Completus, Series Latina* 84.

Cyprian. *Saint Cyprian: Treatises.* Edited by Roy J. Deferrari. New York: Fathers of the Church, 1958.

Cyprian. *Saint Cyprian Letters.* Trans. Sister Rose Bernard Donna. Washington, DC: Catholic University of America Press, 1964.

de Gaiffier, B. "Sermons latins en honneur de S. Vincent antèrior aux X siècle." *Analecta Bollandiana* 67 (1949), 267–86.

Eusebius. *The History of the Church from Christ to Constantine.* Trans. G. A. Williamson. Harmondsworth: Penguin, 1984.

Glimm, F. X., trans. "Shepherd of Hermas." In *The Apostolic Fathers*, 225–354. New York: Christian Heritage, 1948.

Gregory of Tours. *History of the Franks.* Trans. E. Brehaut. New York: Norton, 1969.

Herodotus. *The History.* Trans. D. Greene. Chicago: University of Chicago Press, 1987.

Hippolytus. "Refutation of All Heresies." In *Ante-Nicene Fathers.* Vol. 5, edited by A. Roberts and J. Donaldson. Peabody, Mass.: Hendrickson, 1995.

Irenaeus. "Against Heresies." In *Ante-Nicene Fathers.* Vol. 1, edited by A. Roberts and J. Donaldson. Peabody, Mass.: Hendrickson, 1995.

Isidore. *Etimologias*, edited by J. Oroz Reta and M. Marcos Casquero. Madrid: Biblioteca de Autores Cristianos, 1982.

Jacobus de Voragine. *The Golden Legend.* Trans. G. Ryan. New York: Arno, 1969.

Jerome. *Letters and Select Works in Nicene and Post-Nicene Fathers, V. VI*, edited by P. Schaff and H. Wace. Peabody, Mass.: Hendrickson, 1995.

Jones, Jim. *The Jonestown Massacre.* Brighton, U.K.: Temple Press, 1993.

Josephus. *The Jewish War.* Trans. G. A. Williamson. Baltimore: Penguin, 1967.

Justin Martyr. *Ante-Nicene Fathers.* Vol. 1, edited by A. Roberts and J. Donaldson. Peabody, Mass.: Hendrickson, 1995.

Lactantius. "Of the Manner in Which the Persecutors Died." In *Ante-Nicene Fathers.* Vol. 7, edited by A. Roberts and J. Donaldson. Peabody, Mass.: Hendrickson, 1995.

Lucian of Samosata. "De Dea Syria." In *The Ancient Mysteries: A Sourcebook*, edited by Marvin W. Meyer. NY: HarperCollins, 1986.

Morin, G. "Deux lettres mytiques d'une ascete espagnola," *Revue Benedictine* 40 (1928): 289–318.

Musurillo, Herbert. *Acts of the Christian Martyrs.* Vol. II. Oxford: Clarendon, 1972.

Origen. *Collected Works.* In *Ante-Nicene Fathers.* Vol. 4, edited by A. Roberts and J. Donaldson. Peabody, Mass.: Hendrickson, 1995.

Plato. "Phaedo." In *Great Dialogues of Plato.* Trans. W. H. D. Rouse. New York: Mentor, 1956.

Pliny. *Letters.* Edited by E. G. Hardy. Oxford: Oxford University Press, 1889.

Plutarch. *Moralia.* Trans. F. C. Babbitt. Cambridge: Harvard University Press, 1962.

Prudentius, "Crowns of Martyrdom," http://harvest.rutgers.edu/latintexts/prudentius.

Scott, S. P., trans. *The Visigothic Code (Forum judicum).* Boston: Boston Book Company, 1910.

M. Staniforth, trans. *Early Christian Writings: The Apostolic Fathers.* New York: Dorset, 1968.

Sulpicius Severus. "Sacred History." In *Nicene and Post-Nicene Fathers.* Vol. 11, edited by P. Schaff and H. Wace. Peabody, Mass.: Hendrickson, 1995.

Tacitus. *The Complete Works of Tacitus.* Trans. A. J. Church. New York: Random House, 1942.

Tertullian. *Tertullian: Apologetical Works and Minucius Felix.* Trans. R. Arbesmann. New York: Fathers of the Church, 1950.

Tertullian. *Disciplinary, Moral and Ascetical Works.* Trans. R. Arbesmann. New York: Fathers of the Church, 1959.

Tertullian. *Latin Christianity: Its Founder, Tertullian.* In *Ante-Nicene Fathers.* Vol. 3, edited by A. Roberts and J. Donaldson. Peabody, Mass.: Hendrickson, 1995.

Tilley, Maureen A. *Donatist Martyr Stories: The Church in Conflict in Roman North Africa.* Liverpool: Liverpool University Press, 1996.

Van Henten, Jan Willem, and Friedrich Avemarie. *Martyrdom and Noble Death: Selected Texts from Graeco-Roman, Jewish and Christian Antiquity.* New York: Routledge, 2002.

Virgil. *Aeneid.* Trans. A. Mandelbaum. New York: Bantam Books, 1981.

SECONDARY SOURCES

Atkinson, Clarissa W. *The Oldest Vocation: Christian Motherhood in the Middle Ages.* Ithaca, N.Y.: Cornell University Press, 1991.

Bakhtin, Mikhail. *Rabelais and His World.* Trans. H. Iswolsky. Cambridge, Mass.: MIT Press, 1965.

Barnard, L. W. *Justin Martyr: His Life and Thought.* Cambridge: Cambridge University Press, 1967.

Barnes, T. D. "Pre-Decian Acta Martyrum." *Journal of Theological Studies* 19 (1968): 509–31.

Bilde, P. *Flavius Josephus between Jerusalem and Rome: His Life, His Works and Their Importance. Journal for the Study of the Pseudepigrapha Supplement Series 2.* Sheffield: Sheffield Academic Press, 1988.

Boyarin, D. *Dying for God: Martyrdom and the Making of Christianity and Judaism.* Stanford, Calif.: Stanford University Press, 1999.

Bradshaw, P. F. *The Search for the Origins of Early Christian Worship.* Oxford: Oxford University Press, 2002.

Brown, Peter. *Augustine of Hippo.* Berkeley: University of California Press, 1969.

Brown, Peter. *The Cult of the Saints: Its Rise and Function in Latin Christianity.* Chicago: University of Chicago Press, 1981.

Bynum, Caroline Walker. *The Resurrection of the Body in Western Christianity, 200–1336.* New York: Columbia University Press, 1995.

Camporesi, Piero. *The Incorruptible Flesh: Bodily Mutation and Mortification in Religion and Folklore.* Trans. T. Croft-Murray and H. Elson. Cambridge: Cambridge University Press, 1988.

Cantarella, E. *Pandora's Daughters: The Role and Status of Women in Greek and Roman Antiquity.* Baltimore: Johns Hopkins University Press, 1987.

Carroll, James. *Constantine's Sword: The Church and the Jews.* New York: Mariner Books, 2002.

Chadwick, Henry. *Priscillian of Avila.* Oxford: Clarendon, 1976.

Davidson, Linda Kay, and Maryjane Dunn-Wood. *Pilgrimage in the Middle Ages: A Research Guide.* New York: Garland, 1993.

de Lacger, L. "Saint Vincent de Saragosse." *Revue d'histoire de l'église de France* 13 (1927).

de Maille, Marqui, and Genvieve Aliette. *Vincent D'Agen et Saint Vincent de Saragosse: Étude de la "Passio S. Vincentii Martyris."* Melun: Libraire D'Argences, 1949.

de Ste. Croix, G. E. M. "Why Were the Early Christians Persecuted?" *Past and Present* 26 (1968): 6–38.

Dixon, S. *The Roman Mother.* Norman: University of Oklahoma Press, 1988.

Feldman, L. H. *Jew and Gentile in the Ancient World: Attitudes and Interactions from Alexander to Justinian.* Princeton: Princeton University Press, 1993.

Feldman, L. H., and G. Hata, eds. *Josephus, Judaism and Christianity.* Detroit: Wayne State University Press, 1987.

Flint, Valerie I. J. *The Rise of Magic in Early Medieval Europe.* Princeton: Princeton University Press, 1991.

Fowden, Elizabeth Key. *The Barbarian Plain: Saint Sergius between Rome and Iran.* Berkeley: University of California Press, 1999.

Frend, W. H. C. *The Donatist Church.* Oxford: Clarendon, 2000.

Frend, W. H. C. *Martyrdom and Persecution in the Early Church.* Grand Rapids, Mich.: Baker Book House, 1981.

Frend, W. H. C. *The Rise of Christianity.* Philadelphia: Fortress, 1984.

Frend, W. H. C. *Saints and Sinners in the Early Church.* London: Darton, Longman and Todd, 1985.

Freud, Sigmund. *Interpretation of Dreams.* Trans. J. Strachey. New York: Avon Books, 1965.

Gallonio, Antonio. *Tortures and Torments of the Christian Martyrs.* Trans. A. R. Allinson. Paris: Fortune, 1903

Garcia Rodriguez, Carmen. *El culto de los santos in la España romana y visigoda.* Madrid: C.S.I.C., 1966.

Geary, P. J. *Furta Sacra: Thefts of Relics in the Central Middle Ages.* Princeton: Princeton University Press, 1990.

Goldstein, Sidney. *Suicide in Rabbinic Literature.* Hoboken, N.J.: KTAV Publishing House, 1989.

Grant, Michael. *The Jews in the Roman World.* New York: Scribner, 1973.

Hall, John R. *Gone from the Promised Land: Jonestown as American Cultural History.* New Brunswick: Transaction Books, 1987.

Heine, Ronald J. *Montanist Oracles and Testimonia.* North American Patristic Society, vol. 14. Macon, Ga.: Mercer University Press, 1989.

Humphries, Mark. *Communities of the Blessed.* Oxford: Oxford University Press, 1999.

Hunt, E. D. "St. Stephen in Minorca: An Episode in Jewish-Christian Relations in the Early 5th Century AD." *Journal of Theological Studies* ns 33 (1982): 106–23.

Jacquart, Danielle, and Claude Thomasset. *Sexuality and Medicine in the Middle Ages.* Princeton: Princeton University Press, 1988.

Kiefer, O. *Sexual Life in Ancient Rome.* New York: Dorset, 1993.

Kruger, Steven F. *Dreaming in the Middle Ages.* Cambridge: Cambridge University Press, 1992.

Langan, John. "The Elements of St. Augustine's Just War Theory." *Journal of Religious Ethics* 12 (spring 1984): 19–38.

Le Goff, Jacques. *The Birth of Purgatory.* Trans. A. Goldhammer. Chicago: University of Chicago Press, 1984.

Le Goff, Jacques. "Christianity and Dreams (Second to Seventh Century)." In *The Medieval Imagination,* trans. A. Goldhammer, 193–242. Chicago: University of Chicago Press, 1985.

Le Goff, Jacques. *Time, Work and Culture in the Middle Ages.* Trans. Arthur Goldhammer. Chicago: University of Chicago Press, 1980.

Levenson, Jon D. *The Death and Resurrection of the Beloved Son: The Transformation of Child Sacrifice in Judaism and Christianity.* New Haven: Yale University Press, 1993.

Lieu, J., John North and Tersa Rajak, eds. *The Jews among Pagans and Christians in the Roman Empire.* London: Routledge, 1992.

McDannell, C., and B. Lang. *Heaven: A History.* New Haven: Yale University Press, 1988.

Merrill, Elmer Truesdell. "Tertullian on Pliny's Persecution of Christians." *The American Journal of Theology* (1918): 124–35.

Minois, George. *History of Suicide: Voluntary Death in Western Culture.* Trans. Lydia Cochrane. Baltimore: Johns Hopkins University Press, 1995.

Murray, Alexander. *Suicide in the Middle Ages: The Curse on Self-Murder.* Oxford: Oxford University Press, 2000.

Murray, Jacqueline. "Mystical Castration: Some Reflection on Peter Abelard, Hugh of Lincoln and Sexual Control." In *Conflicted Identities and Multiple Masculinities: Men in the Medieval West.* New York: Garland, 1999.

Nickelsburg, G. W. E. *Resurrection, Immortality, and Eternal Life in Intertestamental Judaism.* Cambridge, Mass.: Harvard University Press, 1972.

Oberhelman, Steven M. *The Oneirocriticon of Achmet.* Lubbock: Texas Tech University Press, 1991.

Pagels, Elaine. *Adam, Eve, and the Serpent.* New York: Random House, 1988.

Pagels, Elaine. *The Gnostic Gospels.* New York: Vintage Books, 1981.

Pagels, Elaine. *The Origin of Satan.* New York: Random House, 1995.

Peters, Edward. *Torture.* Oxford: Basil Blackwell, 1985.

Plumpe, J. C. *Mater Ecclesia: An Inquiry into the Concept of the Church as Mother in Early Christianity.* Washington, DC: Catholic University of America Press, 1943.

Potter, Jack M., May N. Diaz, and George M. Foster, eds. *Peasant Society: A Reader.* Boston: Little, Brown, 1967.

Price, S. R. F. "The Future of Dreams: From Freud to Artemidorus." In *Before Sexuality: The Construction of Erotic Experience in the Ancient Greek World*, ed. D. M. Halperin, F. Zeitlin, J. J. Winkler, 365–88. Princeton: Princeton University Press, 1990.

Reavis, Dick J. *The Ashes of Waco: An Investigation.* New York: Syracuse University Press, 1998.

Rejak, T. "Dying for the Law: The Martyr's Portrait in Jewish-Greek Literature." In *Portraits: Biographical Representation in the Greek and Latin Literature of the Roman Empire*, edited by M. J. Edwards and S. Swain. Oxford: Clarendon, 1997.

Rousselle, Aline. *Porneia: On Desire and the Body in Antiquity.* Oxford: Basil Blackwell, 1988.

Russell, Frederick H. *The Just War in the Middle Ages.* Cambridge: Cambridge University Press, 1975.

Salisbury, Joyce E. *The Beast Within: Animals in the Middle Ages.* New York: Routledge, 1994.

Salisbury, Joyce E. *Iberian Popular Religion.* Lewiston, N.Y.: Edwin Mellon, 1985.

Salisbury, Joyce E. *Perpetua's Passion.* New York: Routledge, 1997.

Salisbury, Joyce E. "'The Bond of a Common Mind': A Study of Collective Salvation from Cyprian to Augustine." *Journal of Religious History* (June 1985): 235–47.

Salisbury, Joyce E. "The Origin of the Power of Vincent the Martyrs." *Proceedings of the PMR Conference* 8 (1983): 97–107.

Sanders, E. P. *Jewish and Christian Self-Definition.* Philadelphia: Fortress, 1980.

Scarry, Elaine. *The Body in Pain.* New York: Oxford University Press, 1985.

Schoedel, W. R. *Ignatius of Antioch: A Commentary on the Letters of Ignatius of Antioch.* Philadelphia: Fortress, 1985.

Scholer, D. M. ed. *Women in Early Christianity.* New York: Garland, 1993.

Segal, Alan N. *Rebecca's Children: Judaism and Christianity in the Roman World.* Cambridge: Harvard University Press, 1986.

Snyder, G. F. *Ante Pacem: Archaeological Evidence of Church Life before Constantine.* Macon, Ga.: Mercer, 1985.

Stark, Rodney. *The Rise of Christianity: A Sociologist Reconsiders History.* Princeton: Princeton University Press, 1996.

Tabor, James D., and Eugene V. Gallagher. *Why Waco? Cults and the Battle for Religious Freedom in America.* Berkeley: University of California Press, 1995.

Tedlock, Barbara. *Time and the Highland Maya.* Albuquerque: University of New Mexico Press, 1982.

Thurer, Shari L. *The Myths of Motherhood: How Culture Reinvents the Good Mother.* New York: Penguin, 1994.

Trigg, Joseph Wilson. *Origen: The Bible and Philosophy in the Third-Century Church*. Atlanta: John Knox, 1983.

Valle, Rafael Heliodor. *Santiago en América*. Mexico: Santiago, 1946.

Van Henten, Jan Willem, and Friedreich Avemarie. *Martyrdom and Noble Death*. New York: Routledge, 2002.

van Hooff, Anton J. L. *From Autothanasia to Suicide: Self-Killing in Classical Antiquity*. New York: Routledge, 1990.

Weinstein, Donald, and Rudolf M. Bell. *Saints and Society: The Two Worlds of Western Christendom, 1000–1700*. Chicago: University of Chicago Press, 1982.

Wharton, A. J. *Refiguring the Post Classical City*. Cambridge: Cambridge University Press, 1995.

Wiedemann, Thomas. *Emperors and Gladiators*. New York: Routledge, 1992.

Wilken, R. L. *John Chrysostom and the Jews: Rhetoric and Reality in the 4th Century*. Berkeley: University of California Press, 1983.

Yadin, Y. *Masade: Herod's Fortress and the Zealots' Last Stand*. London: Weidenfeld and Nicolson, 1966.

INDEX